T0300324

ROUTLEDGE LIBRARY EDITIONS:
WORK & SOCIETY

Volume 14

EDUCATION VERSUS QUALIFICATIONS?

EDUCATION VERSUS QUALIFICATIONS?

A Study of Relationships Between Education, Selection for Employment and the Productivity of Labour

Edited by
JOHN OXENHAM

Routledge
Taylor & Francis Group

LONDON AND NEW YORK

First published in 1984 by George Allen & Unwin (Publishers) Ltd.

This edition first published in 2024
by Routledge
4 Park Square, Milton Park, Abingdon, Oxon OX14 4RN

and by Routledge
605 Third Avenue, New York, NY 10158

Routledge is an imprint of the Taylor & Francis Group, an informa business

© 1984 George Allen & Unwin (Publishers) Ltd.

British Library Cataloguing in Publication Data
A catalogue record for this book is available from the British Library

ISBN: 978-1-032-80236-7 (Set)
ISBN: 978-1-032-83541-9 (Volume 14) (hbk)
ISBN: 978-1-032-83548-8 (Volume 14) (pbk)
ISBN: 978-1-003-50986-8 (Volume 14) (ebk)

DOI: 10.4324/9781003509868

Publisher's Note
The publisher has gone to great lengths to ensure the quality of this reprint but points out that some imperfections in the original copies may be apparent.

Disclaimer
The publisher has made every effort to trace copyright holders and would welcome correspondence from those they have been unable to trace.

Education versus Qualifications?

A Study Of Relationships Between
Education, Selection For Employment
And The Productivity Of Labour

Edited by JOHN OXENHAM
The Institute of Development Studies, University of Sussex

London
GEORGE ALLEN & UNWIN
Boston   Sydney

George Allen & Unwin (Publishers) Ltd,
40 Museum Street, London WC1A 1LU, UK

George Allen & Unwin (Publishers) Ltd,
Park Lane, Hemel Hempstead, Herts HP2 4TE, UK

Allen & Unwin, Inc.,
9 Winchester Terrace, Winchester, Mass. 01890, USA

George Allen & Unwin Australia Pty Ltd,
8 Napier Street, North Sydney, NSW 2060, Australia

First published in 1984.

British Cataloguing in Publication Data

Education versus qualifications? – (Unwin education books)
1. Education   2. Degrees, Academic
I. Oxenham, John
370.11   LB1027
ISBN 0-04-370148-5
ISBN 0-04-370149-3 Pbk

Library of Congress Cataloging in Publication Data

Main entry under title:
    Education versus qualifications?
(Unwin education books)
Bibliography: p.
Includes index.
1. Industry and education – Addresses, essays, lectures. 2. Manpower
policy – Addresses, essays, lectures. 3. Curriculum planning – Addresses,
essays, lectures. 4. Educational planning – Addresses, essays, lectures. I.
Oxenham, John.   II. Series.
LC1085.E375   1984   370.11′3   84-6418
ISBN 0-04-370148-5
ISBN 0-04-370149-3 (pbk.)

Set in 10 on 11 point Times by Fotographics (Bedford) Ltd

Contents

Acknowledgements

This book is the result of trust and co-operation. The trust was offered by the bodies which provided the funds for the research which forms the core of the discussion. They are the Commonwealth Secretariat Youth Programme, the Economic and Social Committee for Overseas Research of the British Ministry of Overseas Development (now Overseas Development Administration), the Ford Foundation, the Nuffield Foundation, the Swedish International Development Agency and the Swedish Agency for Research Co-operation with Developing Countries. We acknowledge with much gratitude their generous support.

The co-operation involved institutions, researchers, facilitators and respondents in six countries: Ghana, Hong Kong, Malaysia, Mexico, Sri Lanka and Sweden. While gratitude is owed and offered to all of them, particularly heavy debts require to be named: the Centre for Development Studies at the University of Cape Coast in Ghana, through Mr J. Kwasi A. Boakye, currently its director, shouldered the entire responsibility for the field research among employers and schools; the assistance of the Curriculum Development Centre and the Examinations Syndicate of Malaysia enabled a study of educational processes for curriculum design, through classroom teaching to final examinations. In addition, the Kuala Lumpur office of the British Council helped with invaluable background information and technical discussions; in Sri Lanka, too, the Curriculum Development Centre, the Ministry of Education and British Council gave similar help, while Miss C. Deraniyagala, of the National Institute of Management in the Ministry of Labour, took major responsibility for research among employers; and Professor Torsten Husén and his colleagues, of the Institute for International Education at the University of Stockholm, not only drew attention to and made available considerable data but also helped with refining and interpreting its implications.

Considerable supplementary information is owed to a study

commissioned by the Jobs and Skills Programme for Africa (JASPA) of the International Labour Organisation: it covered eight anglophone African states.

Much of the preparation and editing of this book was done at the Max-Planck Institute for Human Development and Educational Research in Berlin, thanks to a most generous sabbatical period granted to me by the Max-Planck Society. I am particularly in the debt of Professor Dr Dietrich Goldschmidt, my sponsor, and of his wife Mrs Ursula Goldschmidt, and his colleagues Mmes Pohlenz and Sanchez, for their comprehensive support, sustenance and encouragement.

Mrs Maureen Dickson has had the long-drawn-out chore of arranging for the typing of the drafts and finished version. To her and her colleagues' patience, good humour and speed we are all in debt.

JOHN OXENHAM

Part One

Interactions between Employment and Education: the Impulse from Employers

Chapter 1

Educational Reform and Selection for Employment – an overview

RONALD DORE and JOHN OXENHAM

THE PROBLEMS OF REFORM AND RELEVANCE

Why is educational reform so difficult? The question applies quite
as much to the richer industrialised states as it does to the less-well-
off states of Africa, Asia and Latin America. However, the
emphasis of this book is on the latter group, because their
resources are scarcer and the need for understanding
correspondingly more pressing. The question can be made more
particular: why do programmes of pre-vocational or vocational
education or attempts to make education 'relevant' meet with such
strangely restricted success? Sinclair and Lillis (1980) have
catalogued projects, ambitiously announced, which have simply
dwindled to a few faithful and obscure centres. Although their list
ends in the mid-1960s, the story continues as the following
examples illustrate.

In 1966 the Kericho Conference in Kenya produced the idea of
village polytechnics to train young school-leavers for self-
employment (Sheffield, 1969). By 1978 the polytechnics numbered
220 with an estimated enrolment of 22,000 students. But the
graduates from the primary schools of that year numbered just
over 280,000, while the following year's new enrolments in the
general secondary schools – both state and Harambee – were
around 110,000. Village polytechnics have evidently not taken
Kenya by storm. Further, many of them look suspiciously similar
to ordinary schools (Court and Ghai, 1974). Again in the
mid-1960s Patrick van Rensburg began his production brigades in

Botswana. His idea seems so sound that the puzzle is why it has not been more widely adopted. More pointed is the query why the brigades seem to have perished in Botswana itself – after more than a decade of interest and promise (Knox and Castles, 1982). In contrast, the ordinary general secondary school has flourished and multiplied.

'Education for self-reliance' was announced by President Nyerere in Tanzania early in 1967. Schools were to become production units and excellence was to be judged on moral and practical, not solely academic, grounds. Ten years later production seemed well below hopes and the criteria of moral and practical excellence were so applied that only academic excellence appeared to carry any weight (ILO, 1978). Less ambitiously and with less fanfare, Ghana in 1969 launched a pilot-project in continuation schools. Pupils in the last stages of the ten-year course in elementary education were to receive instruction in local crafts from local craftsmen. The programme is now nationwide but not yet universal. However, a longitudinal study of its graduates suggests that they differ not at all in their orientation or fate from the graduates of the ordinary school (Boakye, 1977, 1983).

China began its Cultural Revolution in 1966, with educational reform as a central, even spectacular, feature. As in Tanzania, production and moral excellence were to be the touchstones of scholastic success. By the end of the 1970s the process had gone into reverse – a later chapter in this book examines the reasons. In 1972 under a socialistic government and the stress of an insurrection attributable in part to high unemployment among well-educated youth, Sri Lanka embarked upon a novel scheme of pre-vocational studies for secondary schools. The idea, as in Ghana, was to connect schools with the livelihoods actually practised in their neighbourhoods. But, like the Tanzanians and Chinese, the Ceylonese went further and tried to connect success in pre-vocational studies with general scholastic success. Early reports suggested widespread and good acceptance among teachers and pupils. Yet a change of government in 1977 brought the scheme virtually to an end (Wanasinghe, 1982).

Attempts at similar reform have been frequent in Latin America as well. Later in this book the reasons why Mexico's efforts in primary education appear rather unsuccessful are discussed. Elsewhere Brooke (1982) has looked at Brazil, and Avalos (1978) has given an obliquely cheerless impression of the Peruvian reforms. More generally, the World Bank seems to be retreating from projects in diversified secondary education (Lillis and Hogan, 1981). In short, educational reform and educational 'relevance' continue to this day to be beset by difficulty and uncertainty. The observation is as true of socialist states, whatever the mix of their socialism, as it is of mixed economy and capitalist states. So the source of difficulty appears not to lie in the political system.

The Goad to Relevance

Before it is – or, more likely, the several sources are – sought out, however, there is a prior question to be settled. Why are attempts to make education more 'relevant', that is, more closely related to vocations and production, so widespread and so persistent? There seem to be two main answers, unemployment and migration to urban areas. The cardinal point is unemployment among the educated.

In the early years of school systems unemployment appears among primary school graduates – those with between five and seven years of schooling. Later it breaks out among those with junior secondary, or eight or nine years of education. Then it begins to affect secondary school-leavers and eventually even university graduates. It is deemed deplorable, if only because it represents a waste of the resources, public and private, which have been devoted to each year of schooling. Politically, of course, it could be a source of civil unrest and revolution – and was, indeed, regarded as a prime-factor in the insurgence which occurred in Sri Lanka in 1971.

Two additional phenomena frequently aggravate the frustration over the situation. In many countries natural resources and other opportunities for productive livelihoods lie unutilised, at the same time as many educated people are without work. An often-quoted example is the failure of food and other agricultural production to keep pace with population growth in many states of Africa, despite the availability of much arable land and the presence of numerous educated unemployed. Secondly, in a number of countries educated unemployment coexists with acute shortages of skilled manpower: foreigners have to be imported to do critical jobs even while local people are jobless. A consequential and natural feeling is that there must be something wrong with education. If only it could be put right, educated unemployment would not exist and productive opportunities would be better utilised – and the risk of political disturbance allayed.

This feeling about the wrongness or irrelevance of education is reinforced by another observation. Excessive migration from rural to urban areas is a well-known worry to governments and development planners – for reasons that need no explanation here. Among the migrants, the educated appear to be signally over-represented: an educated person is rather more likely to desert the village than is someone who never went to school (see, for instance, Gould, 1982). This suggests that his or her education is not fitting him for life and a livelihood in the village: it is irrelevant to rural conditions. The importance of this point is, of course, that in most countries most people live in rural settlements; only relatively small minorities are town-dwellers. So education in schools is apparently unhelpful to most people. If it could be reoriented and reformed, the urban drift might be slowed and the rural areas derive 'arger benefits from the education of their young.

A further consideration – less urgently felt, perhaps – is that some sections of the population fail to utilise educational opportunities properly. Either they do not enrol their children at all, or they do not ensure their regular attendance, or they allow the children to leave school prematurely. In part, their reasons are economic: they cannot afford the direct costs of schooling or to forgo the labour and earnings of their children. However, there are other reasons besides. The school may not appear economically relevant, for their children might make satisfactory livings without any school education at all. An example of this is those boys in Botswana and Lesotho who do not go to school, because they expect eventually to earn good money as miners in South Africa. Moreover, the school may appear culturally irrelevant, even hostile to traditional values and customs. Examples can be drawn from Islamic societies, where both boys and girls – but particularly the latter – have been withheld from schooling. If these latter objections could be met through reorienting and reforming the school's curriculum, the utilisation of education would greatly improve.

With these sorts of argument to support them, the forces for educational reform should surely have been more successful than the literature indicates. If the suggestion is correct that the causes of disappointment are not to be found in the political system, where might they lie? As a first step let us note that, whatever their differences, the socialists, capitalists and eclectics among the developing countries do share four characteristics which might help explain their problems with reshaping education.

Educational Weaknesses

The first, most obviously, is a relatively weak system of schools with a high proportion of poor schooling. Large proportions of the teachers are still either untrained altogether, or below official standards. Among teachers who are trained, there is often low morale, low professional commitment and a simple unwillingness to do the job properly. Low pay, poor working conditions and poor prospects are cited as causes. The teachers who are good tend to be badly distributed, for their very quality propels them to a few urban schools peopled by the children of the better-educated groups. The consequence is that most schools which are rural and serve the less-educated groups, tend to be staffed by less competent, less committed and less permanent teachers. Two factors compound the already bad situation. First, the textbooks, teaching aids, equipment and even the buildings themselves tend to be poor, scarce and badly distributed: they make the task of teaching even more difficult. Secondly, the services of supervision, support and in-service training tend to be weak and erratic: there is no reliable channel through which reform can be effectively communicated and sustained. Hence, the development of reform is slow, unpredictable and often disappointing.

Educational reasons such as these are easily identified and can be readily tackled. So they tend to deflect public attention away from the other three common features, which lie outside the schools and universities, and are indirect in their influences and cannot be easily handled. Indeed, if they are to be broached at all, they require engaging not just a single agency, like a Ministry of Education, but virtually the entire polity and economy. These three factors interact and need to be seen as a package.

Dual Economy and Inequality

There is, first of all, what used to be called the dual economy. A small 'modern sector' of government services and large-scale industry, commerce and transport offers wage, salaries and working conditions which are comfortable and assured, with long-term hopes of improvement and security in old age. In Africa and Asia only a few states have more than 25 per cent of their labourforces in the modern sector. The states of Latin America tend to have higher averages but are still well short of the industrialised states, where wage/salary employment absorbs 90 per cent and more of the earning population. Contrasting with the modern sector is family and self-employment – in which great majorities of populations are engaged. Incomes and conditions range all the way from the illiterate millionaire in his mansion and Mercedes motor car to the subsistence cultivators and landless labourers, who can scarcely keep their families alive. While this spectrum is indeed wide, the mass of a population tends to cluster much closer to the landless labourer than to the millionaire. Average conditions show much uncertainty in earnings (or harvests), prospects and old age, together with rather poor working, living and health circumstances. The contrast naturally generates a strong desire to escape from ordinary forms of self-employment to the modern sector. To be sure, exceptions can be found. Some people prefer the independence and freedom of self – or household – employment to the restrictions imposed on a wage or salary slave. Others have actually used the modern sector to launch themselves into handsomely remunerative forms of self-employment. Through securing well-paid jobs, they have been able to accumulate the capital and connections to set up business on their own. Offsetting these exceptions, however, are the pressure and persistence of applicants for salaried work, and the long pensionable careers of most employees of civil services and large corporations. The majority of the self-employed seem to be reluctantly self-reliant, like the young people in Monrovia, who frankly confessed to their hopes of a government job (JASPA, 1980, p. 35 *et seq.*).

Equality of Opportunity and Mobility

The second of the three features is the virtually universal acceptance of the concepts of socioeconomic mobility and equality of opportunity. No one needs to stay in the place where he or she was born: that aspect of feudalism is dead. On the contrary, everyone is entitled to try to improve his income and standard of living. Indeed, governments are obliged to promote such efforts. And this improvement is most conveniently achieved by moving out of old forms of self-employment into the better forms of modern employment. The move is well expressed in the perspective plan for Tanzania for the period 1981–2000:

According to the 1978 population census, the number of salaried employees in the country was around 800,000 people. This figure is about 8·2 per cent of all people in the working age group (15–64 years) . . . By the year 2000, salaried employees should not be less than 30 per cent. (Government of Tanzania, 1981, p. 17, para. 69)

If a socialistic, egalitarian government sees progress in these terms, the tendency for the individual to do likewise will presumably be rather more powerful.

Not to be underestimated in this context is the moral link between mobility and equity. To attempt to achieve, say, equality of income, while restricting social mobility, would be regarded as simply discriminatory and unfair. For example, if a policy were announced to raise the incomes of peasants to equality with those of skilled industrial workers on the one hand, but on the other insisted that the children of peasants remain on the farm and have no access to industrial training, public response would likely be hostile in the extreme. Poverty in self-employment coupled with claims to social mobility then, can be expected to generate insistent demands for whatever facilitates mobility.

Qualifications and the Schedule of Correspondence

The last common feature is the formal, institutionalised link between education and jobs in the modern sector. It is universal across the political spectrum and most explicit in states which, like Tanzania or the German Democratic Republic, plan their education in terms of high-, middle- and low-level manpower. The link is simply that entry to most – and certainly the best – modern jobs depends on a minimum level of schooling. It has been elaborated into a schedule of correspondence between level of job and level of education. The higher a job is ranked in terms of responsibility, emoluments and prospects, the higher the level of schooling deemed necessary for it. The practice rests, of course, on a belief that the process of schooling progressively and cumulatively fits people for functions in the modern sector. The practical corollary is that, in all states, the school is used *to sort young people into an order of eligibility for the modern sector, and not simply to educate them.*

Educational weakness, economic dualism, the drive for

mobility and the qualification system are, then, the context for efforts at educational reform. However, the bearing of the last three has not usually been adequately recognised. China, Sri Lanka and Tanzania exceptionally acknowledged their force and tried to grapple with them. Incomes were to be made progressively less unequal and inequalities of opportunity and access ironed out. But China alone tried to ensure the success of its educational reforms by discarding this link entirely. It confronted a central contradiction: while 'relevance', scientific curiosity, creative problem-solving, the dignity of practical skills and labour were all praised and encouraged as essentials of education, not one of these played the least part in selection for either further education or jobs. So the Chinese broke the link between schooling and jobs. That they were impelled to recreate a link later did not so much invalidate their insight as question the extremes to which they took the break.

The Dilemma

More important for present purposes, the Chinese highlighted the dilemma which is the core of this book. If it is, indeed, the case that schooling as currently practised is necessary and indispensable for the development of the modern sector, and if it is equally true that longer experience of schooling does fit people for more responsible functions, then it follows that using the school to assort and select people is legitimate and sensible. It also follows that those who are good at school – the academically able – are likely to be good also in the modern sector.

On the other hand, the Chinese believed – with corroboration not only from the Ceylonese and Tanzanians, but also from reports out of Kenya (ILO, 1971), Ghana (Foster, 1965) and elsewhere – that precisely because the schools were used to select manpower, their processes seemed actually to suffocate the qualities most needed in educated people – initiative, creativity, the capacity and will to be 'prime-movers of development', co-operativeness and a wish selflessly to serve.

The dilemma was deepened by the ill-effects appearing to ripple out wider than the school and employed manpower. They were seen to exacerbate open unemployment; to push qualifications for jobs higher than necessary; to create pressures to distort educational expenditures; and to encourage social division.

Exacerbating Unemployment

By making people eligible for selection to the modern sector, but not guaranteeing it, the schools were fuelling hopes and expectations which could not readily be fulfilled. The reason was simply that the schools were growing faster than the modern sector. Before the days of the 'dual economy', adolescents would have been found some productive role within the economy of either the family or the local community. However, the existence of the modern sector and its apparent, indeed projected, growth encouraged calculated unemployment: better to queue even a long time in unemployment than to miss a modern sector entry through being too busy in self-employment (Blaug, 1969). The incidence of the educated unemployed in India, Sri Lanka, the Philippines and more recently in several states of Africa and Latin America seemed to prove the point.

Escalating Qualifications

Two associated consequences then combined to produce yet another ill. The surplus of educated people means, of course, more candidates per job available. That makes the task of selecting employees more cumbersome, awkward and expensive for employers. Their line of least resistance is simply to raise the educational qualifications for jobs – consequence 1. The unintended but real knock-on effect is naturally to raise the demand for higher education – consequence 2. Qualification escalation, then, demands more resources for schools. Where resources are scarce, it presses towards a reallocation of educational resources to higher education.

Inequity and Misallocation

What seems to happen is that the more influential families find it hard to get jobs for their children. For the latter to improve their competitive position, more education is necessary. So they press for more opportunities for higher education. Governments and their civil service, who include the influential, find it hard to resist such pressure. Since the resources for simple expansion cannot be found easily, they tend to allow some reallocation from primary or basic schooling towards the secondary and tertiary stages. This has the effect both of retarding the universalisation of primary education and of preventing its qualitative improvement. The first is an offence against equity, for virtually every state has accepted and declared that primary education is a basic need and right of every citizen. The second is an offence against efficiency, for sound primary schooling is a prerequisite for sound further education. This is the double ill-effect of open unemployment and qualification escalation. If it were counterbalanced by the emergence of more productive citizens able to compensate the unschooled for their deprivation, the cost might be worthwhile. But too often, it was alleged, the most obvious results were not only the enlargement of educated unemployment; worse, public authorities were pressed further to create even unnecessary employment to keep the educated busy. At least three states – Egypt, Somalia and the Sudan – even took the step of guaranteeing a state job for every university graduate. Elsewhere around three-quarters of university and even secondary graduates are absorbed into public posts. So national resources were diverted to swelling bureaucracies with educated workers, who were reluctant to work.

Social Divisiveness

A further evil seemed to follow. Because schooling was (and is still) not universal and because secondary and tertiary schools were available to progressively fewer and fewer, the educated were *ipso facto* selected and by definition an elite. Many of them appeared to feel that their elect status not only separated them from the masses, but also entitled them to special privilege – in which sentiment they have often been supported by their societies. At the same time, the majority of the better educated seemed to be drawn from the economically better-off social groups. In effect, educational privilege was reinforcing economic privilege for many and creating it for a few newcomers. It was deepening and legitimating social divisiveness.

In a word, using the school as a selector was not only defeating manpower development, it was setting up a syndrome of economic, social and political ill-effects as well. Few educators, social observers, or politicians would contest this, although they might regard it as inescapable.

The Balance of the Dilemma

On the other hand, China apart, no state – developing or

industrialised, capitalistic or socialistic, free market or centrally planned, elitist or egalitarian – has tried to separate selection from schooling. This naturally raises the issue of the balance of the dilemma: might the uses and conveniences of schooling with selection outweigh the syndrome of disadvantages? Let us look at the advantages. In the first place, however bad the effects of selection, manpower of sufficient quality has after all been produced to enable pretty rapid economic growth in most states. Secondly, an earlier paragraph remarked that, in most states, schools and universities had been expanding faster than their modern sectors. It would seem to follow that, if the modern sectors had been less sluggish, there would be no problem. Young people would be schooled, selected and allocated smoothly, with no deplorable repercussions in either the schools or the economy. Relatedly, if development in the agricultural and other rural sectors had been pursued more vigorously, their disadvantages against the modern and urban sectors would be less marked. Pressure on the modern sector would then be less severe, the repercussions in schools less regrettable. That is, selection as such is not the problem. It is simply distorted by larger distortions in a society. Quite apart from these considerations is the plain fact that no better or even equally good alternative exists: the school has to go on selecting, because nothing else can. Obviously parallel is the possibility of inertia: selection by scholastic performance works sufficiently well to make alternatives unnecessary.

Each of these points in favour of the status quo can be countered. To be sure, a fast-growing economy can eliminate open unemployment. On the other hand, no economy seems to have grown fast enough to avoid qualification escalation, as Chapter 2 will substantiate. Qualification escalation may be tolerable as a consumption good in states wealthy enough to afford it and, indeed, it may not affect equity. Nevertheless, it can be questioned even there in terms both financial and human. Does it represent an optimal allocation of the resources which can be spent upon education or on human resource development? Does it represent an optimal use of the time, energy and intelligence of the young people compelled to escalate?

Within the schools there are strong impressions that anxiety about selection, in the form of examination marks or school grades, are almost as destructive of educational values in Britain, Japan, or the USA as they are in Ghana, Mexico, or Sri Lanka. This is an issue which later chapters will examine more fully.

As for alternative mechanisms of selection, it is more likely that non-awareness and inertia have impeded the search for alternatives than that such alternatives cannot be devised. It is probably no coincidence that the society which has moved furthest in mass education, the USA, is also the society which has experimented most widely in alternative methods of personnel selection. An easy and plausible inference is that, where education becomes ineffective in selection, human inventiveness can devise ways round the problem.

Setting out the pros and cons may be useful in clarifying the issues. However, it cannot help resolve the dilemma, unless empirical evidence is brought to support one side or the other, and to give some idea of where the balance might lie. That is the task attempted in this book. It departs, in this chapter, from a consideration of the need for occupational selection in societies, from the simplest subsistence communities to the most complex industrial and commercial megastates and traces the evolution of selection procedures. In attempting to explain why selection now seems to distort education, especially in developing countries, it offers a scheme of diagnosis for the 'diploma disease' or 'paper-qualifications syndrome'. There follows an examination of the assumptions underlying the diagnosis, with some associated considerations.

THE EVOLUTION OF OCCUPATIONAL SELECTION

Having outlined why there is concern about the relationships between salaried employment, selection for it and schooling we now explore more fully the notions of occupational selection and education. Both are necessary to any society and both take on different forms, depending on the nature of the society. Every individual needs either to make a living or to be supported. Consequently, every individual needs to learn the skills appropriate to the way he/she keeps alive. Precisely what choice of livelihood an individual has or what combinations of skills he can adopt again depends upon the society of which he is a member. As societies change so do the range of occupations and skills available; and also the channels and institutions through which they can be learned and mastered. Societies tend to shift from rather simple forms of organisation to somewhat more complex ones and it is possible, therefore, to view the process as a species of

.1 A Schematisation of Social Evolution

‘ociety	Emergent or dominant forms of occupational selection	Occupational training	Making a living
al/tribal ‘ral economies’	inheritance	informal family training	self-sufficient fa‑ production plus reciprocal statu‑ exchange
›-industrial	inheritance plus sending to apprenticeship	some general education; apprenticeship training as extension of family training	sale of goods an‑ services in the m‑
‘capitalist	ditto, except that certain levels of general education may be required for entry to apprenticeship or institutional training	formal institutional training either to supplement apprenticeship or before career entry	sale of goods an‑ services in the m‑
‑aucratic (late ‑alist and	almost exclusively certificated through	pre-career vocational training plus formal in-career	by entry into wo‑ organisations fo‑

evolution. Table 1.1 offers a schematic history of this social evolution.

Most evolutionary schemes are ethnocentric. They are generally produced by Europeans, or by those with roots in Europe, and try to schematise the history of 'Western civilisation'. This one is no exception. However, there is no suggestion that all societies progress through these stages, or that – as Japanese historians, for example, have been prone to suggest about Japan's century of industrialisation – the Western pattern is in some sense a 'normative' one and others (somehow deplorable) deviations. Late-developers have advantages as well as disadvantages – though in the education–employment field, as we shall suggest, mostly disadvantages.

There is no suggestion either that a society must be of only one type at one time – wholly feudal or wholly bureaucratic. On the contrary, part of the problem of social and economic development is that one section of a society moves into a later stage, while others linger in an earlier. Some developing countries still have whole geographical areas in the first stage of largely self-sufficient family production, inheritance of occupation and little or no formal schooling; while large sections of their capital and other cities are well into the bureaucratic stage. The Indian *jajmani* system, where all the farmers pay an annual bag of rice as a retainer to the barber and another few cupsful every time they are shaved – the price regulated by tradition rather than by the market – persists, even though India is the world's tenth largest industrial power, with public and private bureaucracies notoriously sensitive about the schedule of correspondence and, too, its own transnational corporations. Because of this variety of subsocieties within a single state, Table 1.1 refers not to an exclusive form of occupational selection, but rather to 'emergent or dominant forms'. However, in a thoroughly industrialised state, such variety is likely to be much narrower. In Britain, for example, perhaps the only example of an inherited occupation, with training for the job within the household and income based on a tax on the community, is the monarchy.

A lot is, of course, left out of Table 1.1. Most important is the progressive specialisation of occupation. The simpler the society, the more people have to learn several skills to maintain their livelihood. A woman might need not only to grow and cook her own food, but also to brew beer in exchange for services or to weave fabrics for her family's use. A man might have to be not only a farmer, but also a hunter and soldier. On the other hand, even in a very complex society – or in a bureaucracy – a single occupation or set of skills might yield an insufficient livelihood. The second job or 'moonlighting' is well known everywhere. Government clerks and teachers may struggle to supplement their meagre pay by giving private tuition or running a night-stall in the local bazaar. That notwithstanding, there does seem to be some correspondence between the degree of industrialisation (or bureaucracy) and the degree of specialisation of occupation – and from there to specialisation and institutionalisation of training.

In the tribal, 'natural', or subsistence economy there are few occupations, so that occupational selection is mainly a matter of inheritance and learning the skills from one's family. Even in such societies there are a few specialists – the midwife, the medicine-man, perhaps the blacksmith, or a particularly skilled producer of spears. Such people could decide to transmit their skills and lore only to their own children, in keeping with the rest of their community. Or they might detect an unusually gifted youngster outside their family and offer to induct her or him in their secrets. This would likely be done by adoption, assimilating the transmission of skills to the normal family pattern.

Through the next stages of proto-industrial and early capitalist societies the main story is the growth of markets and the acceptance of changeable prices. A monarch may open hospitals or plant trees for nothing; that is part of his duty reciprocating his subjects' duty to provide his income through taxes. On the other hand, a famous personality, like a film-star, might require a fee for the same services – and the size of the fee will vary with the fame of the film-star.

No one envisaged the sale of that sort of sophisticated service when the first tentative markets began – as markets of goods; of food surplus to families' domestic needs; of cattle (and other chattels like slaves); and cottage-industry products. The idea of fluctuating market prices for services came later, but soon barbers were selling haircuts and leg-amputations, herbalists sold cures and priests indulgences. Hordes of the poor sold only their labour, day-length packages of fetching and carrying and earth-moving services. But all set the asking price for their services with a sharp eye to the competition and the strength of likely demand.

The growth of markets – soon vastly accelerated by the invention of money as a generalised means of exchange – is, of course, a consequence of the division of labour. Families come to specialise. And they *can* begin to specialise only because occupations became technologically more productive: 50 per cent of the population can have specialist jobs outside agriculture only when the remaining agriculturalists have become clever enough at their jobs to grow sufficient food and fibres for two families instead of one. And their getting cleverer means that there is more to be learned. People become more self-conscious about their occupations. Parents teach their children the family trade more systematically. This opened up the possibility of taking other people's children, too, as formal apprentices; two could be taught almost as cheaply as one, and the extra lad was helpful in the work. Apprenticeship thus comes to supplement heredity as a mechanism of occupation *selection*. It needs to, because we are talking about an economically progressive society in which some specialities are expanding and others contracting – and, in any case, some people have a lot of children and some have none. With these changes come other developments in the institutions of education.

Reading and writing first form part of a specialist apprenticeship in most societies for priests. When priests marry, and the occupation is hereditary, as in recent centuries in Japan, it can be a family apprenticeship like any other. But where priests are celibate, as in Catholic Europe or Buddhist Tibet, they need other arrangements. Monastic institutions have specialist training branches, which provide the first schools and universities. Table 1.2 schematises the evolution of educational institutions.

When the society was able to afford specialists in teaching the young, and the first non-vocational schools appeared, they were usually of three kinds. First, there is the expansion of the religious schools out of some Protestant notion that laymen as well as priestly specialists benefit from direct contact with the scriptures. The temple schools in Burma and Thailand and the Koranic schools in the Middle East – as well as the schools John Knox planned to make universal and compulsory in Scotland in the sixteenth century – come in this category. Secondly, they – often the same institutions playing a different role, as in the case of the European universities – served to transmit the status-validating culture of an upper class. Societies with a relatively advanced division of labour become stratified societies. As the state develops and provides means for the peaceful co-ordination of society, superseding continuous military coercion, the upper classes, patrons of the priests, turn to the more secular, politico-

.2 A Schematisation of the Development of Educational Institutions

	Family	Educational institutions — General schooling	Vocational schools
...ribal, industrial	does both moral, manual and intellectual training	rudimentary, for upper classes	rudimentary for priests
...pitalist	ditto, less general education, more intensive special education (for own or imported apprentice children) as occupations become more specialised	high culture for upper, 3 Rs for lower, classes	proliferation of i to supplement apprenticeship
...ratic	general, especially moral, education only	national educational system with promotion to higher levels supposedly by merit not class; general education achievements certified, and readable as measures of	in-career apprent supplementation decline; pre-care qualifying course (entry by general- education qualifi

philosophical and literary traditions which priests have developed (or, as in Europe, preserved from earlier periods of high civilisation). They seek in the mastery of these skills and graces both the wisdom to be rulers and the urbanity that makes them plausible as rulers. Schools may well prove the most convenient way they can get priests to pass on this high culture to their children.

The third kind of school appears, when written records and contracts and written communications become used for a sufficiently wide range of occupations for it to become worthwhile to run schools for the apprentices of those occupations – either on a commercial basis or as a by-product of religious schools. The schools can give a basic common training in the 3 Rs with economies of scale which cannot be achieved in families. There comes a kind of threshold turning-point – it has been suggested that it is when literacy reaches about a 40 per cent level – when enough people *are* literate and numerate for the formal institutions of society – the way laws are promulgated in public notices, official forms of marriage, and so on – to be based on the assumption that everybody *is* literate. Then, rather than literacy being a positive advantage, illiteracy becomes a positive disadvantage, and a strong fillip to the expansion of such schools is given.

Meanwhile the first vocational schools develop: in the first instance, as a supplementation of apprenticeship. Usually medicine and law lead here. Starting with the odd anatomy lecture arranged *ad hoc* for all the local apprentices, when there was a convenient corpse to be cut, the courses become more formalised – as medical science progressed and there was a steady increase in the amount of medical knowledge. It becomes possible, then, to *systematise* and teach more economically by books and lectures, rather than in clinical, on-the-job practice. The system is extended, as surveying, accountancy and the various branches of engineering developed their own stock of specialised knowledge, providing formal courses to supplement the learning of those undergoing apprenticeships.

At this point comes the second big change in the story. Through the transition from subsistence and traditional exchange to the early capitalist dominance of markets, all the learning has been either learning to be good or learning to *do* a job. And because there was usually a direct market test – the doctor did not get fee-paying patients unless he had learned to do the job well enough to establish a good reputation, an engineer could not expect contracts unless he had learned to build bridges that did not fall down – learning to do a job was real and earnest. If you went to the Royal College of Surgeons, you might get a certificate of membership when you had completed the course, and it looked fine in the waiting-room and helped to attract patients. But it was whether you remembered what you had learned there, after the final examination, that determined whether you kept the patients. So students were concerned about what they were learning and how much it would help them to do their job.

The big change is the growth in bureaucracy and large employing organisations. Coinciding with it is the first emergence of 'job-holding', of the tenured career job with stable salary and prospects as a way of life. The possibility is introduced that *learning to get a job* becomes a motivation for study, displacing the skills of the job itself. In Britain the crucial period was the middle of the nineteenth century. Bureaucracy started, as always, in government service. The civil service gradually ceased to be simply a field for the exercise of patronage. Instead, the careers of the able were protected and recruitment came to be based on merit. The finishing-touch was added to the process in 1867 with the establishment of examinations to test merit – examinations which came to have a dominant effect on university curricula. The army similarly lost the contours derived from its feudal origins and became a service that one joined as a life career, as did the police force.

So appeared a new category, the 'job-holders'. In countries where the market principle was as deeply ingrained as in England, and where the steady growth of capitalism and agriculture over a period of centuries had firmly entrenched the idea of the weekly labour contract – entailing no obligation to continue the relationship beyond the following Monday – job-holding did not immediately spread beyond the public sector; but spread it did. Banks; universities; the areas of manual work where seniority rules for promotion were firmly established, like steel and railways; the management bureaucracies of the big enterprises, such as Shell, ICI, and Unilever, which developed in the first half of this century – all evolved career structures predicated on the assumption that one joined the organisation at the earliest possible age and, barring accidents, could expect to remain in it until one retired.

This change coincided with the steady growth of scientific knowledge and the continuing rationalisation, systematisation and formal recording of the accumulated wisdom of various occupations. It became possible to provide formal classroom vocational training which was (or was claimed to be) in part a short-cut alternative to learning on the job, and in part a provision of basic theoretical understanding, which on-the-job training alone could never provide.

These two transformations: the growth of bureaucracy and the growth of classroom alternatives to apprenticeship, had the following consequences.

Consequence 1: The body of theory taught in these courses provides the basis for a *licensing examination*. This becomes much more formal and objective, than, say, the previous practice of bodies like the Institution of Civil Engineers after its foundation in 1818: it judged whether a man was fit to be allowed to call himself an engineer by having its membership committee talk to him for half an hour about his professional understanding and achievements. The concept of professional licensing was seen to be so universally convenient that, once the idea of formal paper tests was accepted, the practice spread. Today the British City and Guilds provide qualifications with some measure of licensing function for almost anything from probationary care to circus management. The practice helps the potential customers of professionals and is convenient for employing organisations. Not least is it useful to professions themselves. They can restrict entrants to maintain a scarcity of their services, enhance their good name, and raise their fees and salaries.

Consequence 2: The vocational courses – as they became more systematised – were transformed from being a supplementation to apprenticeship for those already accepted as future practitioners into *pre-career* courses for those hoping to be accepted. This is presumably because:

(*a*) for subjects (like engineering and medicine, especially) which require a good deal of theoretical learning, there are advantages in continuing the rhythm of concentrated schooling established in the secondary school – particularly for subjects which require a deepening of cumulative skills – acquiring a mathematical fluency, for example;

(*b*) the costs are shifted clearly on to the aspirant (or the state) and are not at the partial charge of employing organisations;

(*c*) the training course provides also a *selection* function. Those lacking in brains or diligence can be weeded out. This becomes especially important for those science-based professions which are so complicated that only a relatively small proportion of the population could ever learn to do them well. They need to tap the right 'pool of ability'.

Consequence 3: For those professions in particular – for example, medicine, engineering, or metallurgy – the need to reduce failure rates, and the waste and friction involved, leads to an attempt to select *entrants* to vocational courses – making sure that one has only adequately prepared people from the right pool of ability to begin with. This is usually done by taking the results in basic school-subject examinations as proxy measures. The 'pool of ability' aspect comes to be taken care of by requirements about the *number* of subjects and about grades of performance; and the 'adequate preparation' requirement by sometimes specifying the subjects that need to have been studied (for example, mathematics for engineers). The paradigm for these procedures in Britain (for African and Asian examples, see Chapter 2) was the institutional requirement of the General Medical Council soon after it was established in 1858 that doctor apprentices should 'pass an examination in Arts'. It was concerned that too many country doctors were 'rude mechanicals' who were getting the profession a bad name.

Consequence 4: Especially in societies like Britain where professional bodies have a very high degree of autonomy the various professional bodies seek competitively to raise their admission requirements. (And even in the majority of societies where these matters are very closely regulated by the state, then the professional body, far better organised than the customers, is often the strongest single influence on policy.) In other words, qualifications escalation sets in. The justifications and rationalisations for this will be explored in Chapter 2.

Consequence 5: There is a parallel and closely related development in the selection of employees who need no specialised qualifications: performance in general education subjects is increasingly used as a selection device. A large range of jobs – general management, lesser supervisory, planning and clerical, which require some sort of 'ability to think' and to formulate thoughts on paper – multiply with the growth of bureaucracy and ask only for a *level* of education, without specifying the *content* of it.

Two factors seem to explain this. While the principles of such jobs are common across organisations, their detailed content and execution depend largely on the employing organisation. A carpenter or electrical engineer will do roughly the same work in the same way, wherever he works. A manager or clerk will also do roughly the same work, but the procedures or conventions to be observed and the situations to be dealt with may vary considerably from one organisation to another. What can be learned *before* the job is minimal. Most of the learning has to be done *on* the job. Consequently, only general skills of literacy and numeracy, and logic – applicable in all situations – are needed before selection.

The second factor comprises the changes in both social conditions and social values. The expansion of large employers couples with their ability to offer better wages and conditions to reduce the attractiveness of employment with family, friends and small firms. Placing young people in employment – allocating them – becomes a matter of wider search and competition, rather than local negotiation. Consequently, those who give the prizes are pressed to develop public rules for the winners. Simultaneously, the development of scientific rationality, the urge to run businesses as rational organisations, combines with the increasing value given to social mobility and meritocratic ways of running society – getting the best man for the job. This combination encourages employers to invent objective, impersonal and easily measurable ways of selecting employees. Aspects such as 'personal qualities' become too slippery, and give way to the more concrete educational qualifications. However, since no specific vocational qualifications can be devised, general education qualifications come in handy. At the same time, since jobs are arranged in hierarchies of, say, clerks, senior clerks, supervisors and managers, it seems logical that those in the upper ranks should be asked for better, or at least higher, general qualifications than those in the lower.

Here the 'pool of ability' or screening by ability justification may be a little more open. A third of the employing organisations notifying vacancies for graduates to university appointments boards in Britain say that they are open to graduates in any subject – it is somebody of 'graduate level' they want. A strong and genuine 'adequate preparation' consideration is still involved in so far as they assume that all university courses involve certain kinds of mental training – in solving problems, analysing data and formulating thoughts. But in asking for someone of 'graduate level' they are also stipulating someone 'bright enough, and capable enough of orderly effort, to get a degree'. The British navy put the ambiguity nicely in an advertisement for graduate officers 'with a degree in either Science or Humanities': 'We see your time spent at university as time spent making up your own mind, thinking for yourself. And we know you don't get a degree without a good deal of intelligence and concentration.'

Employing organisations are, of coure, engaged in the same kind of competition as professional bodies – indeed, in the *same* competition: banks recruiting 16- or 18-year-old trainees are competing with the training courses of the accountancy profession at universities and polytechnics. The same tendency for continuous upgrading of requirements naturally occurs. A striking British example is the way in which the executive grade of the Civil Service, open in theory to 18-year-olds, now predominantly recruits graduates.

Consequence 6: The above discussion of the motives of the professions and employing organisations has been in terms of a contrast between adequate preparation considerations and pool of ability considerations. Ability was implicitly equated with IQ and whatever else it is that helps people to get good grades in literature and maths and geography. This is, however, not quite the only ability in question. In the 1860s it was generally assumed in Britain that education beyond the 3 Rs was always likely to be limited to the children of the middle class. So the General Medical Council, when it decreed the need for a level of arts accomplishment, was perfectly well aware that it was hoping to get a 'better class of people' to be doctors. Social screening was deliberate.

As Britain has slowly moved towards meritocracy, the level of general education reached – and even more performance grades achieved – has become more a function of brains (and application) than social status. Consequently, education requirements have become a more reliable filter for the former than for the latter. Social-status filters operate now in the interview process, rather than in requirement-setting, and the education background indicators of social status are now more of *type of school* (private school or not, for instance) than of formal achievement levels. Nevertheless, there still remains a correlation between social class and achievement levels.

Rational Disaster

So much for the story of how our complex of educational and

employment institutions, and the recruitment institutions which link the two, have evolved over time. Knowing how things have got the way they are is a precondition for judging whether the institutions we have represent a rational response to the challenges for which they were designed, or whether we have problems.

The view taken by and large in this book is that they do not, and that we do have the problems sketched earlier. It is necessary, though, to stress that the problem is not the individual student or individual employer or individual profession. Indeed, each of these individually devises a solution rational for itself. However, the individual's actions combine with those of others to work against the interests of all. It is the classic problem of aggregation and the gap between individual and collective goals. A telling example can be drawn from monetary inflation. In a time of inflation it is rational for the individual to convert his unstable money into stable goods. But if all individuals attempt this at once, inflation is immediately worsened and their money loses even more value even more rapidly. They accelerate the situation they fear and wish to avoid.

Something of the sort has happened in the relationship between the three elements that we are examining: the need for capable people for jobs (demand for goods); the preparation of capable people (supply of goods); and educational qualifications (the monetary denominations by which demand is guided to select from supply). However, monetary inflation and its repercussions cannot be put right by individuals: action is needed on the whole economic system. Similarly, counteracting the ill-effects of selection upon education will require action on the whole pattern of incomes, status and linkages between jobs and education.

THE CASE OF DEVELOPING COUNTRIES

Earlier we pointed out that a single state may simultaneously exhibit several phases of occupational selection between the tribal, proto-industrial, early capitalist and bureaucratic forms of society. The phenomenon is frequent among the developing countries and operates to exacerbate the impact of selection through education. The reason is simply that their contact with industrialised states, whether through colonial experience or voluntary commerce, has foreshortened the evolution of their education-employment institutions. The 'bureaucratic' pattern of selection for organisational careers by educational qualifications was not a slow, late growth coming after centuries of 'proto-industrial' and 'early capitalist' phases, when most people were making their living by selling goods and services in active markets, and the first schools developed to provide them with the skills they needed to do so. Instead, colonial or 'modernising' governments introduced transplants of *fully developed* bureaucratic systems into economies which were still, in the terms of Table 1.1, in the feudal/tribal stage. Thus (1) the first entrenchment of the market system, and (2) the appearances of the first bureaucracies and the first generations of salaried jobs, and (3) the first schools, all appeared simultaneously.

The effect was that schools in these countries were born into a bureaucratic age and linked almost indissolubly to bureaucracies. Schooling was about salaried jobs from the very beginning. There were no proto-industrial, early capitalist-period schools in which the traditions of schooling for personal development could have developed. Further, since the most coveted first salaried jobs were clerical and sedentary and required general not vocational education, schooling was from the beginning divorced from obvious occupational skills – and helps explain much of the opposition to vocational and pre-vocational courses, which we noted at the beginning of this chapter. Schooling then was not about learning to *do* jobs, only about getting or qualifying for jobs. No necessary connection existed between what had to be learned and what would eventually be done.

Entrenching this divorce has been the widespread failure of modern sectors to keep pace with educational expansion. The ensuing qualifications escalation has discredited any notion that 'adequate preparation' has anything to do with qualifying for selection. When a Calcutta shoe-store owner advertises for a shop assistant and stipulates 'MAs only need apply', nobody can possibly believe that his young ladies sell shoes better because they have been to school for seventeen to eighteen years. The consequence of this divorce is that the *substantive content* of what is learned is universally degraded. A ritualised and mechanical learning is substituted for the kind of learning which would form both productive manpower and humane citizens.

A special effect is discernible in those developing countries with a low level of cultural differentiation between the social classes. They have had no early schools to perpetuate the culture of an upper class and to legitimise its status. Accordingly, the school at first provides a genuine equality of opportunity – at least in those places where it is available. Meritocracy is established easily without having slowly and ambiguously to disentangle itself from principles of hereditary ascription. In other words, arguments from 'the pool of talent' or 'screening by ability' are more genuine. They are not adulterated by 'social screening' – at least until people in the modern sector begin to transmit their privilege to their children. However, while the absence of such social-class considerations is helpful in some ways, even more importance is given to marks, grades, class of degree, or whatever to denote performance in scholastic learning. Even though the learning is publicly acknowledged to be unrelated to the content of jobs, its rituals have to be faithfully, even feverishly, observed, because it is only merit that counts. Conversely, if perversely, where systems of privilege take the form of positive discrimination and some children are offered assured futures independently of scholastic performance, learning can stop. The reason is simply that advancement is defined as the only purpose of school; if it can be secured without actually learning, why learn? Examples range from job reservation for Bumiputera in Malaysia to the effects on bright high-school American blacks of being guaranteed places at Harvard.

THE 'DIPLOMA DISEASE'

The distortions and dislocations which have been described are termed the 'diploma disease' (Dore, 1976) or, more recently, the 'paper-qualification syndrome' (JASPA, 1981, 1982). Figure 1.1 sketches its anatomy in an attempt at a graphic summary. Like all models, it greatly oversimplifies. Nevertheless, for present purposes, let it be called the diploma disease, or DD, diagnosis. Let us look at some of its salient assumptions.

The first is indicated by boxes 6, 13 and 7. It is that the abilities competences and characters which can be developed by schooling are *all* relevant to work efficiency in both salaried jobs and self-employment. Indeed, the boxes suggest that the failure of the school to foster the right attitudes and motivational patterns as much as cognitive abilities is one of the factors contributing to failures in economic and social development. This is by no means to argue that the failure totally inhibits all development. Japan, Kenya, Malaysia, Mexico and Singapore, to name only a few, are sufficient denial of any thesis of that nature. All have school systems with severe, acknowledged and deplored problems in these terms. Yet all have achieved respectable, even envied, rates of economic growth and some improvements in social well-being. None the less, it does imply that among other, possibly more powerful factors, the quality of human resources does affect the quality of development; and that the quality of human resources can be affected by the quality of schooling. (The limits to that assumption are examined in a later chapter.)

The second assumption is given in box 5: it suggests that, when assessment, teaching and learning are all oriented to selection, there is an irresolvable incompatibility with good education. As Chapter 7, 'Combating the diploma disease', demonstrates, the impression is caused by the simplification necessitated by a diagram. It may well be possible to combine efficient selection with excellent education: doubtless numerous examples could be shown. That notwithstanding, the evidence from at least Mexico, Malaysia, Sri Lanka and several African states does strongly suggest that matching selective assessment with good education is a very difficult business.

The third apparent assumption is that there might be a universal, identical and irretrievable downward spiral to complete educational and social disaster. Such is not the actual case, of course. To offset that impression let the statements in the boxes read more as hypotheses. For example, box 1–box 2: the greater the differentials between salaried and self-employment, the stronger the public preference for salaried employment; and box 3–box 4: the more rigidly that eligibility for salaried employment depends on scholastic attainment, the stronger the public demand for schools and universities.

Such a reading allows, of course, for converse hypotheses. For example, boxes 1–2: the narrower the differentials between salaried and self-employment, the weaker the public preference for salaried employment (or the greater the willingness to develop self-employment); and boxes 3–4: the less eligibility for salaried employment depends on scholastic attainment (or the more diverse the channels for eligibility), the weaker the public demand for schools and universities.

The figure, then, attempts not only to illustrate the course of the 'diploma disease', but also to identify points where its force might be resisted. It implies that the closer the resistance to boxes 1 and 3, the greater its presumed power to arrest the disease. The importance of this should not be missed, for it asserts that the being and workings of the educational system are determined more by the economic system than by educational philosophy. This is by no means a new view. It needs to be expressed, however, to balance the first assumption that schooling can affect the quality of human resources or manpower. The implication is that the economic system has a substantial effect on the influence of the schools.

Mentioning the economic system requires that two other dimensions be mentioned also, the social and political. Figure 1.1 does this, indeed, in boxes 10 and 11, but only tangentially, and conflates the two. It misses the interactions between the economic, social and political spheres in affecting the educational. The figure seems to posit what might be called a utopia of equal economic and educational opportunity, and equal access to and utilisation of both. In fact, as is well documented, there are inequalities of opportunity between the sexes, between richer and poorer social groups and between people living in different areas of a state. Concomitantly there are inequalities of utilisation: some social groups appear less anxious than others to use schools, or even to secure salaried employment; some appear much more determined. Where there is competition for opportunity, political influence may be brought to bear. Consequently, in some states the education of richer groups is subsidised out of the taxes paid by the poorer, while what education the latter get, is little and wretched (Jallade, 1977). Elsewhere the rich may shoulder part of the burdens of the poor and differences in educational quality may not be so glaring. However, underlying Figure 1.1 is the hypothesis that the more severe the diploma disease, the more will social and political factors conspire to favour the richer and better-placed and to discriminate against the poorer and less powerful. That is, while the figure puts the emphasis on the effectiveness and efficiency of education, it has an accompanying – if latent – concern for equity also.

INVESTMENT IN HUMAN RESOURCES

In its further assumptions and hypotheses Figure 1.1 invokes a number of ideas about the relationship between education (in the form of certified schooling) and employment. Boxes 6, 13 and 7 imply agreement with the concept of *human capital*, namely, that spending money to put people through the process of schooling is an investment in productive skills and qualities, which will in time turn a profit on the expenditure (see, for example, Schultz, 1961; Denison, 1962; Psacharopoulos, 1973, 1980). The notion is, of course, related to the considerations of adequate preparation discussed earlier. (It is helpful to bear in mind here that 'productive skills and qualities' do not only mean literacy, numeracy, knowledge and horizons of interest, skills of reasoning and manipulating data, but also obedience, co-operativeness and the ability to communicate. There are also economic, psychological and social dimensions to human capital (Blaug, 1974; Inkeles and Smith, 1974).) This is, of course, the assumption on which manpower plans and educational expenditures are based. However, the human capital idea and the schedule of correspondence, in box 3, suggests that progressive investment in educating a person leads to a similarly progressive development of competences. This is what is supposed to move employers to ask for higher education for higher jobs. On this, some of the boxes in Figure 1.1 signify hesitation.

Qualifications by Surplus Supply

Box 9 in Figure 1.1 hypothesises that employers escalate qualifications, simply because there are too many educated people and not because the jobs need a substantively higher level of skills. It implies, then, that employers are using scholastic attainment merely as a convenience to ease their task of selecting employees, to cut down the number of candidates. Here the figure sides with those who have suggested that the level of qualifications for a job may be less a matter of human capital or productive skills, and rather one of the supply of qualifications (OECD, 1970; Psacharopoulos and Sanyal, 1981). In doing this the figure necessarily exposes its agnosticism about box 3. It recognises that a schedule of correspondence is, indeed, operated by employers. (Chapter 2 discusses the point at greater length.) Nevertheless, it does not necessarily go along with the human capital concept in ascribing the correspondence to real and measurable increments in productivity generated by education. By hinting that there may be no intrinsic link between qualifications and jobs box 9 hints also that the schedule of correspondence in box 3 may be factitious, a convenience with no empirical justification.

Screening by Ability

A loose link between education and jobs could be acknowledged, and the schedule and escalation still justified on the ground that the more educated do jobs better, either because of their education

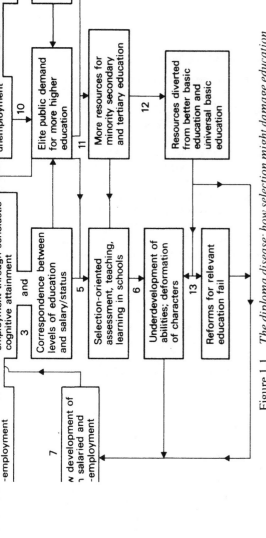

Figure 1.1 *The diploma disease: how selection might damage education and development.*

or because their education shows them to have greater general ability and other useful qualities. If the first reason is advanced, that is solely human capital, of course. If the latter is the case, then screening theory comes into play (Arrow, 1973; Wiles, 1974). This suggests that people do vary in their abilities, but employers have few means of telling who has what abilities. The process of schooling gives young people at least an opportunity of displaying their abilities: those with greater abilities tend, first, to do better at school, and secondly to go further in school. It is possible that what is taught and learned in school may not actually develop abilities. Nevertheless, it is enough that the abilities are identified and sorted out. It then makes practical sense to allocate the higher abilities to the higher jobs in a schedule of correspondence, whatever the real effects of the school and university. Clearly, too, qualifications escalation would be a necessary accompaniment to a wider provision of education. For as schooling spreads, so the more able go further up the educational ladder. To secure the same ability for a particular job, then, necessitates a higher educational prerequisite for it. By supposing a loose link between qualifications and jobs Figure 1.1, or the 'DD diagnosis', allows for the operation of both human capital (or 'adequate preparation') and ability screening (or the 'pool of ability').

Social Screening

At the same time, there are suggestions that many employers are interested not merely in ability, but also, and perhaps rather more, in social background (Collins, 1972; Bowles and Gintis, 1976; Carnoy, 1974). The critical element here is not the characteristics as such but the fact that their incidence is closely related with social background. For example, the characteristics which are thought to mark out future top managers and decision-makers seem to be concentrated oddly among rich and powerful social groups. There is a remarkable correspondence between the social background of a person and his position in salaried employment. The better off and more influential a person's family, the more likely he or she is to have a well-paid post in the managing or controlling echelons. Equally remarkable is the correspondence between social background and educational attainment: the better placed a person's family, the further he or she is likely to go in the educational system. This appears to be quite as much the case in socialistic as in capitalistic systems, and was indeed something the Chinese Cultural Revolution tried to combat. So an ambiguity arises: are the social characteristics the product more of social background or of education? If social background is more powerful in forming the characteristics than the school, is education being used merely as a device for perpetuating privilege?

At this point a brief diversion is needed to take note of private education. In some countries private schools and possibly universities are the preserve of relatively small groups of better-off people. In part they help transmit the culture of the rich, and in part they enable the rich to sustain superior scholastic levels. They could be viewed as facilitators of social screening, because they actively combine the cultivation of cognitive and desired social characteristics. Elsewhere, private establishments can be generally of poorer quality than the state's and act almost as shelters for the less successful children of the rich. Attendance at them could well be disadvantageous. The actual role of private education, then, differs from society to society.

More important for present purposes is that, where state schools and universities are the better or only channel, children who already have some social advantage will tend to predominate in the upper levels. A corollary of this is that poor people of high ability are likely to have less education than rich people of low ability, and hence to have less access to the upper echelons of salaried employment. A further corollary, then, is that while educational merit *appears* to be a basis for selection, what is *really* being selected is social class. This is the consideration of social screening. It can be introduced deliberately, as in the case of the British medical profession cited earlier. It can occur more by understandable preference than by malicious discrimination, as when some applicants are more compatible in language, outlook and culture with the employers than are others. It might occur because certain social characteristics – self-confidence, polished manners, influential social connections – are sincerely thought to help effective performance in the job. Besides these innocuous possibilities, however, there is also a more questionable political dimension: the ruling classes might arrange and allocate salaried employment in a way which appears to be rational and fair but in fact permits them to load the dice in favour of their own children, and thus in favour of the retention of economic and political control by themselves and their successors.

It is important not to draw too black and white a view here. Social considerations are likely to weigh more heavily in societies which have long-established, clear patterns of class differentiation, like the countries of Europe, Latin America and parts of Asia, for instance. They are likely to be much less important in those countries, say, of Africa, where the new elite classes have had only a couple of decades to develop. (Ethnic or tribal aspects may enter, but that is a separate issue.) But even where class stratification remains relatively strong there may be a sufficient measure of social mobility to permit a plausible appearance of selection by merit. In Britain, for instance, the Conservative Party is often thought of as the party of the rich and privileged, closed to those of humbler background. However, in the past forty years three of its leaders – including the two most recent – who have become prime ministers of the country have been the sons and daughter of ordinary tradespeople. This fact may well persuade people that British society esteems merit more than social class. More routine and widespread, of course, is the effect of mixing social classes in schools. Although the majority in the upper levels of state schools may be children from advantaged homes, the minority by definition is drawn from humbler backgrounds. Because it is the minority, its members will tend to be drawn into the culture of the majority and in this way acquire the social characteristics which employers are said to seek. This avenue of mobility would certainly be offered as evidence that merit was the real criterion of advancement. Further, where salaried employment is expanding, people of ability have to be recruited, whatever their social background. It has also to be borne in mind that even within the richer classes there is competition for employment and position: a person of the requisite social background but with less than the requisite education can be displaced by a person of identical background with the required education.

In boxes 10 and 11 the 'DD diagnosis' suggests that social screening probably does operate, along with ability screening and human capital. However, the diagnosis is agnostic on the issue of whether the richer and more powerful social classes actually arrange a system which favours them, while appearing to be accessible to others; or whether employers operate social screening deliberately to protect and entrench their own social classes; or whether the system is essentially reasonable and the richer classes maintain their position simply by being able to afford to take more advantage of educational opportunities.

THE BALANCE OF CONSIDERATIONS

The preceding suggests that the relationship between education and employment is not simple or straightforward. The diagnosis in Figure 1.1 certainly assumes considerations of 'adequate preparation', which themselves have cognitive, psychological, social and psychomotor dimensions. It also assumes the factors of underlying ability and social class. Uncertainty arises only over the relative weight of each and the circumstances under which that weight might change. A concrete example here may help. An employer may have ascertained that a certain set of functions cannot be satisfactorily executed by a person with less than a certain level of education E, and that people with E perform adequately (human capital). Yet because E graduates are so numerous, he fears an unmanageable flood of candidates, so sets the qualification at F (surplus supply). Even at F there are so many candidates that he demands evidence of outstanding performance – on the ground that the more distinguished the performance, the higher the quality of a candidate (screening by ability). At the same time, since the set of functions involves dealing with top management, the employer prefers candidates who speak 'his language' (social screening). All four considerations would have played a part in this employer's calculation, but it would be hard to say which was most powerful. Still, the presumption might be that, had there been no surplus supply, human capital and social screening would have outweighed screening by ability. And if only one E graduate had presented herself, but without quite the right social background, presumably human capital would have been the touchstone – on the rigid assumption that less than E education would certainly have been insufficient. (How rigid that assumption might be is explored in Chapter 2.)

The balance between the considerations is not of serious interest to the individual employer. It is however, of considerable interest to governments and planners genuinely concerned with the topics mentioned earlier: educational improvement, the quality of human resources and the allocation of national resources between different forms of education, social equity and educated unemployment. Why it is important to examine each case closely for the balance between factors may be seen by following through the implications of each one singly.

If considerations of *human capital* and adequate preparation were the *only* ones which motivated employers, as many theorists about the economics of education assume, then:

- employers are interested in capacity to do a job above all other considerations
- and irrespective of ability and despite remarkable exceptions, people with more education tend to do more demanding jobs better
- thus, the schedule of correspondence between education and jobs is justified
- and different levels of manpower do, indeed, need different amounts of schooling

then it follows that manpower planning is well founded as are the practices of selecting by scholastic attainment and giving some people a great deal of education – even when basic education cannot be provided for everybody. Efficiency has to be given priority over equity.

Conversely, the educational, social and economic ill-effects which appear to follow have then to be accepted as part of the cost of the system of salaried employment. They are deemed, in effect, to be not only necessary evils, but actually a lesser ill than might follow in the absence of such a system. If, on the other hand, employers were seeking only a convenient way of selecting among a *surplus supply* of applicants, the structure of qualifications for salaried employment would merely reflect the educational attainments of the available labourforce. There would be no necessary or even close connection between a job and its educational prerequisites. Human capital would be only a minimal consideration and the schedule of correspondence largely a convenience for discrimination or screening. The escalation of qualifications would in principle be open-ended, limited solely by a society's ability to pay for more and more education for everyone. *In extremis* a doctorate could become the minimum qualification for a clerk and post-doctoral studies necessary for all who aspired to higher posts. In reverse, if the educational policy and resources of a people led them to provide only six years' general education for everyone – followed by specialist occupational studies – salaried employment would necessarily make do with that. Governments, then, would have no anchor for educational or manpower policy. It would also follow that the argument for education as investment in socioeconomic development would be weakened, with the possible consequence that the importance of scholastic institutions in national budgets would decline.

Similarly, if employers were concerned solely to *screen for ability* the role of school and university would be called into question: they would simply be serving as costly filters, doing little or nothing to develop their students' potential. It would be more sensible to invent cheaper ways, first, of separating out the potential managers, researchers and technicians, and subsequently of realising their potential. The point is, though, that while it would be more sensible for 'society' as a whole, it might not suit the individual employer. From his point of view, identifying the more able is more easily and cheaply done through those selected for extra schooling, than through, say, taking a batch of primary school graduates on probation and gradually culling them. The facts that the state arranges to pay for most of the schooling and that it is not the employer who directly suffers the effects on education or unemployment encourage the use of the school as a convenient filter. The fact remains that from the point of view of the whole of society, the use of qualifications exclusively as a proxy measure of ability – for screening for ability alone – would call much of school education into question, and entail both misallocations of resources and inequity.

Misallocation and inequity of an even worse kind would be implied if employers were intent exclusively upon *social screening*, without the least consideration for what schools are presumed to do to the minds and characters of their pupils. The whole apparatus of differentiated schooling would be called into question. So, too, would the intelligence and cunning of the employing and ruling classes. For educational systems cost money and at least part of the cost has to be contributed by those classes themselves. To be sure, in most societies the cost may well be successfully shifted to the main and poorer body of taxpayers. Even so, where private education is widespread the ruling classes carry most of the cost themselves. Indeed, in states like the federal republic of Germany, the USA, Britain and others the rich who use private education not only have to pay for their own education, they have also to contribute to the state schools which they do not use. If, then, they knowingly used the schools simply to provide facades of rationality, fairness and equal opportunity, they would be paying a high price indeed. The question would arise, why could they not find cheaper ways of maintaining their positions? A more pointed question would also present itself: when competing among themselves, why do the rich allow scholastic considerations to enter, if they really believe them valueless? The inference would seem to be that the implications of *pure* social screening render the idea absurd. Social screening can be shamelessly practised only where customs of heritable occupations remain strong. Where meritocracy, social mobility and equal opportunity are widely held values, even the ruling classes seem to believe in some degree of 'adequate preparation'-cum-'ability screening' to assist their social preferences.

All the same, acknowledging that social screening is probably a factor in occupational allocation does, of course, have implications for any society which wishes to minimise it. One simple implication is that some form or other of social screening is likely to persist, if only because the social aspects of human capital or adequate preparation are not always easy to separate from the educational. The socialist European and Chinese experiences seem to bear out this view. The problem would be to restrict social screening as a minimal residual consideration, after requirements of ability and preparation have been fully satisfied.

From the foregoing discussion, it is clear that none of the four considerations, which the diagnosis posits as possible causes of the diploma disease, seems acceptable *a priori* in its pure and exclusive form. None seems able to explain fully what is happening, but each seems to have some weight.

Assessing approximately what part is explained by which consideration under what circumstances is the intent of the next two chapters. The first asks employers why they actually use schooling as a basis of both qualifications for jobs and differentiation between candidates. The second examines evidence on whether schooling is in any way associated with the quality of performance in a variety of jobs.

AN EDUCATOR'S VIEW?

The discussion so far has been in terms of education and selection from the point of view of employers and such governments as might be interested in combining the formation of good-quality manpower with the efficient use and equitable distribution of resources and opportunities. There is another viewpoint, that of the educator in the school, polytechnic and university. How is his or her job affected by the schedule of correspondence? Does he or she see the quest for qualifications as a frustrating cramp upon good education? Alternatively, does he or she see it as an aid to motivation, effort and perseverance? It is possible that, without at least the opportunity of selection for salaried employment, young learners would simply not find it worthwhile to learn at school. In such circumstances, learning in schools might be damaged even more than when constrained by selection. Even if the balance of evidence favoured dissociating selection from education, the educators themselves might see that as a greater evil. This concern will be explored in Chapters 4, 5 and 6, when the focus of discussion moves from selection and job performance to education.

Chapter 2

Employers, Jobs and Qualifications

JOHN OXENHAM

> In a free market the salaries of technicians would rise
> relatively to those of skilless and mediocre graduates in arts,
> but since the government, the principal buyer, bases relative
> salaries on tradition rather than on scarcity, the market
> situation cannot right itself. (W. Arthur Lewis, 1977)

THE QUESTION

Before the main question of this chapter 'why do employers use
scholastic qualifications for recruiting employees?' is approached,
four definitions need to be clear. What is meant by employers,
qualifications, recruiting and employees in the present context?

Working Terms

Employers The word *employer* may call up the picture of the
chief of an enterprise, an individual person, usually a man, who
makes well-informed and rational decisions about the people he
will or will not employ. He runs a firm and he wants it to be well
run and profitable. And, certainly, there are large numbers of
employers of this kind, with enterprises ranging from shops to
factories and with from one to a couple of hundred employees.
However, they are currently perhaps not the most influential. The
bureaucracies, large corporations, government enterprises and
public services now employ important proportions of those who
are in wage and salary employment. In socialistic or centrally
planned states, of course, public employment outweighs private.
   These large-scale employers normally have personnel divisions,

which are charged with co-ordinating policy on salaries and qualifications. In many states the public services are regulated by a central body, sometimes called a Public Services Commission, and are from time to time reviewed by special, *ad hoc* and temporary commissions which overhaul their structures, qualifications for entry and promotion, salaries, and so on. In some states, such as Mexico, there is no such central body. Appointment to public bodies and services can be a matter of political patronage. Even in such states – as President Echeverría's 1971 administrative reforms for Mexico illustrate – there is an increasing trend towards regularising practices and criteria for engaging and paying employees.

The point here is that *employing organisation* would be a more accurate term than employer in the context of this chapter. Given that all such employing organisations have special divisions to strive for rationality and consistency, clear-cut answers on the determination of qualifications can reasonably be looked for.

Qualifications The word *qualification* can mean the licence for a pilot to fly an aeroplane or for a plumber to put in a drainage system. In such cases it designates a specific and restricted set of skills and knowledge for the purposes of particular occupations. Qualification can also mean the simple completion of a level of schooling and, perhaps, a standard of performance. The skills and knowledge acquired can be applied to parts of a wide range of occupations and so constitute a 'general qualification'. A young person with six O levels* in Sri Lanka is qualified to start work as a clerk, a cashier, a ciné-operator, a receptionist, or a shop assistant. If among the six O levels he or she can count three credits (superior marks) in English, Sinhala, Tamil, or mathematics, then he is qualified to start as an assistant manager in a cinema.

At the same time, the *general qualification* also has an important role as a prerequisite to qualifications for specific occupations. O levels may admit a person to training as a secretary or electrician; A levels – two more years of schooling – with very high marks are required for training as a medical doctor; and a university degree may be required from a trainee-manager or

*Before 1975, the O-level course entailed ten years of schooling; in 1975 it was renamed the National Certificate of General Education and reduced to nine years. In 1977 O level and ten years were restored. In 1981 proposals were made to extend the O-level course to eleven years.

chartered accountant. The majority of young people looking for employment or training have only general qualifications to offer. The majority of jobs open to them require only general qualifications, while access to virtually all officially recognised occupational or professional training depends also on having some general qualification. Accordingly, the word qualification in this chapter will denote 'general qualifications'. Where it does not, a special note will be made.

Recruiting Employing (and training) organisations take at least two steps when they want to get new employees (trainees). They, first, delimit a pool of potential employees within the total labour-force, and then from that pool select the people who appear to fall least short of their requirement. The preliminary delimitation – by education, age, sex, experience, or even by family connection or social group, as with the scheduled castes and tribes of India – is what is meant by *recruiting*. The process of choosing within the delimited pool will be called *selection*.

Employees Because the prime interest of this book is the quality of education and how it is affected by the education system's links with salaried employment, the natural focus of this chapter is how employing organisations recruit and select among young people just leaving school or university. *Employees*, then, indicate young people with general qualifications who are just starting to earn their own livings in salaried employment with large employing organisations.

EDUCATION: DIFFERENCES AND INEQUALITIES

Selecting between people – preferring some over others – means that employers accept pragmatically that there are *differences* between people: some have carpentry skills, others have accounting skills. They also accept, rightly, that there are *inequalities* between people: some carpenters are more precise than others, some accountants are more accurate. This chapter will be asking what differences do different levels of general qualification make to the qualities, skills and knowledge that are sought by employing organisations? For example, in Mexico there is a three-year difference in schooling between *secundaria* (a nine-year qualification) and *preparatoria* (twelve years). In what ways does this difference affect whatever is sought in the generally qualified? Then, within a level, what does inequality of performance signify for the employer? For example, in Sri Lanka the government valued a *distinction* at O level 50 per cent higher than a credit and 87·5 per cent higher than a pass (Deraniyagala *et al.*, 1978, p. 39). How are inequalities in scholastic performance interpreted in recruiting and selecting employees?

In particular, why are general qualifications the very first instrument used to delimit the pool for selection? (The habit was noted in Chapter 1.) To illustrate its universality examples are offered from a number of countries. In Liberia an administrative technician is required to have completed high school (12 years) before being permitted to take an aptitude test, while an assistant administrative officer has to show a completed general degree (16 years) (Government of Liberia, 1978). Technical attendants in Tanzania are required to have completed primary school (7 years) to be eligible for an interview or aptitude test, while assistant technicians need form VI (13 years), with passes in physics or mathematics or chemistry (Government of Tanzania, 1975). Six other anglophone states of East and West Africa set out their conditions for entry to their civil services mainly in terms of educational attainment, and the same is doubtless true of the remaining anglophones and the francophones as well (JASPA, 1981). In India and Britain only those with particular grades of (general) university degree are eligible to take the entry examinations and other tests for the higher civil service, while in Kenya aspiring army officers need not just O levels, but a pass in division 2 at least – division 3 was ruled not good enough in 1966. In Mexico drivers had to have nine years of schooling, receptionists needed twelve years and forty-one out of fifty jobs advertised by multinational and large Mexican concerns stipulated minimum educational qualifications (Brooke *et al.*, 1978, pp. 24, 115). Hallak and Caillods (1980) found in both Panama and Indonesia that education was a particularly important criterion for recruitment, and that higher-ranked functions required higher qualifications.

Apart from substantiating the universal importance of pre-career qualification, the examples also expose the universality of the assumption that increased schooling tends to increase suitability for what is deemed more responsible and demanding work. Varying historical experience and varying political regimes make no difference to this central belief. Given this universality and given the rationality of employing organisations, a reasonable inference is that the assumption is well founded. A reasonable expectation would follow, namely, that there would be close agreement between countries and employing organisations on the detailed composition of the schedule of correspondence between education and jobs.

CONSISTENCIES?

A natural next step, then, is to inspect the consistency between countries and thereafter the consistency between employers. Since primary schooling of between five years (for instance, India) and seven years (for instance, Kenya) has been dropped from the schedule of correspondence almost everywhere, and since junior secondary, or middle schooling of between eight years (for instance, Sri Lanka) and ten years (for instance, Zambia) is well advanced towards the same fate, a convenient handle with which to start is the general secondary school course. O levels in Britain, and the states it influenced; the *Baccalauréat* in states influenced by France; high schools in states influenced by the USA; and *preparatoria* in states like Mexico, are now the minimum qualifications required for most clerical or junior white-collar jobs. The content of such work does not appear to differ much from country to country. That the same level of schooling should be required for it, accordingly, is reasonable.

However, the same *level* of schooling turns out not to mean the same *amount*. In Sri Lanka O levels take ten years to achieve. In India and Kenya they require eleven. The *Baccalauréat*, high school and *preparatoria* all represent twelve years of schooling. (Indeed, parenthetically, Zambia's Junior Secondary Certificate and Cameroon's *Probatoire* pre-secondary examinations need as much time as Sri Lanka's O levels, but give access to lower-level jobs like clerical assistants.) The difference between the lowest and highest estimates of secondary schooling sufficient for clerical jobs is only two years; but some consideration is needed of what these two years imply.

Most obviously, they represent a 20 per cent further investment of educational effort and resources over the minimum ten years for the execution of much the same job. As will be shown more fully later, they can also represent a large gain in earning capacity: in Kenya, in 1979, two years' difference of general schooling could mean a 20 per cent rise in salary at one level, a 41 per cent rise at the next and a 35 per cent rise at the third stage up, compared with only a 7 per cent rise for two years of work (Government of Kenya, 1979). Similar arrangements could be shown in many other states. They indicate that employers, in particular governments, pay substantially for each additional year of general education. Presumably, they would not require more education than was actually needed to have a job done adequately. Why, then, the two-year difference between states for a given level of education and job?

One possibility is that some school systems are better than others: what pupils learn in ten years in Sri Lanka needs twelve years of teaching and learning in Zambia and Mexico. A second possibility is that the labels secondary, O level and *preparatoria* are misleading. They do not indicate equivalent levels of attainment: O levels in Sri Lanka are inferior to O levels in Zambia, to the high school in Liberia and *preparatoria* in Mexico. In that case, the interpretation could be that the O levels of Sri Lanka enable a person to tackle clerical jobs with bare adequacy, whereas the extra two years in Zambia leave a clerical officer with some capacity in reserve. This is, of course, tantamount to saying that in Zambia and similar countries clerks tend to be over-qualified and that the schedule of correspondence is not exact. Obviously, a third explanation is that equivalence of clerical jobs across the states is as false as the equivalence of educational level. Clerks in Sri Lanka, perhaps, operate more like clerical assistants than clerical officers in Zambia and so need only ten years for their O levels, whereas the Zambians do need twelve. At present there is no way of saying which interpretation is the more reliable. The chief point, however, is that either in its educational descriptions or in its job descriptions, the schedule of correspondence, when viewed across states, appears inconsistent.

A refinement in inconsistency appears among states which operate centralised, standardised examinations. The USA, Mexico, the Philippines, Liberia and some others permit each school to graduate its own pupils, subject to general guidelines on standards. France, Britain, Sri Lanka, Malaysia, Zambia, the Cameroon, Senegal and many others have national examination systems which elaborately test whether schools and pupils have satisfied national standards. Ghana and three other West African states* sponsor the West African Examinations Council to standardise their O level and other examinations on a regional

---

* The Gambia, Nigeria and Sierra Leone. Liberia is also a member, though late joining, but with its American tradition, does not follow the O- and A-level pattern.

basis. With the first group, the general guidelines permit such latitude that exact comparisons between schools and particular subjects are almost impossible. With the other two, on the contrary, such comparisons can be – and are – easily made, between schools and subjects and, most critically, between individual pupils. A consequence is that, in the first group, qualifications for clerks are set simply as high school or *preparatoria*. In the latter two groups requirements can be more specific. Tanzania and Zambia demand simple completion of the secondary course for eligibility as a clerical officer, but the latter offers a 10 per cent premium in salary for 'three O levels including English language' (Government of Zambia, 1975, p. 17). Sri Lanka demands a minimum of six O levels of which four must be credits, that is, with marks of at least 50 per cent, and of which one must be mathematics and a second either Sinhala or Tamil or English and achieved in *two* sittings (Deraniyagala *et al.*, 1978, p. 39). The Gambian civil service asks for either four O-level passes at *one* sitting, including mathematics and English, or if mathematics is failed, five O-level passes again at one sitting and still including English. Sierra Leone similarly asks for four O levels, but Ghana, with the same WAEC O-level system, wants five O-level passes including English. Kenya's civil service sets out a range of alternatives for aspiring clerical officers:

> 6 East African Certificate of Education passes with 2 credits; 5 East African Certificate of Education passes with 2 credits (*sic*); The E.A. Certificate of Education with 4 credits or 4 'O' levels in the General Certificate of Education (as distinct from the East African). (Government of Kenya, 1973, p. 3)

These variations and trade-offs in educational attainment are puzzling to square with the idea of the relatively homogeneous set of functions performed by clerical workers. Perhaps the schedule of correspondence denotes only a loose and variable fit between job and education. But how loose and how variable is an important issue, if not for efficiency and productivity in jobs, at least for the volume and allocation of resources for education.

More open inconsistency is found when the same job title calls for different levels of education, directly indicating requirements for a different amount of schooling. In Panama, Mexico and the Philippines managers in all kinds of occupation are now expected to have university degrees, which entail at least sixteen years of school and study. In Britain, however, young people with A levels (thirteen to fourteen years of schooling) are still eligible to be managers, even in very large multinational firms. Hallak and Caillods (1980) found the education of managers in Indonesia to be even more modest: the average had only 11·5 years' schooling and, although there were variations between sectors of activity, very few had university degrees. Indonesian managers, then, manage with four to five years less education than do their Philippines or Mexican and Panamanian counterparts. The magnitude of this difference is better appreciated by recalling that most states deem six years a sufficient primary schooling and that in most states only a minority of young people get more than primary schooling.

As the Indonesian situation hints, the variations of qualification around a particular job title are even wider within states. The qualifications demanded by employers in the capital city can be higher than those required in the provinces. In addition, managers were found with between six and eighteen years of education, and bookkeepers and secretaries with between six and fifteen years of education. In Panama secretaries and accountants had an average education of 8·42 years (but could range between 6 and 14 years) (Hallak and Caillods, 1980). Messengers in Mexico were found to need between six and twelve years' schooling, and technicians between nine and sixteen (Brooke *et al.*, 1978, p. 24). These huge differences might be explained simply through employers using a single label to cover varying sets of functions. For example, warehousemen in Mexico were asked for anything between twelve and sixteen years' education. But one position was for a large warehouse with a high turnover and a computerised inventory, whereas others were for very small depots indeed. Similarly, salesmen may be asked for between nine and sixteen years of education, but some will be peddling bread and confectionery, while others selling drugs to pharmacists and doctors. The differences in knowledge and skills required need no amplification. The differences of educational requirements would seem to follow naturally.

While certainly plausible in such instances, the explanation is hollower when applied to typists, office assistants, cleaners and other job titles, where the range of job content is rather narrower. It becomes even more hollow when examined within the framework of a single employing organisation. Deraniyagala *et al.* (1978, p. 67) found groups of clerks under a single supervisor doing the same kind of job. Within a single group education could range from eight to fifteen years, although the mean difference was 3–2 years. They also found groups of managers operating under a supervising manager. Again education could range from eight to fifteen years and the mean difference was wider than for clerks, 4·4 years. Similarly, in Mexico Brooke *et al.* (1978, p. 89) found groups of workers doing identical jobs under one supervisor, but with differences in education which ranged from two to five years in the case of a group of map draughtsmen to ten years in a group of sales managers. A group of timekeepers differed by as much as six years and a group of computer programmers by eight years in their educational attainment.* Brooke also found among ten organisations that of the nineteen jobs with more than one vacancy, fourteen were filled by candidates with more than three years' difference in education; six of them took applicants with more than seven years' difference! These posts were not offered by several different employers, each was in the gift of a single organisation. In Ghana, too, nineteen groups of clerks differed within themselves by an average of 6–2 years' schooling (IDS, 1980, p. 15).

Since such a variation of educational attainment is found on the same job under a single supervisor and the same employer, the notion of a schedule of correspondence becomes nebulous indeed. Two other aspects contribute to this. One is the converse, that is, people of equal educational attainment are found spread through a number of jobs within a single hierarchy: university graduates with fifteen to seventeen years' education can be found as clerks, executives and managers within one employing organisation, and so can secondary school-leavers with ten or twelve years' education. The second aspect is that the general qualifications required for a job tend to rise over time, even within one employer. This is attested by Berg (1970) for the USA; Brooke *et al.* (1978) for Mexico; Deraniyagala *et al.* (1978) for Sri Lanka; Hallak and Caillods (1980, 1981) for Indonesia, Kenya, Panama and France; JASPA (1981) for eight East and West African states; Psacharopoulos and Sanyal (1981) for Egypt, the Philippines, Sudan, Tanzania and Zambia; Salmi (1981) for Morocco; Srivastava and Oxenham (1978) for India; and Watts (1973) for Britain. Unless the functions of a job are actually becoming more

---

* Whether educational differences had an impact on performance on the job is a question examined in Chapter 3 by Angela Little.

difficult, the slippage would suggest that their correspondence with a particular level of schooling is slight. Further examination of this issue of *qualification escalation* will be pursued a little later in this chapter.

Yet another aspect dissolving the solidity of the schedule of correspondence is the observation that the specification of minimum qualifications varies along a number of dimensions. Hallak and Caillods found in both Panama and Indonesia that sector of activity, size, status and modernity all seemed to affect educational requirements more than did the actual contents of the job:

> Whereas in Textiles and Hotels the 'mode' of the statistical distribution of education for managers is 14 years, in Construction and Trade it decreases to 12 years. The 'typical' technician in Construction has had 12 years of education; in Textiles he would have 8 years of schooling. (Hallak and Caillods, 1980, p. 177)

Further, the larger the undertaking, the higher the educational qualifications for a particular job, a feature Stolzenberg (1978) found to be true of the USA as well. Somewhat correspondingly, firms with only one owner tended to be less demanding than partnerships, which in turn were less demanding than limited companies, although the jobs to be done were roughly similar. (See Panchamukhi, 1978, for a similar situation in India.) Also the more 'modern' the firm, the higher the educational level of its workers (all other things being equal).*

One inference from these variations would be that there really is little correspondence between job functions and scholastic level. Alternatively, if there is indeed such a correspondence, so that more educated employees are more suitable, and if the job titles do indicate much the same job content, then the economic sector, ownership, size and modernity of an employing organisation systematically affect the standards of suitability it is willing to

---

* A composite coefficient of modernity was constructed, taking into account the production system (in industries), the system of selling, the method of stock control and the systems of accounting and materials handling in the case of trade, and the age of equipment and system of accounting in the case of services. Three broad categories were formed, modern, semi-modern and traditional (Hallak and Caillods, 1980, p. 69).

tolerate in its employees. That is, certain sectors, multiple ownership, limited company status, larger size and more modern operations would tend to demand higher standards of suitability (whether of productivity, efficiency, or other characteristics will be explored shortly) than would other sectors, single ownership, smaller size and less modern operations. Both inferences may prove to be partially true. There may be some – but a very loose – correspondence between schooling and jobs. Simultaneously, the tolerance of employers may be affected by the factors listed. Which is more true under what circumstances is, however, a question which cannot yet be answered.

Because people with identical educational qualifications work at different levels of an organisational hierarchy, they naturally earn different levels of salary. However, if people with equivalent qualifications are working at roughly the same job, differences of salary should either disappear or at least be significantly narrowed, even in a free market situation. A closer correspondence between jobs and salaries can be expected. However, the appearances here, too, are of wide variability. A particularly interesting case is that of Mexico. The beginning salaries were ascertained for a range of jobs open to inexperienced young people under thirty-three different employers. For any given job, the difference between the lowest and highest salaries offered was never less than about 20 per cent and could widen to as much as 75 per cent (Brooke *et al.*, 1978, p. 24). Since a difference of 20 per cent in starting salary could represent up to six years' service, it appeared that, even for almost identical job content, there was no consensus among employers about what would be an appropriate salary.

A similar inference is suggested by a contrast Hallak and Caillods (1980) found between Indonesia and Panama. In the first managers' salaries seemed to be governed mainly by the characteristics of the employing organisation, whereas in the latter they were related more to the manager's own personal characteristics. Skilled workers, on the other hand, had their salaries governed in Indonesia by their professional training, that is, by personal characteristics, but in Panama more by the characteristics of the employers. The inference is that in free market economies, characterised by heterogeneity among employers, aggregate and average appearances of neat correspondences between jobs, salaries and education actually mask considerable untidiness and possible inconsistency. If so, the determination of qualifications for jobs would seem to be less a matter of systematic evaluation, and more a function of random circumstance and perhaps arbitrary decision.

DETERMINING QUALIFICATIONS

The next step, then, is to look at exactly how employers do determine the educational qualifications for jobs and what factors they take into account when doing so. A naïvely technocratic view might suppose that the following stages would be undertaken:

(1) analyse the job to be done into its component functions;
(2) test what levels of general schooling and special training are required to cope with the functions;
(3) assess what other qualities are needed for the smooth execution of the job within the environment and ethic of the organisation;
(4) assess whether further schooling or other qualities might be required for promotion, if promotion and a career were part of normal employment;
(5) recruit according to the findings.

Such a view would have to assume further, of course, that an employer had the resources to undertake the exercise and that the organisation was of a sufficient size and complexity to be able to offer promotion and a career. These additional assumptions are reasonable here, for the organisations in question are civil services and large corporations, whether public, private, local, or transnational.

But the technocrat would still be disappointed. Of the seventeen civil services examined, only one, Liberia's, appeared to have actually undertaken such an exercise on a comprehensive scale. A second, that of Mexico, had been instructed to do so on a department-by-department basis. But only four of seven departments interviewed by Brooke (1978) had begun to implement the instruction, and none had followed the five stages rigorously. The remaining fifteen civil services appeared content to live largely by tradition.

Of the twenty-six private employers interviewed by Brooke (1978) in Mexico, only six (23 per cent) had introduced some form of job evaluation. This assessed jobs in terms of know how, problem-solving and accountability, and produced maximum and minimum salary levels. Only after the salary was fixed did educational qualifications enter in the form of a question: what sort of education is this salary likely to attract at this time? Education, then, was determined not by the needs of the job, but by the 'market' and the going rate.

This minority of Mexican private employers used the salary to determine the educational requirement. In direct contrast are the public services of the former British colonies, which were examined. Without exception, they use education to determine salary. An attempt to change that approach was hinted at by the Ndegwa Commission of Kenya in 1970–1 in para. 122 of its report:

> His pay is therefore that of the pay scale set for that particular Job Group, based on job factors for those occupations. That is, his pay reflects the job requirements, not the particular qualifications of the individual. (Government of Kenya, 1972)

The extent to which the commission was able to implement that principle is reflected in the arrangements for clerical officers, job group D. The first point of the salary scale is for persons who are promoted from junior clerical officers in job group C. Their educational qualifications are either seven years' primary or nine years' junior secondary schooling.* To these are added several years of experience plus a level of performance which justifies their elevation to a higher job group. If, however, they were to succeed in getting four O levels or their equivalent through evening classes or correspondence school, they would by that fact alone and irrespective of experience or performance, be eligible for promotion to the third point of the salary scale, two steps higher. This offers an improvement of 9 per cent in gross pay and the equivalent of actually working as a clerical officer for two years. Of course, young people with four O levels, straight from school and without any clerical experience at all, also enter at the third point. Thus, they are being paid for their qualifications, not for the job.

Similarly, the seventh point on the scale is open to people who have completed their A-level studies but failed their exams. The ninth point is for those who have actually passed their A levels. The important feature to keep in mind is that the promotees, the

---

* In 1973, two years after the commission sat, the Directorate of Personnel Management declared the junior clerical officer grade obsolescent, so that no further recruitment to it was permitted. Using it here is simply an illustration of the commission's thinking.

O-level leavers and A-level leavers would all be in the same job group D, have the same job title, clerical officer, and execute the same clerical functions. But in sole virtue of his educational qualifications the A-level leaver would enjoy a *38 per cent* salary advantage (1979 scale) over the promotee from job group C.* Essentially, then, a particular employer has constructed a schedule of correspondence between education and salaries, independently both of the job to be done and of proven competence to do it. Why this should happen is again a point to be discussed later.

Somewhat in between the Mexicans and Kenyans was an important public corporation in Zambia, INDECO. It carried through an intensive nine-month analysis of all the jobs in the organisation. Manual and cognitive areas were distinguished, and the latter separated into eight subareas, which were allocated a total of 700 points. Of these, 'education and training' received only 110 (15·7 per cent), ranging from 5 points for four years of primary schooling or basic literacy and numeracy to 110 points for a doctorate in a required specialisation. Each point, of course, had an effect on the grading and salary of a job. However, when it came to determining what education was required for what job, the difficulties were such that three committees were established to reach independent but, it was hoped, harmonious conclusions. Unfortunately, the three sets of recommendations did not concord with one another, so that resort was had to an averaging or compromising procedure (JASPA, 1981, Vol. 1, pp. 215, 220). Although this was a more thoughtful and conscientious process, the outcome can scarcely be deemed technocratic. Nor can it be said to reaffirm confidence in the schedule of correspondence.

In Ghana and Sri Lanka fourteen state corporations and sixteen private firms (entire samples) confessed to not having undertaken any painstaking attempt to correlate education and job functions (IDS, 1980, p. 7). In Kenya, Tanzania and Zambia this proposition was put to sixty-seven employers and supervisors:

'My organisation has scientifically assessed how much schooling a person really needs to do every job in it.' Only just under a quarter agreed, 30 per cent in Tanzania, 25·8 per cent

* For similar instances, see Deraniyagala *et al.*, 1978 (Sri Lanka); JASPA, 1981, Vols 1 and 2 (seven other African anglophone states); Oxenham, 1974 (Indonesia); and Panchamukhi, 1978 (India).

in Kenya and 15·4 per cent in Zambia. Very nearly two-thirds in all three states denied that their organisations had done any such thing. Similarly, in India just under two-thirds of a group of fifty-one employers agreed, with hardly any difference between public and private sectors: 'There is no close relationship between the level of education and job functions' (JASPA, 1982, p. 142; Srivastava and Oxenham, 1978)

AN OUTSTANDING EXCEPTION

It will be recalled, however, that one civil service did undertake to investigate the correlation between jobs and educational qualifications: what were the bearings of its results? In the five-year period 1974–9 (note how late and recent the date!) the Civil Service Agency of the government of Liberia, with American assistance – but with not always willing co-operation from ministries and departments – executed a programme of job interviews and desk audits of the way jobs were actually done. It also questioned supervisors on level of performance from different members of staff. From all that data it attempted to determine the minimum knowledge and abilities required for a job to be performed efficiently. On the basis of these painstaking gleanings the Agency developed batteries of tests derived from actual job functions to determine whether candidates had the minimal attainments necessary to learn a job readily and to cope with its basic tasks. The most important conclusions seemed to be:

- for the clerical and subprofessional groups, few people with less than twelve years of schooling (high school), could cope with the tests, even though many with only grade 9 schooling were found actually doing the jobs satisfactorily. A majority even of high school graduates failed the tests and the variability among them was very wide. Among the graduates of rural high schools, the pass rates were reported to be as low as 3 or 4 per cent. Consequently, a level of schooling completed by only 10 per cent of an age group could not be treated as earning automatic eligibility for even junior clerical employment. Taking into account the surplus availability of High School graduates and the average test performance the Agency decided to ignore the less educated people already in posts (or rather to deem them exceptions), and to set the completion of high

school as a prerequisite for even applying to take the clerical aptitude tests;
- in regard to the administrative group, a university degree of any kind was found to be a minimal requirement for the work of such functionaries as assistant administrative officer or assistant staff analyst. People with less education were unable to manage the tests. Even more important, it appeared that learning at a university, even though divorced from any particular job, did enable people to undertake such functions more readily than less schooling coupled with experience in related but lower job groups, like the clerical. Furthermore, although the functions of a supervisory clerk could be successfully attempted by a high school clerk only after several – five and more – years of experience, they could equally successfully be attempted by a university graduate straight out of college and with no experience of clerical work. On the other hand, university graduates were found to be just as fallible and variable as the high school graduates on the tests of occupational suitability: large proportions of them failed;
- in the fiscal group and among statisticians, as elsewhere, cases were found of people already in place with less than the formal qualifications and none the less performing their jobs satisfactorily. However, they were also deemed exceptions who could not justify altering the requisite qualifications.

If this Liberian experience can be taken as a reliable guide, several important general inferences are possible:

- in the clerical, fiscal, subprofessional and administrative groups there is, indeed, an ascending order of difficulty in the functions to be performed. The job hierarchy appears justified;
- competence in the higher functions appears to include competence in the lower. Conversely, competence in the lower functions (at least in principle) may be a precondition or preparation for competence in the higher. It would follow that there is a gradient of developing (that is, related but also differentiated) skills between the lower and higher functions. Consequently, it should be possible to progress from lower to higher by working at the former, while growing familiar with the latter. For example, a clerk working for a subprofessional could learn to do the latter's job. By extension the notion of a

career from clerk to supervisory clerk to subprofessional to assistant administrative officer would be sound;
- each of these four groups of job functions does appear accessible to persons with only general schooling. Conversely, the skills learned in general schooling and university are *occupationally* relevant to this particular hierarchy of functions;
- further, there does seem to be a correspondence between level of scholastic attainment and capacity to undertake higher job functions, without prior direct experience of the lower; schooling appears both to enhance and to extend job capacity in a continuous and cumulative way;
- not only that, but schooling would appear to develop capacity more rapidly and more surely than does experience on the job. This inference is drawn from the apparently low proportions of, say, grade-9 graduates who can satisfactorily discharge clerical functions, or grade-12 graduates who can handle administrative functions. This would mean that, with age and other factors held equal, people with more schooling would tend to have higher job capacity than people with more job experience. If so, appointing, say, a university graduate with sixteen years of general eduation directly as a supervisory clerk in preference to a high school clerk with four years of job experience (sixteen years' education and job experience) would seem justified.*

This series of inferences tends to strengthen human capital theory. It also bears out the commonsense of employers who have not tried systematically to match jobs and education, but who have relied on their own experience and that of their colleagues and competitors. Further, it tends to vindicate the European, perhaps particularly British, traditional belief that general education is occupationally valuable.

On the other hand, account has to be taken of the fact that many high school and university graduates fail the clerical and

---

* This is, in fact, a custom general among the public services, except Mexico's. There are posts which are open either by promotion to people with lower educational qualifications or by direct entry to people with higher educational qualifications. In all cases the minimum number of years of work necessary to earn promotion is greater than the extra years of schooling necessary for direct entry. Often two to three years of experience are equated with only one year of extra school.

administrative aptitude tests. Since the Civil Service Agency had decided that competence at the aptitude tests is so much a function of schooling, that those without a pre-set level of schooling cannot be permitted even to attempt the tests – whatever their job experience – a reasonable expectation would be that everyone with the required level would pass the tests. No inconsistency would arise, if the proportions failing were so small as to be exceptional. But the proportions are high: 75 per cent and sometimes more (Government of Liberia, 1980, p. 9) in the cases of rural high school graduates, and high enough among university graduates to have moved the President to intervene arbitrarily to protect them and the university's reputation. It appears that successfully completing high school and university does not guarantee the requisite job capacity, even though the graduates share the same skills and are, indeed, certified to do so.

If the certificates are reliably standardised, the puzzle may have two parts. One comprises the skills which are acquired through schooling and which are necessary to a particular range of functions; and which would be mastered by everyone who graduated successfully. The other part comprises personal aptitudes, which cannot be created by schooling but which, when present, are incidentally developed by it. Persons with basic aptitudes but insufficient schooling could not be adequately developed on the job – nor could persons with sufficient schooling but lacking in aptitude.*

However, the assumption of standardised certificates can be responsibly relaxed and a clue to an easier answer taken from the performance of the rural candidates. Scholastic attainments vary widely between schools, but are masked by the policy of allowing each school a dominant say in the assessment and graduation of its students. Up until 1964 each school had the total say, as schools in the USA, Mexico and some other states do. However, public dissatisfaction with the variability (and unreliability) of schools brought about a system of centralised examinations, which nevertheless left two-thirds of the weight in the hands of the schools. Despite accession to the West African Examinations Council in 1978, the schools retain this proportion of control in assessment and graduation.

* The possible case of a high school graduate who fails the clerical aptitude test, but then goes on to acquire two years of university study or a full degree, and thereafter to enter the subprofessional or administrative grades, or as a supervisory clerk, cannot be investigated, as none such had been encountered by 1980.

Their persistent variability can be given in two illustrations. The University of Liberia does not accept graduation from grade 12 as evidence of automatic eligibility for higher studies. Instead, it applies its own tests of attainment in only English language and mathematics. In 1979 only 11 per cent of the candidates could cope successfully; in 1978 even that proportion declined to 6·7 per cent. Further, despite the test, the quality of student accepted is such, '. . . that, in any given semester, about one-third or more of the students are either on probation, under suspension or been dropped for poor performance' (Government of Liberia, 1979, pp. 30, 32).

The second illustration is taken from the Ministry of Education, which in 1980 recruited people to be trained as instructors in physical education. It, too, did not take their scholastic attainments for granted – even though certified by itself – but applied a test of ability in English language. Table 2.1 compares the scores on the test with those given by the schools for graduation in English language. It will be seen that, while there is a wide difference between 'accepted' and 'rejected' candidates on the special test, there is scarcely any difference in the school graduation mark. In short, the schools could not be trusted.* A similar situation obtains in Mexico. That is to say, the variation on the CSA tests arises not from schooling as such, as from the variability in the quality of schooling. If the quality of schooling were more even, performance on the tests would be more predictable. While this response might suffice for the schools, it cannot serve to explain the variability in the graduates of the university, unless that institution, too, is to be mistrusted.

Table 2.1   *School Marks and Test Scores of Job Applicants, 1980*

	N	*Mean test raw score (max. 177)*	% *(100)*	*Mean school mark for English (100)*
Accepted	40	135·25	(76·4)	80·5
Rejected	29	76·48	(43·2)	76·8
		Diff. 58·77	(33·2)	3·7

At the same time, the issue of varying educational quality within a state resurrects the issue of educational quality between states.

* This explains the public pressure for stricter, more centralised examinations in Liberia, even as other West African states deplore and attempt to counter the ill-effects of such examinations.

Although Liberia is a member of the WAEC, the examinations for
its schools operate on a different design and level from those of
other members. On the one hand, it is contended that the British
pattern for the O- and A-level examinations is culturally
incompatible with the pattern of assessment borrowed from the
USA. Less kind, on the other hand, is the rumour that Liberian
schools fear that the standard of the O-level examination is too
high for their students. Indeed, an informal comparison of
examination papers suggests that what above-average Liberian
students achieve in twelve years is attained in seven to nine years
elsewhere in Africa. If accurate, two important indications follow.

First, the belief in many states that eleven to twelve years of
schooling are needed for the competent performance of clerical
functions will be misguided. Somewhat less would do, at a
considerable saving in educational costs and salaries. Secondly,
and even more important, is that as the quality of education is
improved, levels of educational requirements should be lowered
not raised – which is, of course, in flat contradiction to the
universally observed escalation of qualifications. But some
support for it comes from an in-house study – unfortunately
confidential and unpublished – by an Anglo-American multinational firm which considered converting its managers in Britain
into an all-graduate body. Before making its decision, it arranged
for its occupational psychologists to measure its non-graduate
managers against their graduate colleagues on a number of
managerial dimensions. The differences were so negligible that it
continues to recruit both A-level school-leavers and university
graduates as trainee-managers.* Whereas the Liberian experience,
on an apparently low and unreliable educational base, suggested a
linear and accelerating trajectory of learning for administration
and management,† the multinational firm's experience, on a
relatively high and more standardised base, intimated a levelling

* In accord with the multinational's finding are the outcomes of studies done by
the Industrial Training Research Unit in Cambridge, England. Working with the
Administrative Staff College at Henley over a period of seven years the Unit derived
profiles of people successful in management teams. A considerable list of
psychological traits was identified, but level of education did not appear among the
important attributes (Jay, 1980).

† The Liberian government emphasises this view by its salaries policy. From
mid-1980 a high school clerk entered at $2,400 per annum, a university graduate
with a bachelor's degree at $6,000, a master's degree at $10,000 and a doctorate at
$14,000. In studytime ratios the figures would run 100 : 133 : 150 : 175. In entry-
salary ratios they would read 100 : 250 : 417 : 583.

off of accumulation-by-general-learning after A levels. Consequently, while the CSA felt obliged to insist on sixteen years of Liberian education as a minimum for its managers, the multinational found it could get by on fourteen years of British education.

Much less systematic, but none the less interesting, support for the CSA comes from two technical trainers/employers, one Liberian, the other from Sierra Leone. One recruits and trains automobile mechanics, the other a range of craftsmen. The Liberian employer had in 1978 decided to restrict recruitment to high school graduates, even though the head of training was himself a graduate of only grade 10. This decision was supported by the trainer. He found, first of all, that on the technical and mechanical aptitude tests introduced in 1979, grade-12 candidates tended to do well, while those with graue 9 had difficulty. On the course the high school recruits mastered both knowledge and practical skills more swiftly than their less schooled coursemates. This head of training acknowledged that, if the tests had been used in 1970 when he was recruited, he would probably have failed. Nevertheless, the new requirements of high school plus good performance on the aptitude tests was, he felt, the correct policy (JASPA, 1981, Vol. 2, p. 196).

Similarly, in Sierra Leone a co-ordinator of an apprenticeship scheme declared:

Some Form III (10 years of schooling) pass our aptitude tests and some Form V (12 years of schooling) fail them. In training, however, the Form IIIs are weaker in grasping training, both theoretical *and* practical, so we have had to hive them off to a special 'Learners' group. (JASPA, 1981, Vol. 2, p. 260)

Now, in Sierra Leone scholastic performance and certificates are relatively well standardised by WAEC. What this trainer implied, then, was that there are indeed two parts to the puzzle. Form III with aptitude but insufficient schooling, and form V with schooling but insufficient aptitude, were both inadequate for his purposes.

The importance of these two instances lies in this. The Liberian CSA had found a correspondence between general education and capacity for clerical and administrative functions. These two employers said that they found a correspondence between general education and capacity for not just mental but manual functions as well. If they are correct, the inference is that general education is relevant to all occupations. Their thinking might favour, but their evidence does not stretch to, the further inference: in any hierarchy of occupations does more general education increase capacity to undertake the higher functions?

On balance, then, the general soundness of the schedule of correspondence seems to be supported by the Liberian studies. However, there are two clear caveats. First, the actual amount and quality of schooling necessary for particular functions apparently remains dependent on local circumstances. These will vary within and between states. Secondly, the needs of jobs are not the only factor which determines general scholastic qualifications. The numbers of educated people available (supply) and, at least for public services, political considerations also affect the matter.

ELEMENTS IN QUALIFICATIONS SETTING

The substantial Liberian effort notwithstanding, the showing so far is that the bulk of employers – governments included! – do not have any well-tested means of relating educational qualifications to job functions. Instead, the impression is that the process of determining educational requirements is very particularistic. However, six elements seem to be common to most employers' calculations, even though their salience varies from employer to employer. These elements are: (1) the skills and responsibilities associated with the job; (2) the salary previously associated with it; (3) knowledge of the educational level likely to be attracted by such a salary; (4) an assessment – rough and stereotyped – of what can be expected from this educational level; (5) latitude for altering the salary; and (6) some knowledge of what the prevailing practice is among other employers. However, very few employers indeed have these elements cut, dried, carefully sorted and weighed: rather, they rely mainly on rules-of-thumb, experience, general wage usage and ears-to-the-ground. The responses of some employers in Kenya, Tanzania and Zambia illustrate the situation. It will be recalled that only minorities of them were willing to claim that their organisations had scientifically assessed what the educational requisites for jobs should be. Three further propositions were put to them, and are set out along with the employers' reactions, in Table 2.2.

Similarly, 62 per cent of Srivastava and Oxenham's (1978)

Indian employers agreed that there was no close relationship between the level of education and job functions; and an even larger proportion, 84 per cent, agreed that the levels of education found within particular occupations were more a function of the educational levels available than of the actual needs of employers.

Table 2.2 *Determining Qualifications for Jobs – Employers' Responses*

Proposition	Kenya N=31 (%)	Tanzania N=10 (%)	Zambia N=26 (%)
In most organisations assessing what educational qualifications are really needed to do a job properly, is mainly guesswork AGREE	41·9	50·0	61·5
When organisations set the educational qualifications for a job, they mostly follow what other employers do AGREE	58·1	50·0	61·5
For many jobs there is no relationship between the minimum educational qualifications required and the actual tasks to be done AGREE	94·8	50·0	50·0

Source: JASPA, 1982.

Preferring the More Educated

Now, in most states, the less-schooled far outnumber the more-schooled, if only because secondary education is accessible to minorities. The virtual admission, nevertheless, that the more-schooled are given jobs within the capacity of the less-schooled, taken together with the universal escalation of qualifications, raises the question whether employers give preference to the more-schooled irrespective of whether or not they need them. The answer is that, by and large, they do: 70 per cent of Brooke's Mexican employers acknowledged the case (Brooke *et al.*, 1978), and similar inclinations were found in the eight African states surveyed by JASPA (1981). Public employers even tend to pay more to people with more schooling, even though they are doing the same jobs as people with less. A legitimate question is why this should be so. Lest there still be a lingering expectation of a tidy answer, these two quotations are salutary. In regard to industrialised countries,

> It is no longer helpful to think of employers as a single type with uniform objectives and methods of operation ... The assumption about motivation ought therefore to be specific to the type of employment and employer under consideration and no single assumption will prove satisfactory for all cases. (OECD, 1974, pp. 103–4)

In regard to developing countries,

> Recruitment and promotion criteria will not only vary by occupation within the same company but also for the same occupation, they will vary from one type of undertaking to another and the same employer for the same job will change his attitude over the course of time to take into account changes in the quality of available manpower. (Hallak and Caillods, 1980, p. 81)

An obvious, intuitive, response to why employers prefer more-educated employees is that they tend to do jobs better. Chapter 3 tests that hypothesis in a range of actual job situations, but here the concern is rather the perceptions of the employers. As predicted, the employers do not permit a simple answer. Brooke's Mexican employers defended no such belief (Brooke *et al.*, 1978). Half of Srivastava's 51 Indian employers denied it (Srivastava and Oxenham, 1978), and so did a quarter of thirty-one employers in Kenya and nearly half of twenty-six employers in Zambia. On the other side of the coin, of course, half the Indian employers, half the Kenyan, 42 per cent of the Zambians and six out of ten Tanzanian employers agreed with the proposition. That is, in nearly all the countries researched, employers differ sharply among themselves on whether the more educated tend to do jobs better.

Limits to the Preference

Before this puzzle is unravelled further, it will be advisable to remark that the preference for the more educated is neither invariable nor unlimited. Indeed, as the Finniston Report of 1980 showed for Britain, many employers, particularly smaller ones, may on the contrary be prejudiced against them. Lehmann and Verhine (1982) report also that, for blue-collar skilled work, Brazilian employers do not seem to take scholastic education into account. To illustrate the limits of the preference elsewhere the work of Brooke and Oxenham (1978) in Mexico and Deraniyagala *et al.* (1978) in Sri Lanka will be used. The files of ten and fourteen organisations respectively were scanned to ascertain whether people with more than the minimum educational qualifications were more likely to secure a job than people with only the minimum. Table 2.3 reproduces what they found.

Table 2.3   *Distribution of Jobs between Those with Minimum and More than Minimum Qualifications: Mexico and Sri Lanka, 1975*

Minimum Education	No. jobs	No. interviewed	Applicants with more than M.E.	Engaged with more than M.E.
Mexico			(%)	%age of jobs
Primaria	44	107	93 (86·9)	40 (90·9)
Secundaria	120	515	394 (76·5)	79 (65·8)
Preparatoria	34	164	93 (56·7)	19 (55·9)
Overall	198	786	580 (73·8)	138 (69·7)
Sri Lanka O levels	162	460	113 (24·6)	48 (29·6)

Sources: Mexico: Brooke and Oxenham, 1978, p. 41, table 12; Sri Lanka: Deraniyagala *et al.*, 1978, p. 39, table 7.

In Mexico, for all the jobs, the proportion of overqualified applicants called for interview was greater than the proportion with only the minimum. This is particularly true of the jobs requiring lower qualifications. Nevertheless, the candidates with only the minimum, once interviewed, had an equal, even slightly better, probability of selection than the overqualified. It is to be noted, too, that there were actually jobs available for people with six and nine years of schooling, (*primaria* and *secundaria*). By contrast, the Ceylonese employers offered jobs only to those with at least ten years' education (O level). On the other hand, they, too, did not allow the minimally qualified to be outweighed by the overqualified. By proportion the latter were only one-third their proportion in Mexico. However, their probability of selection was slightly greater and – not shown in Table 2.3 – increased with overqualification, in terms of both amount of education and quality of (standardised) academic performance. While an O-level applicant had a 32 per cent chance of selection, an A-level one had 39 per cent and a university graduate 50 per cent. An above-average O-level applicant had a 35 per cent chance, and an above-average A-level one a 55 per cent probability of selection. None the less, the major point is that the minimally qualified are not totally displaced by the overqualified; on the contrary, they can compete relatively successfully.

A few more points need to be made, which are not revealed by Table 2.3. In the Mexican example all the posts available, and in the Ceylonese 70 per cent of them, could have been staffed by overqualified people. Yet the twenty-four employers chose not to do so. Even more telling is that those selected with more qualifications are not necessarily those with most qualifications. In Sri Lanka half the university graduates were rejected. In Mexico for twenty-nine 'middle administration' posts, even though the educational qualifications of the selected ranged from nine to sixteen years' education, about half of them had between only nine and twelve, and two candidates with postgraduate studies (18+ years) were rejected. It appeared that choices clustered fairly closely to the minimum qualifications. The inference is that, if all other things are equal, extra education may be an advantage. But those other things are still important and can outweigh extra education. The balance between schooling and other qualities is again in evidence.

Finding that employers tend to keep close to the minimum qualifications raises two by-questions, however. First, is there a fixed or predictable point at which extra education becomes 'over-qualification' and is, therefore, to be rejected? Secondly, if the slightly overqualified are admitted (and bearing in mind that the minimum qualifications are virtually admitted to be both arbitrary and unstable), is there any room for the slightly *under*qualified, those with a bit less than the minimum?

Overqualification

The answer to the first question seems to depend on three factors: the degree to which the overqualified are competing for jobs; whether the employer is public or private; and the degree to which a society has grown resigned to seeing the educated accept jobs for which they are conventionally overqualified. Where competition is severe and resignation longstanding, as in Sri Lanka, 'over-qualification' does not seem to be a disqualification at any point. Nevertheless, employers both public and private still voice misgivings. Where educated unemployment is a relatively recent phenomenon, as in Mexico, there may be open resistance to engaging excessively overqualified people. Although, as shown above, some employers took wide spreads of qualifications for particular jobs, Brooke encountered seven others, all private, who set *maximum* as well as minimum requisites (Brooke *et al.*, 1978). Their most common reason for so doing was that overqualified individuals could be counterproductive: they became frustrated too easily. However, it was not – as might be supposed – boring, repetitive tasks which caused the discontent, but rather impatience for promotion. Similar opinions were heard in Sri Lanka, but were overridden among the public employers by the necessity of giving the educated something to do. In short, there was no real bar at which overqualification became excessive: it all depended on whether a particular employer at a particular time felt that the overqualified would be disruptive.

It is of particular interest that the employers did not claim that the overqualified would be either better or worse on the job, as such. Their circumspection is reflected in the disarray among the Kenyan, Tanzanian and Zambian employers who were asked to react to the statement: 'An overqualified person usually performs disappointingly.' Table 2.4 records their discordant uncertainty. Much more important than the 'job' effects of the overqualified are their 'social' effects and the repercussions of their temporarily disappointed aspirations. Nevertheless, allowances for them were very elastic.

Underqualification

Attitudes about admitting the underqualified were, on the other hand, much more rigid. The public employers of Mexico, as well as two private ones, were ready to acknowledge that patronage

Table 2.4 *Responses to Statement: 'Overqualified Persons Usually Perform Disappointingly' – Employers in Kenya, Tanzania and Zambia*

	Kenya N=31 (%)	Tanzania N=10 (%)	Zambia N=26 (%)
Agree	45·2	20·0	57·7
Disagree	29·0	30·0	19·2
Uncertain	25·8	50·0	23·1
	100·0	100·0	100·0

could override minimum education qualifications. Otherwise, once qualifications had been set, people with less could not be considered. This applied, too, where qualification escalation had occurred: once the minimum had been reset, the old qualification was dropped entirely. This did not mean that the employers all believed that the underqualified would be inadequate. Given their own admissions on the fluidity, if not arbitrariness, of educational requisites, they could not be expected to be so dogmatic. Indeed, only half those in Kenya, Tanzania and Zambia were prepared to agree that 'If a person with less than minimum qualifications is selected, poor job performance will follow'. It was much more a pragmatic matter of drawing a line, for whatever reasons, and sticking to it in order to avoid argument and pressure for exceptions.

Superior Social Skills

The question why employers lean to preferring more-educated persons may now be resumed. Brooke *et al.* (1978) and Deraniyagala *et al.* (1978) asked their Mexican and Ceylonese samples respectively what differences they noted between people of different educational levels. The manner in which the employers generally responded, suggested that they really had not thought about it much. Some actually seemed to fumble for an answer. Not only was there scarcely a mention of 'higher productivity' or some equivalent phrase, but there was no mention of superior occupational skills; and only 12 per cent of the Mexicans mentioned superior knowledge (not necessarily occupational). On the other hand, 30 per cent (the largest single group but still a minority) stated that the really significant difference lay in *presentación* – that is, bearing, personal presence and manner, or 'image'. But is *presentación* a product of schooling or of social class? Four of the twenty-six private Mexican employers (15 per cent) were frank: they used education partly as a social filter. In their view the culture of a person is the outcome much more of family background than of schooling. For higher cultural level to coincide with higher schooling, then, there must be a concomitant belief in a process of attrition in the schools: those of low cultural status are eliminated in the early stages of schooling. The fact that in 1970 only 24 per cent of an age group were even entering lower secondary school in Mexico supported such a belief, of course.

A further four employers not only shared this view, but also went on to complain that with the expansion of schooling, educational level could no longer guarantee cultural background. A department store lamented, '... you find educated people without any culture. They have a certain degree of knowledge but beyond that, nothing' (Brooke *et al.*, 1978, p. 56). Such a sentiment would, of course, augur an escalation of qualifications in an effort again to narrow the social pool of recruitment.

The Ceylonese employers showed rather less concern with social background, but it was still in the minds of the ten private concerns. 'A good all-rounder' from a 'first-rate' school would be preferable. One personnel manager said that boys from these schools,

... are usually from families who have influence in society, and their school friends are also going to have influence in society. So they are going to be useful to the organization. And also they can hold their own, when they go out to meet members of the public. They know how to mix with proper people. (Deraniyagala *et al.*, 1978, p. 38)

However, these remarks on social background, even though voiced by considerable minorities, need to be kept in perspective: they do not imply cruder forms of narrow social patronage. While political influence was acknowledged by the public employers of both samples, only two of the Mexican private employers and none of the Ceylonese said that social connections – as distinct from general social background – were important. Educational level was the critical criterion, even though it might itself be influenced by social considerations. None the less, the observations of Hallak and Caillods (1980) in Indonesia and Panama and Sanyal in the Philippines and Wells (1982) in Botswana do suggest that the greater the competition for employment, the greater the importance of social connections in addition to social background and education. At least the suspicion of such a situation can be detected among the Kenyans, Tanzanians and Zambians of whom 39, 20 and 58 per cent respectively were prepared to agree that; 'For their more responsible positions, employers seek personnel who come from their own social group.'

Potential for Development

As surprising as the infrequency of claims of greater productivity was the relative infrequency of claims that the more educated had more potential or were at least more trainable. Only five of the Mexican employers made remarks like 'With more schooling you understand things faster and you have already accustomed yourself to learning', and the frequency was even less among the Ceylonese group. But they echo the judgements of the Liberian and Sierra Leone trainers mentioned earlier.

However, among Kenyan, Tanzanian and Zambian employers the weight of response went the other way. Fewer than half were prepared to agree that 'Even if they are equal in ability, intelligence and energy, the person with high qualifications will in the long run be more productive than the person who works his way up on the job'. Few Mexicans or Ceylonese hinted that level of education indicated underlying ability. For example, 'The assimilation [of training courses] goes with ability and those with ability have had more education'; or

> 'We give people jobs in accordance with their schooling; the more schooling they have had, the more likely they will be able to do high jobs. Those that have been able to finish school are more on the ball.'

In contrast, a majority of the Kenyans, Tanzanians and Zambians (99, 80 and 65 per cent respectively) believed that 'The more schooling and university a person has had, the more ability he or she is likely to have' and even larger proportions in Kenya and Tanzania (74 and 90 per cent respectively) concurred that 'The school and university improve everybody's abilities'.

At the same time, there were strong currents of feeling that 'average intelligence' denoted suitability for clerical and analogous jobs, while those with 'above-average intelligence' should be groomed for management (JASPA, 1982, p. 147 *et seq.*). Clearly, the African employers had greater faith in the selective and grooming powers of the school than did their Ceylonese and Mexican counterparts. Again, then, local circumstances seem to affect employers' judgement on the uses and effects of schooling.

Equally weak – in all the states – were mentions of the extra-curricular effects of schooling. Employers seemed concerned only with the cognitive achievements of language and mathematics. Practical skills, problem orientation, and so on, seemed not to feature in their thinking.

Moral Obligation

Quite apart from issues of productivity, social provenance, potential, or discipline, was an element of moral obligation: somehow the more educated are more deserving – or more likely to cause trouble – than the less educated, and should get some preference in whatever jobs are available. While such an attitude might be expected among public employers, it was found, too, among the private. A civil servant in Ghana, echoed by others elsewhere in Africa, could defend the preference by pointing out: 'These people have been weeping over their exams, not just doing ordinary jobs. They deserve more.' A private paper company in Mexico justified raising its qualifications with the protest: '. . . doctors are now selling medicines – so we cannot go on filling the company with people of secondary education.'

It is fair to note at the same time that, while this view was found in Sri Lanka, as well, a counterargument also existed. Some managers felt it their duty to the country and to socialism to keep places open for the less qualified, while the Salaries and Cadres Commission of 1974 observed that 'it would not be correct to deprive candidates with [O levels and A levels] of an opportunity of being considered for assignments for which they are academically qualified' by giving preference to those with a degree (Government of Sri Lanka, 1974, Pt II, p. 4).

The interest of this sense of obligation is that it is a little at odds with the image of the private enterprise as an organisation dedicated exclusively to economic rationality. Capitalists, too, can apparently act from compassion. They can also act from vanity or pride. Three of the companies in Mexico were concerned to have a fully professional image, partly in order to improve their prestige and standing with their clients. To this end they had begun a process of 'professionalisation', that is, demanding full university qualifications from their senior personnel. Their attitude is reflected among the professions in Britain (listed by Watts, 1973) and those in Ghana, Sri Lanka and elsewhere (see, for instance, Godfrey and Bennell, 1980), which interpret educational entry requirements as indicators of social ranking. A more important aspect of these observations is that the overt play of non-technical factors in technical decisions further loosens the correspondence between education and job functions.

PAYING THE MORE EDUCATED MORE

The very vagueness and indecisiveness of these possible explanations of why employers seem, on balance, to prefer the more educated only sharpens another question: why do the more educated seem to be paid more? Are employers really paying for nothing? The answer is again complicated by differences between employers.

An easy distinction can at once be drawn between public and private employers. The public employers can be divided into three kinds. One comprises public services like the Mexican, where each department and agency is apparently permitted to regulate its recruitment and salaries within its overall budget, and where appointments depend largely on political connections. Here qualifications and salaries seem too discretionary (or arbitrary) to warrant much discussion: people appear to be paid more by their political usefulness than by any other criterion.

The second group comprises those public services which are regulated by a central agency. In these, particularly where European patterns are retained, salary tends to be governed by educational qualifications, not actual function. Examples have been cited earlier. Whether the more educated are more efficient or more productive is not a matter which is officially discussed, and certainly not systematically examined. These employers may well be paying for nothing.

Third are the public enterprises, which in their official remits have at least to pay for themselves and preferably create surpluses which can be applied to their own and other development. In some states – for example, Tanzania – they are strictly compelled to keep their qualifications and remuneration in line with those of the public services. Hence, they too tend to pay for qualification, rather than function, and may be paying for nothing. Elsewhere –for example, in Ghana and Zambia – the public enterprises are permitted to regulate their own salaries – and often pay more than private enterprises – but have or tend to retain the structures and hierarchy of the public services. In so far as they select over-qualified people, they, too, tend to pay for nothing. The consequences are not frequently serious, because any losses made are covered by subsidies from the government.

Within the public sectors, then, paying for qualifications is simply customary: its costs have not been reckoned. None the less, where certain cadres once open to the less-schooled have been eliminated and their functions subsumed by the more educated (for example, Ghana, Kenya, Tanzania and Zambia), there is an implicit judgement that the superior efficiency of the latter justifies both the extra cost and the removal of employment opportunities from the former. Concurrence with that judgement was strong, but not overwhelming in Kenya, Tanzania and Zambia, where 71, 50 and 50 per cent respectively of employers' groups *dis*agreed that 'The office ran just as well with primary school-leavers as clerks and secretaries, as it does now with secondary school people doing the same jobs'. Whether the judgement is tested or not, the fact that it is widely accepted is enough to ensure that the 'premium' for extra education will continue to be paid by public employers.

Private organisations, on the other hand, seem less inclined to make the premium automatic. Rather, they are likely to decide on an approximate rate for the job and pay within that rate, whatever the qualifications offered. That is, while they might prefer the more educated taken by and large, they are not willing to pay more for them. But then how is it that the more educated tend to earn more with private employers? This is a product of two common phenomena. One is that private employers, which are comparable to public ones, tend to pay more for jobs (see, for example, Bennell, 1981): it can happen, indeed, that a university graduate doing a bookkeeper's job with a multinational company earns more than a graduate doing an accountant's job with the Ministry of Finance. The second is that, because they pay more, private employers can ask for higher qualifications. Why they want higher qualifications is, of course, the question to which the answer has proved slippery: they just seem to like them, even if they cannot explain precisely why.

PREFERRING GENERAL OVER VOCATIONAL EDUCATION

Employers were equally inarticulate in explaining another preference, that for general over vocational education. There was a hint earlier that general education appeared a sound preparation not only for clerical and administrative jobs, but also for those demanding more specifically occupational skills. Indeed, the higher a job in a particular occupational hierarchy, the greater the amount of general schooling required for it. For example, dispensary assistants need less schooling than nurses, who need less schooling than doctors, before they are admitted for training for their jobs. Concomitantly it is frequently impossible to be promoted from one level to a higher in an occupational hierarchy by virtue of experience and further on-the-job training. As a Sierra Leone Salaries Commission remarked, no amount of experience would enable a dispensary assistant to become a fully qualified medical doctor (Government of Sierra Leone, 1957). Further, even where such promotion is possible in principle, it is both infrequent and inhibited by competition from more-educated people eligible for direct entry at higher levels. The consequence is that accepting vocational training, rather than general education at a lower level, may debar a person not just from further general education, but much more importantly from professional advancement as well.

The preference is most readily illustrated by the public corporation in Zambia, which undertook a comprehensive job evaluation. It could be exemplified from other states and employers as well, but INDECO will suffice to make the point. The most obvious and striking feature in Table 2.5 is the disparity of value between 10 + 2 training and 12 (O level) which have parity of time. O level is accorded 25 per cent greater value than the training. Less obviously, the years spent on general junior secondary schooling are accorded 33 per cent more value than those spent on training (two years of training are given half the credit of three years of school). Similarly, two years' training after O level are awarded 10 points; but four years' university education, 30 points. Why functions which require training should be valued less than those which are thought to require general schooling could not be made clear.

Partial exceptions to this tendency were the employers of Mexico. They were willing to accept nine or twelve years' general education only for the most junior clerical posts, which demanded little more than the skills of literacy and numeracy. For anything

Table 2.5 *Comparison of Weights Given to Education and Training in Job Evaluation in a Parastatal Corporation, 1982*

Years of education/ training *A*	Points awarded *B*	Points per year *C (B/A)*	Differential value: points per year* *D*
7 (primary)	10	1·43	—
7 + 2 training	20	2·22	0·39
10 (junior secondary)	30	3·00	0·78†
			0·52†
10 + 2 training	40	3·33	0·17
12 (O level)	50	4·17	0·59‡
12 + 2 training	60	4·29	0·06
16 (degree)	80	5·00	0·36

* The figures in this column are calculated by subtracting the points per year for a lower quantity of education and training from those for the next higher quantity and dividing by the number of years of difference between the two quantities. Thus the differential value per year for 7 + 2 training over 7 (primary) is $\frac{2·22 - 1·43}{2} = \frac{0·79}{2} = 0·3$ points.

† This differential value exists between 10 (junior secondary) and 7 (primary).

‡ This differential value exists between 12 (O level) and 10 (junior secondary).

Source: JASPA, 1982, p. 141, table 30.

higher, they required occupationally oriented studies. Three-quarters of them held that general education at a university was inadequate even for general administration. The proper preparation for administrators or managers lay in accountancy, law, business administration, or in the case of the engineering companies, in engineering itself. Perhaps in response to this not only are Mexican universities overwhelmingly oriented to professional studies, but there are a great number of private colleges offering credentials in 'white-collar' studies (Brooke *et al.*, 1978, p. 21).*

It is not to be thought that vocational studies are unimportant. On the contrary, there is an increasing tendency everywhere for employers to look for – or provide – vocational training after general education. Indeed, 'vocational' university studies seem

* Nevertheless, social background remained important. Brooke *et al.*, 1978, found employers which preferred partially qualified university students to fully qualified diplomates of polytechnics, because of the 'cultural deficiencies' of the latter.

increasingly to be more handsomely rewarded than general studies by public and private employers alike. None the less, that does not explain the paradoxical behaviour of employers in offering professional advancement more surely through general, rather than professional, education at the lower levels.

A second paradoxical point is the attitude of employers to the inclusion of general education in the training of employees. Whereas public employers in Africa and Asia may encourage and assist employees to study for further general qualifications (in their own time) – and recognise eligibility, even priority, for promotion in the event of success – they tend to confine their programmes of in-service training to professional topics. Private employers (see especially Hallak and Caillods, 1980, p. 289) seem to consider post-engagement general education a waste of time and resources.

Why should general education be so important *before* employment, so dispensable after? The apparent inconsistency suggests, perhaps, that what is valued is less the education as such, and more the identification of either superior ability or more desirable social background. Those who go into early and low-level vocational education might be deemed either to be less able academically or from relatively disadvantaged (culturally undesirable) families. Unfortunately, again most employers seem not to have given the issue any careful thought.

QUALIFICATIONS ESCALATION

The tendency to prefer the more-educated concords, of course, with observations that the educational qualifications of those holding jobs seem to be influenced more by the supply of qualifications than by the needs of the jobs. Echoing the OECD (1970) a decade later, Psacharopoulos and Sanyal, surveying five states come to the following 'hint': 'The educational composition of the labour force of a given country is to a large extent supply-determined' (Psacharopoulos and Sanyal, 1981, p. 21). Hallak and Caillods (1980), looking at four further states, draw the same impression. Of Srivastava's Indian employers, 84 per cent concurred with a similar opinion (Srivastava and Oxenham, 1978). One of Brooke's Mexican employers said simply that, as more people with more education were becoming available, not to utilise them would be stupid (Brook *et al.*, 1978).

Taking the uncertain link between jobs and qualifications along with the informal preferences for and the universally increasing supply of the more-schooled, yields an expectation that the formal minimum qualifications for jobs will inexorably raise. The references listed above substantiate that this is, indeed, the case in almost every state investigated.* On the other hand, the limits of the preference and the variations between employers suggest that the process would be slow and uneven. Some employers may prefer to stick to the old qualifications, while others may raise them; in some states the numbers graduating from schools and universities may grow only slightly faster than the numbers of jobs becoming available in the modern sector, whereas elsewhere they may outpace the latter drastically. The following sections look at a few of the factors that seem to influence the pace and degree of qualifications escalation.

Distance Travelled and Quality of Performance

An interesting feature to note in passing is the difference between school systems with decentralised certification (Mexico and Liberia) and those with centralised examinations (WAEC, Kenya, Sri Lanka, and so on). Where the former prevail, employers tend to ask simply for proof of graduation – the amount of schooling or distance travelled is important. Little account is taken of marks or grades. Standardised examinations, however, enable employers, particularly governments, to be more discriminating. They can take the quality of performance into consideration.

In Gambia, for instance, a multinational employer raised the minimum qualifications for clerical jobs from six to eight years' primary schooling to four O levels (11 years' schooling), including passes in English and mathematics. It recruited thereby from a minority of a minority and, in effect, imposed a steeper escalation than appeared at first sight. A double-sieve operated. It seems, then, that – when a level of education is available only to a minority – recruitment is largely by level. As the level is expanded, quality of performance is introduced as a refinement. When even high-level performance is relatively common, the level itself is superseded by a higher one. A classic example comes from Sri Lanka. A public corporation had seven vacancies for production assistants. The minimum qualification was set as six O levels, with credits in mathematics, physics and chemistry. There were 11,000 and more applicants! So the corporation board shifted the

* JASPA (1981) found Somalia to be an exception.

qualifications to A levels and decided that they would remain as the minimum acceptable in the future (JASPA, 1982, p. 54; Deraniyagala *et al.*, 1978, p. 51).

Planned Escalation

None the less, not all escalation is of this variety. Some of it can be said to be part of policy and plan. In Gambia, Ghana, Kenya, Sierra Leone, Tanzania and Zambia (and probably other states with similar histories) the British origin of the public services had imprinted a common assumption: the 'proper' minimum entry for government service was eleven or twelve years' schooling, rounded out with a variable number and combination of passes or credits, but always including English language and most often including mathematics as well. Recruiting personnel of lesser calibre was a temporary measure, to be discontinued as the better qualified became available. So it has been implemented. Minor clerical and secretarial cadres requiring only six to nine years' schooling have been gradually deemed 'obsolescent' or 'wasting', and phased out. In this sense there has not been an escalation, but rather the remedy of a deficit.

More Complex Content

Similarly, with advancing modernisation, changes in the content of jobs or increasing sophistication in techniques might well explain escalation. Employers in Kenya (52 per cent), Tanzania (90 per cent) and Zambia (65 per cent) agreed that 'Qualifications for jobs rise, because changes in the jobs require better-educated people'. The odd feature in that array, however, is the higher measure of agreement in the states, where the modern sector of employment has been stagnating for some years, and the even split in Kenya, where the growth and diversification of such employment has extended furthest. In Mexico, an eminent newly industrialising country, only six out of thirty-three employers (18 per cent) advanced technical change as a cause of escalation. Of these, half offered entirely convincing examples of need, the others seemed a trifle specious: 'Before it used to be completed *primaria* for cleaners, but now they have machines for cleaning the floors, so we have to look for people with a little more [education].' In Sri Lanka no employer mentioned it. The overall impression is that changes in job content explain very little of qualifications escalation.

Supply Pressures

This would mean that most of the phenomenon is caused by pressures not related to job needs. Nearly two-thirds of Srivastava's Indian respondents agreed that escalation reflected a lack of relationship between the level of education and job functions (Srivastava and Oxenham, 1978). Close to 90 per cent agreed that escalation occurred because more and more people with higher qualifications were presenting themselves, while jobs were not proliferating *pari passu*. The Ceylonese were similarly solid in agreement. Of the Kenyan and Zambian employers, 68 and 81 per cent respectively concurred, but they were joined by only 40 per cent of the Tanzanians. The Mexicans were asked what they thought was behind escalation. Fewer than half offered any answers at all, though they acknowledged and documented that it was going on. Only six of them (18 per cent of the whole sample) offered an answer that suggested an imbalance between the educated and the availability of jobs. One, indeed, had a novel interpretation of the idea. New technical and production posts were opening up, but skilled technicians were not available to fill them. The only solution, then, is: 'If you want a topographer, you get an architect; if you want a boiler technician, you get an engineer' (Brooke *et al.*, 1978, p. 63).

Related to the rising numbers of qualified people is the use of escalation to narrow the pool and costs of recruitment. An example of this was given for Sri Lanka and it could be amplified by other instances in that country. However, only half the Indian employers were prepared to agree that 'Qualifications for jobs were deliberately increased to overcome the increasing pressures on jobs' (see Srivastava and Oxenham, 1978, pp. 57–69). And no similar instances were found in Mexico or any of the African states. Evidently Sri Lanka was an extreme case, illustrating that employers' practices will vary according to the pressure of a particular situation – and showing the lengths to which they can be driven.

Professional Status – Conspicuous Consumption

However, the earlier discussion of preference suggests that a further pressure for escalation may be a hankering after prestige. Brooke found seven (21 per cent) of his employers somewhat concerned about having a 'professional' image. Even more concerned are the professional associations. In Sri Lanka they may need to cut down on applicants, too, as the Institute of Chartered Secretaries confessed, but elsewhere it is more a question of maintaining status (and the price of services). The Ghana Bar Association made a university degree compulsory in addition to professional certification, but 'It is however worthy of note that the degree must not necessarily be a law degree'. Similarly, the Ghana Institute of Journalism, while still requiring only five O levels, advertised that some of its members had A levels and even university degrees (see JASPA, 1982, p. 56). No argument is made that these attainments are necessary to the job: they are just 'nice to have'.

Falling Educational Standards

In Sri Lanka, too, came the complaint that qualifications had to rise, because educational standards were falling. There were grumbles also from Mexico about the reliability of educational certificates. Similar dissatisfaction could be inferred from 82 per cent of the Indian employers, who felt that schools and universities had not succeeded in making people productive. Among the African employers, however, there was a good deal less complaint: only 19 per cent of the Kenyans, 30 per cent of the Tanzanians and 35 per cent of the Zambians felt that educational standards were falling; and only 13, 20 and 38 per cent respectively agreed that qualifications were rising as a result. By and large, then, in the states examined, the declining quality of education is not thought to be an important factor in the escalation of qualifications.

Causes Undecided

In sum, although employers almost everywhere acknowledge that the educational requisites for jobs are rising, they do not agree among themselves on what the main causes are. However, majorities, or at least large minorities, seem to think that the phenomenon is not necessarily a bad thing – in Kenya, Tanzania and Zambia 64, 60 and 58 per cent respectively (a rare consensus among the three groups) deemed it decidedly good. At the same time, similar proportions would be prepared to admit that qualifications rise simply because people with higher qualifications are available.

Brakes

Counterbalancing this is the observation that minimum qualifications are not pushed up quite as fast as the higher qualifications appear. Certainly, it is true that in the Philippines, Sri Lanka, Tanzania, Ghana and Mexico qualifications like primary and junior secondary schooling have lost almost all value in securing modern jobs. None the less, it is equally true that, while people with fourteen to sixteen years of education have been competing with some success for jobs open to those with twelve years, the qualifications have not been raised. The earlier discussion on the limits of the preference for the more educated substantiates the point. (Further examples can be found in JASPA, 1982, pp. 107–12.) Why should this be so?

In part, especially among the private employers, it reflects a belief that people with less education can do certain jobs as well as people with more. In part, it reflects a transitional and pragmatic nervousness about the continuing availability and stability of the more educated. Concomitantly there is a suspicion that the more educated will be restless for higher pay and quicker promotion in simple virtue of having more schooling than their workmates. And in part, especially among public employers, where salaries are governed by qualifications not functions, there is resistance to an automatic (and substantial) increase in the cost of a job. There is a connection here with the system of examinations: where the quality of performance can be used as a discriminator, public employers will try to raise qualifications by performance – which entails no cost – rather than by level – which might be expensive.

CONCLUSIONS

The overwhelming impression from the evidence surveyed in this chapter is that there is no neat and universal explanation of how employers come to determine the educational qualifications for jobs. The expectation of consistency within large organisations which try to be rational is disappointed. The almost universal absence of systematic matching makes it more appropriate to think in terms of a theory composed of unexamined assumptions, rules-of-thumb, inertia and narrowly considered responses to changing circumstances. Governments would be subject to such a theory quite as much as other, less influencial employers. Before proceeding further, a summary catalogue of the findings will be helpful:

(1) Virtually all employers believe that schooling, especially literacy and numeracy, does help fit people for work in the modern sector. Here they accord with the concept of human capital and the principle of investing in human resource development. They accept that schooling yields both social and private returns.

(2) Proportions of employers believe that the more schooling people achieve, the fitter they are for the more responsible, better-paid work of the modern sector. Similar proportions, however, have their doubts. The latter regard the schedule of correspondence between jobs and education a factitious and rickety convenience. The former extend the idea of human capital; the latter again suspect the legitimacy of the extension.

(3) Proportions of employers believe that scholastic ability is positively associated with the capacities needed by jobs in the modern sector. They believe also that the process of schooling does tend to discriminate reliably between those more and those less scholastically able and, therefore, between those more and those less likely to work well in the modern sector. Similar proportions, however, suspect that the association is too weak to be reliable. The former support the screening-by-ability theory of schooling, the latter are hesitant. Both, nevertheless, accept the idea of human capital as well: that is, schooling both sorts out and improves abilities.

(4) Considerations of social class do seem consciously, and not always covertly, to affect the hiring policies of many employers. Equally they seem not to affect those of many other employers. What social biases might be revealed by analyses of their workforces are interpreted as the repercussions of the distribution and utilisation of educational opportunities, rather than as the effect of an employer's deliberate policy. However, admission of social bias does not preclude an employer from simultaneous belief in both human capital and ability screening. It is possible to seek an employee combining a particular social class, with a

particular level of education, and a particular quality of achievement.

(5) What qualifications are required for jobs do seem to be influenced by what qualifications are available. However, they are not wholly determined so. The availability of higher qualifications does not necessarily assure the selection of the higher qualification nor, more fundamentally, does it necessarily secure the raising of the educational requisites.

(6) Proportions of employers are prepared to argue that more educated personnel tend to be more productive. Similar proportions, however, are prepared to deny it, while yet other proportions are agnostic.

In sum, there is consensus on only one point, the desirability of some schooling for employment in the modern sector. Apart from that, the relative importance of 'adequate preparation', 'pool of ability', or even 'political screening' and 'social screening', or the 'surplus supply of qualifications' is subject to dispute and variation. The factors which will apparently induce variation are the ethics, prejudices and habits of particular societies and their subsocieties; the ways in which particular occupations, industries and employers are organised; the relative scarcity both of modern sector employment generally and of particular jobs; the relative importance of a post to an employer; and the political climate. In order to make better sense of the evidence let the stance of the employer be adopted. For simplification, let the technocratic assumption be adopted that all factors are equal, except the educational qualifications of candidates for several posts, which have varying importance and remuneration, the educational requisites for which have not been predetermined but which are open to young persons with no previous experience of employment.

Employers are operating in conditions of uncertainty; their agents need to identify those young people who will

(a) perform certain functions adequately;
(b) fit into certain patterns of oranisation;
(c) get on with certain groups of personnel.

They need ways of distinguishing between those more and those less likely to satisfy the three requirements. The advancing bureaucratisation of work creates both the need and the pressure to use rational and impartial ways of distinguishing between the applicants. If, like most employers, this one has not developed ways of its own, its agents must look at what the applicants offer. Certified scholastic attainment presents itself for obvious use. Witness the responses of the Kenyan, Tanzanian and Zambian employers to the statement 'Education is the best information available about a young applicant with no work experience': 97 per cent agreed; there was solid consensus across the three states. Educational credentials are ready to hand. They form a convenient starting-point. To use them to make a first distribution between people, either by performance or by level, is accepted as non-arbitrary and fair. It follows that the schedule of correspondence is similarly accepted as a reasonable instrument of discrimination. Further, if schooling does cumulatively sharpen all abilities, but does not distinguish between endowments of abilities, then it does make sense to use schooling as a first screen. More refined methods can be applied later to identify the job-specific abilities. Naturally, too, it makes sense to prefer those who have both the job abilities and the extra education.

However, because it is indeed a convenience and because there is no tested basis for equating jobs and scholastic attainment, the employer might choose to start his search at the lowest credential presented or, if the supply and price permits, at a higher level. That is to say, the starting-points and operations of schedules of correspondence can differ from employer to employer – and, hence, from time to time, from occupation to occupation, from region to region and from state to state.

Because the employer is using what comes to hand, he can operate satisfactorily, however the educational attainments are certified. Where schools are allowed to graduate their own students and are unreliable, the employer need not press for greater consistency – and, indeed, does not. Instead, employers will simply want evidence of certification, although some will try to identify schools whose credentials can be trused for either cognitive or social, or both, reasons. Where central standardised examinations are conducted, the employer can be more finicky, discriminating between the number of subjects passed, the number of sittings needed to pass, the nature of the subjects passed and the quality of performance in particular subjects. In both cases it is of no relevance to the employer whether primary education means five or seven years' schooling; junior secondary, eight, nine, or ten years; full secondary, ten, eleven, or twelve years; and so on. All that matters is the availability of a legitimate instrument of preliminary discrimination.

Nor need an employer take into account the social consequences of its demands for qualifications. Escalating the requirements of a job from eight or nine years of junior secondary to eleven or twelve years of senior secondary schooling may cost an employer little or nothing – and may perhaps add something to its workforce. That such a step may reinforce public demand for what might be unnecessary schooling and so possibly distort government expenditures further is an argument an employer can counter on two grounds. In the first place, the action of a single employer is not likely to carry much weight in a national economy. Secondly, as has been shown earlier, such a step is likely to be taken only when the supply of the higher qualifications has already reached the proportions of a surplus. The employer is simply recognising an already well-established situation, and is by no means creating a new one.

Similarly, from the viewpoint of theory, the employer also is not interested in the balance of explanation between human capital, ability screening and the surplus supply of qualifications. Whether schooling makes a young person more able, or whether more able young people utilise more schooling, or whatever might be the mix between inherited ability and the effects of school, is not a question which need preoccupy the employer; for its sole purpose is to locate suitable personnel.

However, there is one exception. A government is not simply an employer, it is often the biggest employer in an economy and its behaviour can set and alter trends and conventions. It acts simultaneously as educator and investor of public resources. To the extent that it wishes to act responsibly and equitably in all three roles a government needs continuously to review whether its patterns of resource allocation achieve an optimal balance of advance towards its various objectives. Since supplying educational services is an allocation which takes a major proportion of a government's resources, the balance between the theories is obviously important.

To date, virtually all governments have assumed the validity of the schedule of correspondence and its supporting belief that more and more schooling develops higher and higher manpower for the modern sector. Those which have attempted manpower planning equate a level of manpower directly with levels of schooling: university equals high; secondary school with training equals middle; and primary school with training or simple secondary school equals low. Their recruiting practices and salary scales are consistent with such planning. This has justified and continues to justify policies of expanding secondary and tertiary schooling at great expense, while primary schooling expands rather less rapidly and remains in large part of conspicuously poor quality and efficiency.

If, however, screening by ability were a more reliable assumption, the schedule of correspondence would collapse, along with the entire basis of much current manpower planning. Rationed and differentiated *general* educational preparation would give way to universal and standard general preparation followed by far greater emphasis on careful selection and occupational training. The policy implication would demand a shift of resources from high-quality secondary and tertiary education for a few to high-quality primary schooling for all, and more varied, extensive and flexible occupational training both pre- and in-service.

If, in addition, the surplus supply of qualifications were a more powerful influence on the level of educational requisites than the verified needs of jobs, a government could consider reducing the demand for higher schooling by reducing its own requisites, by ceasing the engagement of even the barely overqualified, or by introducing some form of qualifications tax. Part of the resources so released might be allocated to the development of better methods of identifying the kinds of abilities needed for particular jobs and careers and the development of more efficient institutions for improving the efficiency of manpower.

So much for the viewpoint of ordinary employers and governments. What implications might be drawn for governments as educators, for processes of education and their reform? It seems clear that the link between schooling and salaried employment is uncertain. Using the school to recruit and select employees involves a considerable degree of arbitrariness, and the general qualifications set for particular jobs seem to lack defensible foundations. It follows that, if the diagnosis of the 'diploma disease' is accurate and if education really is distorted by qualification orientation, then distortion is unjustified and needless. It would not be, after all, a necessary evil. On the contrary, the necessity would have been established for dissolving the schedule of correspondence and for insulating education from selection for employment.

Chapter 3

Education, Earnings and Productivity – the Eternal Triangle

ANGELA LITTLE

> education is the principal instrument for providing the skills
> required by the economy and also for improving the overall
> levels of efficiency, productivity, technological and
> managerial performance of the labour force. (Republic of
> Ghana, *Five Year Development Plan*, 1977)

> The contribution of education to development is obvious. It
> shows itself in the formation of qualified individuals; in the
> ability of a people to absorb and produce technological
> innovations and raise the level of productivity on the job.
> (Luis Echeverrîa, President of Mexico, 1973)

> when it is considered how much more competently any job
> could be done with a little more education than a little less,
> educated youth are a national asset in whatever numbers they
> exist. (J. E. Jayasuriya, Professor of Education, Sri Lanka,
> 1964)

The proposition that education is directly related to productivity
is a truism so deeply self-evident that few have thought to question
it. Chapter 1 discussed human capital theory, which is
encapsulated in the quotations above. The theory has entrenched
the belief that more education will lead to increased productivity
in all jobs in all sectors, in all corners of the globe. The belief

sustains and reinforces the activities of education and manpower planners. In turn, these activities perpetuate the belief.

The doubts raised by the considerations of surplus supply, screening by ability and social screening have had little impact on policies for either manpower or education, even though the ravages of the 'diploma disease' are widely acknowledged. As Chapter 1 pointed out, this is natural, if human capital theory is essentially right, that is, if more education through schooling does in truth cumulatively make people more productive.

This chapter* will probe that central belief. It will not, as has been often done, try to measure productivity by earnings in wage/salary employment (see, for instance, Psacharopoulos, 1973, 1980), even though there is a strong and universal positive association between education and such earnings. The reason, as Chapter 2 has intimated, is that the link between educational and salary levels is too often set by arbitrary and variable decisions. Systematic measurements of job needs, performance, or actual productivity are rare. Further, if schooling does enhance productivity, its effects should be traceable not only in salaried employment, but also in self-employment, as Jamison and Lau (1982, p. 3) note in opening their study on farmers and education. Consequently, the focus here will be on two questions: (1) are the educated more productive?; and (2) do earnings closely reflect productivity?

ARE THE EDUCATED MORE PRODUCTIVE?

During the debate about education and income scattered research findings began to question the assumption that more education led to greater productivity. These research studies produced evidence from modern sector employment and from the agricultural economy, and used measures of productivity other than income. For example, Berg (1970) in his provocative book entitled *Education and Jobs: The Great Training Robbery* amassed a number of studies, suggesting that people with fewer years of formal education performed no worse and sometimes even better than fellow-workers with more education. He looked at the relationship for groups of workers *within* several different modern occupations in the USA, including bank clerks and research

* This chapter is an extension of an earlier paper on the same theme; see Little, 1980.

scientists. The measure of productivity of the bank clerks was the number of accounts lost and, in the case of research scientists, a supervisor's estimate. In India Fuller (1972) compared company efficiency ratings and educational levels for workers in two modern factories. In one factory there was no relationship between the number of years spent in formal school education and efficiency ratings while in the other there was a small positive relationship. In Kenya Godfrey (1977) examined the relationship between formal educational qualifications and the performance of candidates on government trade tests in engineering, wood-working, building, tailoring and electrical skills. His data illustrated the 'small significance of schooling in explaining test performance' and reinforced 'widespread doubts about the relevance of what is learned in schools to the jobs that most people end up doing'.

In the agricultural sector, too, some research studies suggested that the impact of education on productivity was not as direct as had once been thought. Chaudhri (1974) examined the relation-ship between educational level and agricultural productivity, measured by gross value of yield of crop per acre at state, district and household levels of analysis for three Indian states. Data analysed at the first two levels showed a positive relation between education and productivity but at the individual household level the results were inconclusive. Heijnen (1968) found that even eight years of primary education had very little effect on the productivity of individual farmers. Heijnen's measure of productivity in his study of farmers in the Mwanza district of Tanzania was the farmers' knowledge of cotton growing techniques, such as knowledge of planting time, spacing and use of fertiliser. The farmers' educational background ranged from no education to standard 8. Heijnen concluded:

the growing methods of the primary school leavers hardly differ from the techniques employed by peasants with less or no education at all. Such differences as do exist can mainly be attributed to the negative influence of the growing practices of some older illiterate peasants, who openly admit that they 'feel too old for these things'. (Heijnen, 1968, p. 150)

These isolated findings reported during the 1960s and early 1970s threw into question the assumed relationship between education and productivity and encouraged us to undertake our own study of that relationship in the modern sector of employment.

Three Modest Studies

The Institute of Development Studies research programme on employers and education included forty-seven microstudies of the link between level of educational qualifications and productivity in private and public modern sector enterprises in Ghana, Mexico and Sri Lanka.

In Ghana we examined the relationship between education and productivity for nineteen groups of clerical workers; in Mexico for ten different workgroups, ranging from security guards to computer programmers; and in Sri Lanka for nine managerial-level workgroups and nine clerical-level workgroups.* Our measure of productivity was a supervisor's estimate.

Supervisors were asked to describe the job carried out by his/her subordinates in detail and to define the qualities of subordinates considered necessary for low and high productivity. Rather than being asked to respond to external, imposed and possibly alien standards, supervisors were encouraged to offer their own criteria of productivity and its determinants. The technique used to elicit these criteria was a sociopsychological technique, known as the 'repertory grid' (Kelly, 1955). After rating subordinates on different criteria, supervisors were asked to give an overall rating of performance. This was used as the measure of productivity. At no time during or preceding the ranking procedure were supervisors given any hint that this was a study of the relationship between education and productivity. Education data on the subordinates were collected later from personnel files, along with data on previous work experience, years with the firm, and so on.

The number of subordinates per supervisor, though generally small, was in most cases large enough to be subject to meaningful statistical analysis. The range in years of education between people doing the same job for the same supervisor averaged 6·2 years in Ghana and Mexico and 3·9 years in Sri Lanka, in all cases a significant proportion of the maximum education cycle.

* The research data in Ghana were collected by Salina Adjebey and Kofi Agyeman; in Mexico by Nigel Brooke; in Sri Lanka by Mahinda Perera and Byron Mook. The Mexico and Sri Lanka country studies are reported in full in Brooke *et al.*, 1978, and Deraniyagala *et al.*, 1978 respectively; the method in Oxenham *et al.*, 1975, and literature and methodological reviews in Little, 1974, 1977.

Results

Table 3.1 shows the correlation between educational level and productivity for the forty-seven workgroups, together with some basic data for each workgroup. Column 1 describes the type of work performed by the members of the workgroup. Column 2 indicates whether the enterprise is from the private sector or the government sector. Column 3 lists the number of subordinates in each workgroup, column 4 the range in years of educational levels of the subordinates and column 5 shows the rank correlation (Kendall) between the education level and productivity measure.

Table 3.1 shows that there is no consistent positive relationship between level of education and productivity for a variety of different types of work. Certainly, there are a few strong positive relationships – the group of Mexican government public relations officers and one group of private sector clerks in Sri Lanka, for example, but the size of coefficients range from +0·71 all the way through to –0·89. The average size of correlation for all forty-seven workgroups combined is +0·023. Of the correlations which do reach statistical significance, four are negative and only two positive.

The simple correlations between education and productivity which we have presented in column 5 of Table 3.1 do not, however, tell us immediately whether there is, or is not, a real connection. Real correlations between two variables are often disguised, because of the confounding effects of other variables. One might expect, for example, that experience on the job would correlate positively with productivity but that experience would correlate negatively with education, that is, that older, more experienced workers would have less schooling. This would be expected particularly in times of rapid educational expansion and qualification escalation. If experience *did* correlate positively with job performance and negatively with education, then any real correlation between education and productivity would be disguised. It is necessary, therefore, to compute a partial correlation, that is, the correlation between education and productivity, holding experience constant. Partial correlations were computed for forty-five of the forty-seven workgroups for which experience data were available. The partial correlations are shown in column 6 of Table 3.1. They too, demonstrate the lack of a consistent, positive relationship between education and

	Sector	N	education	Red.p	exp.	work	Sector	N	education	Red.p	exp.	work	Sector	N	education
k	Government	5	6	0·36	0·18	Map draughtsman	Government	8	2·5	-0·07	-0·12	Clerk	Government	6	7
k	Government	7	6	-0·57	-0·42	Public relations officer	Government	6	4	0·60	0·55	Clerk	Government	4	2
k	Government	12	5	-0·05	-0·01	Timekeeper	Government	7	6	0·21	0·11	Clerk	Government	6	4
k	Government	4	6	0·32	0·71	Price inspector	Government	7	9	0·41	0·40	Clerk	Government	7	2
k	Government	8	5	0·33	0·52	Ticket agent	Private	7	5	0·10	0·10	Clerk	Government	5	5
k	Government	7	5	0·53	0·50	Security guard	Private	6	6	-0·24	-0·23	Clerk	Private	6	2
k	Government	6	7	0·00	0·00	Clerk	Private	8	9	0·26	0·18	Clerk	Private	4	5
k	Government	8	7	-0·32	0·08	Computer programmer	Private	8	8	0·04	-0·25	Clerk	Private	6	5
k	Government	8	6	-0·04	0·06	Salesman	Private	6	3	0·00	0·16	Clerk	Private	8	8
k	Government	8	6	0·35	0·37	Sales manager	Private	6	10	-0·20	0·03	Manager	Government	5	5
k	Government	6	5	0·37	0·51							Manager	Government	4	5
k	Private	5	7	-0·45	-0·47							Manager	Government	5	2
k	Private	15	6	-0·20	-0·12							Manager	Government	5	5
k	Private	5	7	0·29	0·86							Manager	Government	6	5
k	Private	5	7	-0·89*	-0·94							Manager	Private	5	5
k	Private	5	7	0·56	-0·81							Manager	Private	5	4
k	Private	5	7	0·50	—							Manager	Private	8	7
k	Private	8	6	-0·54	-0·31							Manager	Private	5	2
k	Private	8	7	0·15	0·31										

·05 (Kendall)

productivity. The partials range from +0·86 to –0·94, the average size of coefficient being 0·05.*

Critics of our work will immediately point to (1) the unreliability of using supervisors' subjective estimates of productivity, and (2) the fact that a supervisor's own level of educational qualification may affect the way he or she evaluates subordinates. Perception biased by 'qualifications envy' might distort a 'true' judgement of productivity. The first criticism can be countered with data from the Mexican research. In three firms more 'objective' data were available on worker productivity from their respective personnel departments. A private airline company measured the productivity of its ticket reservation agents by the number of airline tickets sold; a government agency measured the productivity of its map draughtsmen by the distance travelled per month, by marker-pens, with a weighting for the type of terrain covered; and a private sector engineering company measured the productivity of its computer programmers by their 'programming velocity'. In all three cases educational level failed to correlate positively with the objective measure of job performance.

The second criticism about the impact of the supervisors' own education level on their judgement about their subordinates' productivity can be examined via the Sri Lankan data. In Sri Lanka data on the educational levels of the supervisors were available. The eighteen workgroups were divided into two groups. In the first group the supervisors' qualification was greater than or equal to the highest subordinate qualification. In the second group the supervisors' qualification was less than the highest qualification in the group. There was no difference in the pattern of correlations between education and productivity between the two groups. In summary, then, our data suggest that the contribution of education to productivity is by no means 'obvious'.

It should be pointed out, of course, that we have not proved that education contributes nothing to productivity. To claim that would be absurd. First, we have been dealing with a restricted range of education levels. In all three countries every member of every workgroup had completed at least primary-level education; in no case were we dealing with people who had no or only minimal education. Secondly, we have been examining a particular range of jobs – clerks, managers, public relations

* The partials must be treated with caution, since sample sizes are very small.

officers, security guards, and so on. We do not know how our findings would generalise across other groups of workers. Thirdly, we have been examining the relationship between education and productivity *within* particular levels of job; we have not examined the relationship *across* different levels of job. Indeed, to have examined the relationship between education and productivity across a range of jobs in an economy (in terms other than income) would appear to be a practical (though perhaps not theoretical) impossibility. How does one compare the real productivity of a clerk with that of a turner or a personnel manager or a shopkeeper?

Fourthly, we have concentrated on the individual characteristics of education and experience, and examined these in relation to productivity. In so doing we have ignored the effects on productivity of factors external to the individual which may be present to different degrees for the different individuals, or else present to the same extent but interacting in different ways with different individuals. Take the example of clerks. Although six clerks may be performing very similar worktasks, office-space constraints may require that two pairs share desks, while the remaining two clerks have a desk each. Productivity differences may simply be related to the amount of space one controls. On the other hand, six clerks may appear to be working under very similar space conditions, a bustling, active, open-plan office. Some clerks may find that this atmosphere 'suits' them, others may find it distracting and would prefer the seclusion and privacy of a smaller room. Occupational psychologists and sociologists have for some time been pointing to the endless lists of organisational factors which can affect individual productivity: for example, decision-making processes and communication links between organisation members; internal promotion prospects determined by performance and not by the personal or political whim of the supervisor; job involvement; job satisfaction; the physical layout of work; and on-the-job training programmes. Individual productivity should not be viewed simply as a product of an individual's past experience and education. Productivity emerges out of an interaction between an individual and a social and physical environment.

However, these four points should not detract from the overall message of our data. The range of modern sector jobs studied does cover widely different functions and responsibilities from routine operations to high-level supervision and planning. It should also be borne in mind that there was considerable overlap between jobs in the educational qualifications of workers. If the relationship between education and productivity is uncertain in this variety of jobs, its nature elsewhere can at least be called into question.

Recent Reviews of the Literature

That the relationship is now seen as problematic is evidenced by a number of reviews which have recently appeared, sponsored by major international organisations. The World Bank has published a review of the available literature on the link between education and agricualtural productivity (Lockheed *et al.*, 1980), on education, income and productivity in urban areas (Berry, 1980) and on primary schooling and economic development (Colclough, 1980); while the International Institute for Educational Planning (IIEP) has reviewed the recent evidence on the contribution of education and training to production in the urban traditional sector of the economy (Hallak and Caillods, 1981). These reviews are synthesised by Lewin *et al.* (1982).

Education and Agricultural Productivity

The review of farmer education and farm efficiency by Lockheed *et al.* (1980) provides a very comprehensive synthesis of the available literature. The authors concentrate on thirty-one data-sets on farmer productivity in low-income regions in Africa, Asia, Europe and Latin America. They examine the relationship between the number of years spent in formal education and agricultural productivity, measured either by crop yield or crop-yield value. Out of these thirty-one data-sets, a positive relation between education and agricultural productivity was demonstrated in twenty-five and a negative relation in six. The authors estimated a mean gain in output for four years of primary education of 7·4* per cent, that is, just under 2 per cent per year of education.

The positive results are impressive but it should be remembered that the measures of productivity vary between studies. Lockheed *et al.* (1980) discuss the problem of comparing studies which examine inter-farmer differences in the *quantity* of output with those that examine the *value* of output, since a value of a crop is dependent on price structures prevailing in a district. It is unclear,

* Jamison and Lau (1982, p. 8) give this figure as 8·7 per cent.

however, how many of the thirty-one data-sets analysed used quality of output and how many value of output. And in those studies which did measure productivity via output value it is unclear whether price structures have been adequately controlled for. Although the studies 'typically' use data from the same locale (in which case one can assume that the price structure is constant), *some* of the studies clearly compared data and, presumably, crop values from different locales (Lockheed *et al.*, 1980, pp. 113, 116).

A separate analysis divided the data-sets into those where the general environment in which the farmer was working was either modern or non-modern. A non-modern environment was indicated by 'primitive technology, traditional farming practices and crops and little reported innovation or exposure to new methods'. A modern environment was indicated by 'the availability of new crop varieties, innovative planting methods, erosion control and the availability of capital input such as insecticides, fertilisers, and tractors or machines, market-oriented production and exposure to extension services'. The results were impressive. The relationship between education and productivity was much stronger under modern than under non-modern conditions: 'The mean increase in output for four years of education under traditional conditions was 1·3 per cent compared with 9·5 per cent under modern or modernising conditions.' The contribution of education to productivity under non-modern conditions, then, is fairly small but under modern conditions its contribution is marked.

These findings represent an important step forward in understanding the role of education in promoting productivity. What they suggest is that there is a statistical interaction between education and factors such as the availability of new crop varieties, fertilisers, exposure to extension services, and so on. The relationship of education to productivity is strong and positive only when certain levels of these other factors are present. In a later study of three data-sets from Korea (South), Malaysia and Thailand Jamison and Lau (1982) confirm the indications discussed above. They estimate that one year of additional education increases agricultural output by the following percentages (ibid., p. 10, table 1-1):

	(%)
Korean farmers using mechanical power	2·22
Korean farmers using no mechanical power	2·33
Malaysian farmers	5·11
Thai farmers using chemical inputs	3·15
Thai farmers using no chemical inputs	2·43

These are important findings in support of human capital theory, particularly as they suggest that there is an increasing and cumulative benefit for every additional year of schooling.

An extended inference suggests, then, that a farmer with a postgraduate degree would be vastly more productive than one with no schooling at all. Unfortunately, the samples of farmers in the three countries appear to have comprised only primary school graduates. Whether secondary and more schooling would have had any similarly cumulative effects is not ascertainable. However, the IDS evidence above would put the possibility in question.

We have here something of a conundrum. Increasing primary education does appear to affect agricultural productivity (even though it is no longer much use for gaining entry to salaried employment). Within salaried employment increments of secondary and tertiary education do not appear to have much effect on productivity. Is there, then, a law of diminishing returns to schooling? Fewer than four years of school are insufficient for an important effect; five to eight years have a noticeable impact; beyond that, does the impact diminish? The question will occur again in a moment.

There is another conundrum. All the studies reviewed in this section have taken as their dependent variable increased agricultural productivity measured either through yield or yield value. An interesting extension to this relationship is provided by studies of agricultural productivity and education in the Philippines by Halim (1976), and in Mexico by Bautista (1981). Halim found that the more educated not only seemed to produce more from 1 ha of land, but also made large incomes in *off-farm* activities. Bautista, on the other hand, found that although farmers with six years or more of primary schooling did not produce more per hectare, their off-farm incomes were again greater. The intimation seems to be that, while there may be limits to the effects of schooling within agriculture itself, advanced schooling may multiply opportunities for increasing incomes. This recalls, of course, the earlier discussion about possible interactions between the person, his/her potential and the environment.

Education and Modern Sector Productivity

However, these positive findings for primary education in modern agricultural areas do not as yet generalise across modern urban areas. Research on the relation between education and productivity in urban areas poses a number of problems, many of which have already been described. Perhaps the most obvious one is the measurement of productivity. Income measures are confounded by many factors other than productivity. And if one confines oneself to more 'objective' measures, then one is compelled to examine the relation between education and productivity *within* particular job categories. It becomes impossible to say whether, for example, a lawyer is more productive than a welder, and then to compare their educational levels. All one can do is to compare the performance of people performing the same or very similar jobs, and to resist the temptation of generalising these findings *across* the entire structure of urban jobs. Comparisons of productivity within jobs have been made in our own research; and also in the research of Berg (1970), Fuller (1972) and Godfrey (1977), described earlier.

Those studies covered a variety of jobs – from bank clerks to factory workers, to trade apprentices and research scientists. Recently a review by Avalos and Haddad (1981) on the impact of teacher qualifications on student outcomes confirmed the mixed results of the earlier studies on the impact of qualifications on modern sector productivity. Higher educational qualifications do not always (or even usually) promote higher levels of productivity.

Other reviews of modern sector productivity fail to find further studies which measure individual productivity other than through the proxy of income level (Berry, 1980). Some studies, however, have attempted to measure productivity at the firm, rather than individual worker, level. Layard *et al.* (1971), for example, compared firm-level output in the electrical industry in England with the proportions of qualified personnel employed. The proportion did not affect firm output, but it did seem to be related to technical change. Newer products were being produced in firms with the highest proportion of qualified personnel. Perhaps this is the important aspect of productivity overlooked by previous studies. Though the more educated may not perform well-defined and static job requirements any better than lesser-qualified peers, they *may* have developed the potential for creative and innovative responses to changing economic conditions.*

Education and Productivity in the Urban Traditional Sector

An attempt to draw together the research on the contribution of education to productivity in the urban traditional sector has recently been made by the IIEP (Hallak and Caillods, 1981). They review studies by the World Bank on education and entrepreneurship in the 1960s; by PREALC† on the informal sector in Paraguay, Ecuador, the Dominican Republic and Mexico; by Nihan on Mauritania and Togo; by Aryee on Ghana and by Van Dijk on Senegal. In none of the studies reviewed was there a clear and direct relationship between educational level and productivity (measured by the firm's income) in a wide range of jobs in the traditional or informal sector.

Of interest, however, is the suggestion from the Ghanaian study that there is, first, a threshold effect, and then a diminishing effect for education. Aryee (1976, 1980) examined the effects of no formal education, primary (six years), middle (ten years) and technical education (fifteen years) on the gross output and gross earnings of heads of manufacturing enterprises in the informal sector of Kumasi, Ghana. The gross output and gross earnings of heads having no education were compared with those having primary, middle and technical education separately. In all cases the comparisons were positive. But only the comparison of middle school education proved statistically significant. The next largest coefficient was provided by technical education. The suggestion here, then, is that the relationship between education and productivity is S-shaped. It is gradual and slight up until middle school level, where it becomes optimum. Thereafter it levels off.

However, the precise level of education which makes a significant impact on productivity also seems to depend on the kind of work in which one is engaged. This point was demonstrated by one of the PREALC† studies in San Salvador. Educational level was related to income but the precise level of

---

* For a very similar conclusion in the British plastics processing industry, see Walsh *et al.*, 1980, p. 79.

† PREALC, Progama de Empleo para America Latina y el Caribe, 1978.

education necessary to bring about a significant rise in income varied by branch of activity. In basic services, for example, having more than three years of education, made a major contribution to income level. In repair and construction services that major change came with the completion of primary education, whereas in regular commerce a significant leap in income occurred both after ten to twelve years of education and then again after thirteen years or more. It is difficult to tell from the report of this study, however, which workers in which branches of activity were considered to be in the modern and which in the traditional sector. Moreover, we are not told whether educational qualifications were a necessary minimum for the achievement of any of the jobs, and if so, whether educational qualifications were tied in an institutional way to income levels. Outside of the agricultural sector then the results for the relationship between education and productivity remain equivocal.

Indirect Evidence on the Link between Education and Productivity

The evidence reviewed so far suggests that the impact of education directly on productivity is mixed, and inconclusive. Data from the agricultural sector are more convincing than from the modern sector. However, a separate set of studies relevant to the question are reviewed below. These examine possible *indirect linkages* between education and productivity. They attempt to answer the question *how* might education contribute to productivity. The studies cited cover (1) the contribution of education to attitudes and values, and (2) the contribution of education to health. Although the links between health and productivity and attitudes and productivity are not examined in any of the studies, both are none the less plausible determinants of increases in productivity.

Education and its Non-Cognitive Outcomes

As our earlier section on the rationales of educational plans showed, education has always been seen as a 'socialiser', as a process which encourages 'desirable' social and political attitudes. Certainly, there does seem to be ample evidence that differences in educational experience are associated with differences in adult attitudes. Inkeles and Smith's large-scale survey (1974) of the values and attitudes held by 6,000 men in Argentina, Chile, India, Israel, Nigeria and East Pakistan pointed to the very strong association of school experience with 'modern' values and attitudes. 'Modern men' were defined as those who

(i) take an active interest in public affairs; (ii) exercise their rights and perform their duties as members of a community larger than that of the kinship network and the immediate geographical locality; (iii) keep to fixed schedules; (iv) observe abstract rules; (v) make judgements based on objective evidence; (vi) defer to authority legitimated not by traditional or religious sanctions but by technical competence; (vii) show a readiness to adapt to innovation; (viii) display a tolerance of diverse backgrounds of others; (ix) display persistent efforts and confident optimism and show little tolerance for fatalism and passivity.

These were the characteristics required of men to work in modern institutions in a modernising world and formed the modern pole of a modern vs traditional scale of individual development. Years of school experience proved to be the most powerful predictor of modernity, when compared with the effects of factory experience and exposure to the mass media. One year of schooling led to median gains on the modernity scale of 1·6 points for rural-origin factory workers and of 1·9 points for urban-origin factory workers.

Others point to a rather different set of attitudes, values and behaviours associated with school experience. On the one hand, punctuality, obedience, conformity, a sense of duty and deference to authority are highly valued in modern large-scale organisations – and are 'reproduced rather faithfully' in the school. On the other hand, attitudes and behaviour such as creativity, curiosity, independence and co-operative groupwork are not highly valued in the typical workplace and are, therefore, not encouraged in schools (Bowles and Gintis, 1976; Illich, 1971; Dore, 1976). Although the empirical base for many of these effects is American, there are a number of sources which offer cross-cultural evidence in support of the general position (see, for instance, Torrance, 1965; Brooke and Oxenham, 1980; Lewin, 1981).

Education and Health

There is considerable evidence on the impact of education and literacy on a number of different health indicators: infant and child mortality, life expectancy and nutritional standards (Cochrane *et al.*, 1980), all of which could be expected in the long term to lead to increased productivity. The evidence on infant and child mortality suggests that a wife's education has a larger total effect on mortality than that of her husband, but that the combined effects of both parents being literate (as compared to having no schooling) may be such as to reduce mortality by up to twenty-seven per 1,000. Secondly, there is evidence that maternal education not only reduces child mortality, but also improves the health of the survivors: children of more-schooled mothers tend to be better nourished.

Health, of course, has at least two separate components. The first is physical health encompassing all the indicators mentioned above. The second is mental or psychological health. Limited evidence from some developing countries in this under-researched area suggests that the level of the mother's education does have an impact on the rate and type of psychological development of the child (Levine, 1980).

Not only is there evidence on the impact of the mother's education on psychological development and nutritional status, there is also evidence on a link between these two dependent variables – nutrition and psychological development. Brozek (1978) reviews the available data and concludes that there is a causal link between the two. However, the supposed causal effect of nutrition on psychological development is not undisputed (Warren, 1973; Palmer and Barber, 1981).

Summing-Up the Effects of Education on Productivity

The evidence on the link between education and productivity to date points to a mixed picture. The data on education and agricultural productivity are reasonably conclusive. Education does seem to make a difference when other factors in the environment are changing simultaneously. The evidence on productivity in the urban sector is too scattered to provide generalisations. The evidence on modern sector productivity is also not compelling. Studies of the urban traditional sector and of the urban modern sector are hampered, because of the difficulty of measuring productivity. However, even if one can show that differences in education are unrelated in the modern sector to differences in productivity, one must *not* conclude that education does not matter. Studies in the modern sector generally involve workers *all* of whom have received primary education. Therefore, it is impossible to examine whether or not primary education has an impact on productivity – only whether different levels of secondary education make a difference.

Other studies on education and attitudes, and on education and health, were cited because of their plausible link in the long term with productivity. The data on the link between education and health were particularly compelling.

DO EARNINGS REFLECT PRODUCTIVITY?

We turn now to the second question posed in the introduction to this chapter. To what extent do earnings data reflect productivity? There are at least two problems associated with using earnings as a proxy for productivity. The first is that earnings are a product of a number of factors other than productivity. The second is that the relationship between education and earnings is often 'institutionalised' in the sense that the possession of a qualification itself entitles one to higher pay without productivity necessarily having to be demonstrated.

Earnings Do Not Necessarily Indicate Productivity

The first problem can be examined with an example from Sri Lanka (Deraniyagala *et al.*, 1978). The salary structure for clerks provides a good example. In one public sector firm there were three grades of clerk with three associated salary scales:

grade 1   Rs 312·50 – 15 × 12·50 – 7 × 15 – Rs 606
grade 2   Rs 425 – 20 × 15 – Rs 725
grade 3   Rs 800 – 10 × 40 – Rs 1200

A clerk entering grade 1 starts at Rs 312·50. The salary rises by Rs 12·50 annually for fifteen years, then by Rs 15 annually for another seven years. Clerks who enter the organisation from the outside are usually appointed to the bottom grade and to a point on the scale appropriate to their qualifications and experience. These decisions are taken *before* a new recruit starts the job, and *before* he or she has a chance to demonstrate his performance ability. Thereafter increments in salary are awarded mainly for seniority and work experience. There are just two ways in which performance and productivity can affect one's salary. The first is that performance on the job can affect the transition from clerk grade 1 to clerk grade 2. Most organisations operate formal efficiency bars in theory. However, in practice the efficiency bar often refers to 'minimum efficiency', rather than 'maximum efficiency'. One would have to demonstrate positive demerit not to be promoted from grade to grade. The second way that job performance can affect income is via increments awarded specifically for merit. Extra increments are sometimes awarded for additional responsibility or for conspicuously good job performance or for obtaining qualifications. Alternatively, annual increments may be withheld for conspicuously poor performance or attendance. In the public sector especially, however, most increments are awarded automatically for simply staying in the job over time.

A study cited by Berry (1980) is instructive here. He cites the work of Medoff and Abraham who studied managerial and professional employees in two large American corporations. A strong positive relationship was found between experience (seniority) and earnings but a very low or a negative relation between experience and productivity as measured by supervisor ratings. Productivity was apparently not tied closely to earnings even within job grades.

It is clear that performance criteria do bear *some* relation to earnings in the sense that salary increments are sometimes awarded for good job performance and withheld for poor job performance. But the other factors which determine the level of earnings other than merit-incremental earnings are many. This is especially true when one is considering the relationship between education and productivity across job categories. Trade union or professional association pressures and international job market pressures are just two of these factors. A third very important factor is the issue of the job itself. Certain jobs appear simply to be more productive than others. That is to say, irrespective of the educational qualifications of the incumbents of the jobs, the jobs themselves determine the level of income one can expect to earn – even when that income is tied closely to actual output. This finding generalises across the self-employment sector and the modern sector (see, for example, Hallak and Caillods, 1981; Aryee, 1980; Brooke *et al.*, 1978; Salmi, 1981).

The Institutionalisation of the Link between Education and Earnings

The second problem associated with using earnings as a measure of productivity and then showing that education is related to earnings, and then arguing that education has 'caused' the earnings, has to do with the 'institutionalisation' of the education–earnings link. The case of clerks again provides a good example, but this time the example comes from Kenya (JASPA, 1981). In the Kenyan civil service there are sixteen separate job grades and associated salary scales. Clerical officers are placed in job group D with an associated salary scale of K£399 – 5 × 18 – 5 × 21 – £594 p.a. The initial salary point is for people who are promoted from junior clerical officer. The third point at K£435 is for new entrants who have just graduated with secondary school EACE* qualification and with no work experience. The seventh point at K£510 is for those who have 'completed form 6 standard of education at a recognised secondary school' but who do not possess the advanced-level qualification, the EAACE.† This means they have either failed or have not taken the advanced -level examination. The ninth salary point at K£552 is for those who do have a satisfactory EAACE. Clearly, from a private economic point of view, it makes sense to stay in school, rather than to get a job. JASPA (1981) considers the cases of three young people, A, B and C, all with the EACE qualification. Imagine a situation where A becomes a clerical officer immediately, while B and C continue to study for EAACE. B completes the course but does not obtain a certificate. C obtains a certificate. At the beginning of the third year after the EACE, A would earn K£471, B would earn K£510, while C would earn K£552. In other words, A would have two increments for two years of satisfactory work, B would have *four* increments for two years of school without a superior qualification, while C would have six increments for the same two years of school plus an advanced-level qualification. One year of education at school, therefore, is at least twice as 'valuable' as one year of education at work and may be even three times as valuable.

In other words, all three would be performing the same job but their pay would reflect their qualifications. It should come as no surprise, therefore, to find that education is correlated with

* EACE – East African Certificate of Education, taken after an eleven-year course of seven years' primary and four years' secondary schooling.
† EAACE – East African Advanced Certificate of Education, taken two years after EACE and so entailing thirteen years of schooling. Both titles are now obsolescent, following the dissolution of the East African Examination Council in 1980.

earnings. Whether their earnings or their education is related to their productivity has, of course, never been examined.

The Link between Productivity and Earnings Defended

These two challenges to the use of earnings as a proxy for productivity – the first that earnings are determined by many factors other than individual productivity, and the second that the link between qualifications and earnings has become institutionalised in some occupations – have, of course, themselves been challenged. Psacharopoulos (1980), for example, argues that the relationship between social productivity and education has been vindicated, because of the several studies (mentioned earlier) on education and agricultural production. In those studies agricultural production, if measured by gross yield rather than by market value, gives a close estimate of real productivity. However, while this may be a valuable comment *à propos* the agricultural sector, it does not necessarily follow logically that earnings are a good proxy for productivity in the modern sector of organised labour and capital.

A second argument might object that the two examples from Sri Lanka and Kenya have been taken only from the public sector, whereas the modern sector comprises also a private sector. While organisations in the public sector may not be profit-maximising, firms in the private sector surely are profit-maximising. Organisations in the private sector would not go on paying a person a high salary if he or she was not demonstrating a supreme level of productivity. There is obviously some mileage in this argument, but even it, too, is vulnerable to an objection based on organisational size. Private sector firms, when they grow in size, become more and more bureaucratic. Functions within them become more and more specialised. Personnel functions become separated from, even alienated from, accounting functions. If the man in charge of organisational profit knows little or nothing about the individuals producing that profit, how can individuals expect to be fairly rewarded for their individual efforts? Of course, as we have said before, a person who clearly falls below a certain minimum expectation and annoys everyone in the process will not be tolerated by the organisation as a whole and will soon be 'cooled out'. But the vast majority of people will be tolerated and few will worry about their precise level of performance. This will be true both in the private and public sectors and may be a function of size of organisation as much as market orientation. The impact of size of firm on the relationship between education and earnings has recently been demonstrated in the USA. Stolzenberg (1978) examined education, earnings and employer size data for a sample of 690 American respondents from the Michigan 1973 Quality of Employment Survey. The earnings rates of return to schooling increased as the size of the employing establishment increased. The rates of return varied from a low of 0·90 per cent where establishment size was small (one to nine employees) to 5·00 per cent where establishment size was more than 500 employees. Might it be that employers in close contact with their employees see less advantage in education *per se* than employers who do not know their employees well, but who need to find some rules for legitimating salary differentials?

CONCLUSIONS

It is likely that the controversy over the contribution of education to productivity rather than earnings will continue throughout the next decade. Doubts about the precise value of certain types of educational provision are already widespread. But those doubts should not be interpreted in a totally negative way.

We hope that the data from our studies and from those others working on education and productivity in the urban modern sector, the urban informal sectors and the rural sectors will be used in a constructive way in the controversy. In particular, the following six challenges and questions seem to flow from these studies.

Getting Qualifications

When employers, large or small, insist on particular qualification levels for particular jobs, what are the reasons lying behind the insistence? If they are asking for a particular level of qualification simply because it is a convenient way of cutting down a large number of applications to a manageable size, then let us not deceive ourselves that this action will necessarily have anything to do with increased productivity in the future. Its main effect will probably be of increasing the pressure from the clients of the education system for more and more qualifications. It will not be the employers' problem, but it will be the education system's problem. If, on the other hand, the employer believes that by raising the education and qualification level he is thereby ensuring a greater level of productivity, then he may be mistaken and would do well to evaluate his recruitment and selection behaviour before actually demanding higher qualifications.

Keeping Productivity and Earnings Distinct

That productivity and earnings are not necessarily the same thing should, by now, be clear. The distinction may not be a useful one for conventional economic planners but it should certainly help those of us who are not economists to understand what the economist is trying to say. For the most part, the economist is talking about the earnings returns to investment in education and not necessarily the productivity returns to investment in education. The latter, of course, are extremely difficult to assess. The distinction between productivity and earnings should also help us to separate out theories about why education is related to productivity from theories about why education is related to earnings. Those two sets of theories have been confused in the past. The confusion which has ensued may turn out to have been due more to the fact that the theories were trying to explain different things in the first place than to major intellectual differences between the theories themselves.

Alternatives for Improving Productivity

We hope that doubts about the strength of the link between education and productivity will stimulate people to question what are the other ways besides education of improving productivity. Education often seems to be given the sole responsibility for ensuring that productivity improves. We listed earlier just some of the organisational factors which can affect it, for example, decision-making procedures, communication links between organisation members, promotion procedures, in-service training programmes, and so on. The list is endless. If the unfulfilled promises of education over the last two decades have anything to tell us, it is that if education is to contribute to productivity, then other factors must also change simultaneously. We saw this point illustrated very clearly in the World Bank review of education and agricultural productivity in non-modern and modern environments. Education did have a contribution to make but only when other aspects of the environment were changing simultaneously.

Education, then, may be a necessary but certainly not a sufficient condition for the achievement of increased productivity.

Redistributing Income

The distinction between productivity and earnings may also help to add a new impetus to the discussion about education and income redistribution. It may help to free the discussion of the effects of education from the causes of income distribution. It may allow for a wider discussion of both the effects of education other than income effects and the causes of income-distribution patterns other than education. It may enable people to take more seriously Jencks's (1979) most recent conclusion from his synthesis of *Who Gets Ahead?* and *Inequality*: 'if we want to redistribute income, the most effective strategy is probably still to redistribute income' (Jencks, 1979, p. 311).

Quality and Quantity in Education

The future controversy about education, productivity and income will also, hopefully, consider the qualitative aspects of the education variable as well as the quantitative aspects. To date all studies on education and productivity have examined only the quantitative aspects of education. Education has been treated as a continuous linear variable. Ten years of one person's education has been considered to be equal in its effects to ten years of another person's education. In fact, the quality of those two ten-year experiences may have differed radically. The cognitive learning outcomes of those two ten-year experiences may have been quite different. One person may have ended up with a package of problem-solving abilities at his or her fingertips. The other may have ended up with a store of useless, irrelevant factual information.

The non-cognitive learning outcomes may also be radically different. A student with ten years of education from one district may be a member of that district's elite. Another student with ten years of education from another district may be no different from his age-peers. In that district all young people may have ten years' education. He may consider himself to be simply one of the educated masses. What impact may these two experiences have on the students' self-esteem; on their need for future achievement; on their attitudes towards peers in the workplace; on their attitudes towards income redistribution; on their need for power; on their need to control others? Like the list of factors associated with increased productivity, this list too is long, and very under-researched. It is time those concerned with education stopped counting the numbers of university graduates produced each year, and started to ask what those graduates have learned – apart from how to get a degree.

An Ideal–Empirical Research Solution

Finally, the only solution to the research question about the impact of a wide range of different educational experiences on productivity in all branches of economic activity lies in a number of widescale 'experiments' in which unknowing employees of wide educational backgrounds are selected for different kinds of work by unknowing personnel officers, who pay employees strictly in accordance with perceived or even 'actual' performance. Then we could really examine the effects of one on the other. Of course, the employers would have to be guaranteed large risk-taking monetary guarantees – just in case the poorly educated were too unproductive. But then again if they were *so* unproductive, the employers would not be paying them very much anyway – or would they?

Part Two

The Effects of
Selection on
Education

Chapter 1 discussed the need for occupational selection and suggested how the present pattern of selection by education evolved. Chapter 2 showed that the schedule of correspondence between jobs, salaries and education was inconstant and even inconsistent, with little systematic, empirical basis to justify it. Chapter 3 went further, demonstrating that attempts to verify the presumed empirical basis have had only limited success. They have raised the possibility of an S-curve or diminishing returns to additional schooling beyond a threshold. That calls into question the validity of the schedule of correspondence. However, all this is simply to say that employing organisations may not be using ideal means to select employees.

Whatever its academic interest, the issue is of practical importance only if what the employers do, really does adversely and severely affect education and prevents the cultivation of thinking, problem-solving, humane citizens and productive manpower. The next three chapters accordingly devote themselves to curricula and classrooms. The first focuses on the educational institutions which are intended to guide, support and assess schools. It examines the extent to which selection might constrain the formulation, implementation and evaluation of improved curricula. The following two are more intent on the users of schools –the pupils and their families – their perceptions of the value of education and their responses to the selection function. They do not, of course, neglect the teachers, who are the interpreters of educational and social values to the pupils.

Underlying all three chapters is the question of the actual mechanism through which the employers' influences are felt. The qualifications which learners earn and educators grant is the proof of eligibility required by employers. Two major patterns seem to govern its distribution, the Sino-European and the North American. In the first students are tested by one or more relatively centralised authorities, which indicate the syllabuses to be studied, lay down the criteria to be satisfied and administer examinations to test what learning has been achieved. The certificates subsequently issued carry a standard value. The second pattern decentralises the assessment of scholastic performance by delegating certification to individual schools. Only regulatory and supervisory functions are reserved to the central authorities. Whether the certificates awarded by the schools have a standard value depends on whether the teaching profession observes the norms closely or the regulating authority succeeds in enforcing them.

A main advantage of centralised examinations for employers, aspiring employees and ambitious educators is that they facilitate comparisons between schools and individuals. It is possible to identify schools which consistently achieve good examination results, can promise their students higher probabilities of success and assure employers of reliable employees. It is also possible to rank students by the quality of their examination results. As examples in Chapter 2 illustrate, examination marks can make a vital difference between earning and losing eligibility for ranges of desirable salaried jobs.

The harm of centralised examinations is said to spring from the restrictions they will impose upon curricula, teachers and students. Teachers are unwilling to teach, students resist learning matter outside the purview of the examiners. For their part, these last are constrained by the techniques available to them and can manage to examine only a tiny part of the field of education. Considerations of local relevance, creativity and practical problem-solving appear to be beyond their grasp. Their almost inescapable bias is to encourage the most mechanical, boring and debilitating forms of teaching and learning. However overdrawn and outdated these objections appear, a study by Lewin and Little (JASPA, 1981, Vols 1 and 2) of examination papers from eight African states suggested that they retain an uncomfortably large measure of substance, even in 1979 and 1980. The old Ghanaian scholastic injunction, 'Chew, pour, pass, forget!', had not yet been discredited by the advances in examinations technology.*

Trusting the schools to certify their own students should, by contrast, free them also to pursue better education. Guided by the broad principles of the central authority, and stimulated by their own professionalism, teachers should be better able to see and respond to opportunities for creative thinking, orienting the syllabus to the local environment and community, avoiding a stultifying reliance on facts remote from their students' lives, and on rote memory and dreary drills. The cost of such liberation might be the loss of some standardisation and the ability to make fine-tuned, reliable comparisons between students and schools. On the other hand, the experience of North America and states which have adopted that pattern intimates that employers are at no loss for selecting employees in ways satisfactory to themselves and to the public at large.

That these desirable consequences do not always follow is demonstrated in Liberia. From a pattern of complete decentralisation the state has retreated to a mixed system, whereby schools control two-thirds of the graduation marks and a centralised examination tests for the remaining third (JASPA, 1981). Public pressure persists, however, for the examination to control half the certification. In Chapter 5 Brooke examines the results of decentralisation in Mexico and the results of easy exams in Ghana: in both cases liberation has not led to the blooming of a thousand flowers. On the contrary, it seems to have facilitated the dereliction of professionalism by teachers.

Its effects on the pupils are less clear-cut but seem to encourage the search for minimisation and easy ways out. More dramatically, liberation

* While Lewin's study of Malaysia in Chapter 4 supports the tenor of this paragraph, Little's analysis of some Kenyan papers in Chapter 7 demonstrates that the bias can be counteracted, albeit with strenuous ingenuity and persistence. Somerset's (1982) account of the Kenyan experience is instructive and fascinating.

from selection for jobs altogether seems to incite rebellion against learning altogether, at least among China's urban students, as Chapter 6 recounts. A grave dilemma appears. If the school is used for selection to salaried jobs, it is either crippled by centralised examinations or debilitated by 'satisficing' or 'minimising'. If it is not used for selection, it loses all meaning for large proportions of its students. Whether the situation is quite as extreme as this formulation would have it will be assessed after the next three chapters.

Chapter 4

Selection and Curriculum Reform

KEITH LEWIN

INTRODUCTION

Sri Lanka and Malaysia are two states which award general scholastic qualifications on the basis of performance in centralised examinations. The level of the examinations, numbers of subjects examined and fine distinctions in the marks achieved are all important ingredients in determining eligibility for particular bands of salaried jobs and opportunities for further education. Allegations that the examination tail wags the educational dog and frustrates all efforts to improve education naturally have long histories in both countries. This chapter tests the allegations, taking the two countries as its main cases but drawing also on experience elsewhere. The particular curricula in which reforms have been adversely affected are innovatory integrated science courses. Analysing their fate provides a starting-point for identifying possible strategies for using examinations more positively to promote effective curriculum reform.

This chapter is organised in five sections. The first provides some contextual background; the second examines patterns of curricular development in the two countries; the third explores the influence of examinations on the curriculum-development process through two detailed case histories; the fourth elaborates on some corroborative studies; and the fifth reaches some conclusions based on the analysis.

THE CONTEXT

In Sri Lanka and Malaysia school examinations were first introduced in 1862 and 1865 respectively. They rapidly became a central feature of both school systems and the number of examinations increased as their value in the labour market began to be recognised (Jayasuriya, 1969; Wong and Gwee, 1972). As an official historical commentary recognised in Sri Lanka, all the examinations

> served one main purpose . . . that of screening the candidates for further education or for middle grade jobs . . . Their strength lay in the impartiality (if not thoroughness) with which they discharged their main function. The screen was applied equally to all. There was no room for favouritism or vindictiveness. The validity of the exam could be questioned on the ground that it paid little or no attention to the powers of imagination (as opposed to mere book-learning) or to many aspects of character (as to mere cognitive performances in the artificial setting of the examination hall) but its bona fides were beyond question. (Government of Ceylon, 1972)

The contemporary importance of educational qualifications in Sri Lanka and Malaysia is readily apparent from some simple analysis of labour market statistics. In Sri Lanka, in 1975–6, there were approximately 329,000 new entrants to the labour market and about 49,000 wage and salary jobs available, as Table 4.1 shows.

Table 4.1   *Labourforce Entrants and Number of Available Jobs, 1975–6*

Level of achievement	No. of labourforce	Available wage and salary jobs	
Below grade 9	157,300	7,500 } 16,400 }	23,900 manual
Completed grade 9	145,000 }	8,400 }	25,400
Completed grade 11 and higher	27,000 } 172,000	17,000 }	non-manual
	329,300	49,300	

Source: Ministry of Education and Ministry of Labour statistics, unpublished; see also Deraniyagala *et al.*, 1978.

On the assumption that students reaching grade 9 aspire to non-manual jobs the imbalance of supply and demand is obvious (172,000 job-seekers for 25,400 jobs). In such saturated labour market conditions where much employment is bureaucratised, there is evidence that employers use educational qualifications to limit the numbers of applicants for jobs and every additional qualification increment does improve the chances of an individual of being selected (Deraniyagala *et al.*, 1978).

Table 4.2   *Manpower Supply and Demand: Malaysia, 1976–80*

Aggregate demand by occupational category (wage and salary employment)		*Aggregate supply by educational attainment*	
Professional/technical	65,000	Diploma/degree	35,000
Administrative/ managerial	12,000	Grade 12/13	18,000
	77,000		53,000
Clerical	59,000	Grade 11	315,000
Sales	32,000	Grade 9	390,000
Service	145,000		705,000
Production	190,000		
	426,000	Some secondary	390,000
		Primary only	260,000
Agriculture	142,000		650,000
Grand Total	645,000		1,408,000

Source: Government of Malaysia, 1976.

In Malaysia similar imbalances have developed, though they have been mitigated by much higher economic growth rates and consequent increases in employment. Table 4.2 illustrates the magnitude of these imbalances. For the 705,000 school-leavers over a five-year period with at least grade-9 qualifications, only 426,000 wage and salary jobs were available. Moreover, 650,000 less-qualified school-leavers were on the labour market during the same period. Income differentials associated with different levels of educational qualification in Malaysia are high, and returns to individuals for acquiring more years of education are substantial (Hoerr, 1970; Wilson, 1972). In 1977 earnings in the public sector in professional and administrative jobs were seventeen times higher than those in manual grades (Government of Malaysia, 1977). In the private sector a 1972 survey revealed that average

118/*Education versus Qualifications?*

managerial incomes were 12·3 times those of unskilled factory workers before non-salary income was taken into account. At this time, starting salaries of honours graduates were approximately twice those of grade 12/13 students, four times those of grade-11 leavers, ten times per capita income and thirty times incomes in peasant agriculture (Lee, 1972).

Obviously, in both Sri Lanka and Malaysia educational qualification has become a major factor in determining life chances. Arguably, then, school examinations have come to dominate social-role selection.

PATTERNS OF CURRICULUM DEVELOPMENT

Systematic curriculum development is a recent activity in most countries. Until the 1970s changes in the curriculum in many education systems were generally accomplished through the issue of new syllabuses to guide teaching, which were frequently closely linked to examinations. These usually consisted of lists of content to be covered, and schools were able to interpret them largely as they chose with little direct guidance.

Curriculum development in Sri Lanka first began to be undertaken more systematically with the publication in 1957 of the *Scheme for Teaching in General Science Grades 6–8*. Materials were developed with UNESCO assistance to provide teachers with detailed guidance on methods and content, and this set the pattern for the next decade. This curriculum-development project failed to live up to expectations and had a limited impact for reasons closely connected with educational selection and qualification:

> Science was the focus of public attention but it was access to and success in the GCE 'O' level that was important, not grades 6–8 ... Science teachers (and scarce resources) were preferentially placed in the expanding 'O' level science classes rather than in the grade 6–8 programme. (Wijemanne and Sinclair, 1972)

One positive outcome of the project was the assembly of a group of educators who had acquired skills in curriculum development. A natural progression from the experience was to extend the work to grade 9 and 10 O-level classes. In line with recommendations of the Commonwealth Conference on Science Teaching held in Sri Lanka in 1963 and the emerging priorities of the government, O-level courses were revised and extensive teachers' guides produced for use from 1964. The materials produced deliberately stressed the clear specification of course objectives to permit the revision of examination syllabuses in line with the recommendations of the teachers' guides.

Within two years of 1964 when the budget estimates first included references to curriculum development as a subheading, spending increased fourfold and 100 educators were assigned to curriculum-development activity in various forms. International agencies encouraged these developments and financed the creation of a Curriculum Development Centre (CDC):

> Development of a Curriculum Development Centre is regarded as a matter of high priority. It would provide a sound basis for diversification of the curriculum, especially in Mathematics and Science subjects. A comparatively small investment should yield a high return. (World Bank, 1966)

A CDC was, therefore, established in 1969 and during its first two years it focused most of its work on senior secondary science and mathematics education. After 1971, it was given the task of designing and preparing new curriculum material for all subject areas and at all grade levels as a result of the introduction of a new educational system (Lewin, 1981). Principles and procedures established for the design, trial, evaluation and implementation of science and mathematics programmes were generalised across the curriculum. New curricula were to be accompanied by new public examinations, and the CDC became involved in the construction of pilot-versions of these. Throughout the 1970s the CDC remained the focus of curriculum-development activity, its fortunes fluctuating with changes in the political climate. During this period the practice was consolidated of establishing course teams to design materials, pilot them in schools and evaluate and modify them, if possible, before national implementation. (Government of Sri Lanka, 1976).

In Malaysia a General Syllabus and Timetable Committee was established on an *ad hoc* basis in 1956 to formulate a common national curriculum, and this set the pattern for the next ten years. Subject specialists fed the committee with details of syllabuses which were approved at periodic meetings. No surveys or investigations were carried out to monitor the effects of this process and the committee was dissolved after approving syllabuses in most subject areas. The General Syllabus Review Committee was established subsequently in 1964 to provide syllabuses for the newly introduced comprehensive education system and functioned in much the same way. The first attempts to institutionalise curriculum-development activity came in 1967, when a meeting of chief education officers recommended the establishment of a special department of the Ministry of Education to oversee and co-ordinate all curriculum activity. The new arrangements introduced as a consequence of this were not adequate to cope with the growing workload involved, and in 1972 the Educational Planning Committee was still able to state that:

> To date curriculum change in Malaysia had been largely ad hoc and piecemeal. Efforts to make changes in the curriculum have not always been satisfactory for a variety of reasons. Amongst the most important are –
>
> • no member of a subject committee is involved on a full-time basis;
> • there is limited provision to develop supplementary instructional materials;
> • there is little or no formal evaluation of projects;
> • there is a limited scope for in-depth study of content and of teaching techniques held in current in-service training courses due to limitations of time, space and available personnel, hence implementation often suffers. (Government of Malaysia, 1972)

At this time there were twenty-three curriculum projects underway within various departments of the ministry and communication and co-ordination were becoming a serious problem.

Plans existed to create a Science Education Centre (Government of Malaysia, 1971) in line with the recommendations of various international conferences. These plans were subsequently generalised to include all curriculum development activities in all subject areas and the proposed centre was retitled the Curriculum Development Centre (Pusat Perkembangan Kurrikulum). The UNDP submission for the establishment of a National Curriculum Centre justified its creation by saying:

Curriculum revision and innovation is taking place currently in Malaysia. Limited but significant action has been taken in the fields of Science and Mathematics at the first and second levels of education. It is now recognised that this activity cannot remain limited to the isolated interests and commitments of individuals within the education system. The establishment of a National Curriculum Development Centre will provide an institutional form. This will stimulate curriculum change, revision and innovation. (UNDP, 1972)

This process culminated in the establishment of a national Curriculum Development Centre (CDC) in January 1973, financed by a World Bank loan of M$2,386,000 approved in April 1972, and a further US$565,150 grant from UNDP covering costs of experts, training fellowships, materials and equipment. A planning team, consisting largely of personnel from the Ministry of Education, had been set up in February 1972 with powers to co-opt specialist advice when appropriate. Local experts in education, mainly from the University of Malaya, were consulted in the preparation of plans.

Like the CDC in Sri Lanka, the Malaysian CDC procedures for systematic curriculum development included the production and evaluation of pilot-materials prior to implementation. It also orchestrated arrangement for the support of new programmes and promoted curriculum reform as an activity that involved all aspects of teaching and learning, not merely the production of syllabuses. Throughout this period the CDC worked largely independently of the Malaysian Examination Syndicate, though personnel from the CDC were involved in the construction of items for some public examinations. The pressures on the syndicate to process large quantities of examination scripts rapidly with limited resources, and to maintain high levels of secrecy concerning assessment procedures, militated against close collaboration with materials-development teams. The longer-term adverse consequences of this for implementation have become more apparent with the passage of time.

Curriculum development in both countries, therefore, moved from *ad hoc* arrangements largely circumscribed by the examination syllabuses, towards an institutionalised process where teams of specialists produced detailed materials and guide-lines for curricula. The examination boards retained their separate identity and continued to design and administer public examinations without close co-ordination with curriculum designers.* Though there were some exceptions to this, these were infrequent.

THE INFLUENCE OF PUBLIC EXAMINATIONS ON CURRICULUM REFORM

The importance of examinations for selection guarantees that their form and content are likely to have considerable influence on attempts to change curricula. Although this is almost an educational truism, few authors have tried to document empirically the effects of such influence. By considering case histories of two curriculum innovations in Sri Lanka and Malaysia it is possible to establish, in some detail, what these effects have been in particular instances.

Before undertaking this, it is necessary to recognise that 'influence' is not easy to measure and necessarily depends on interpretations of events and motives that are not always susceptible to rigorous analysis. Nevertheless, it is possible to build a substantial case concerning the kinds of effects on curricular reform that public selection examinations have had by developing a tapestry of inferential data which considers different aspects of the curriculum-development process. In so doing it has been necessary to separate out two different kinds of influence and focus each case history on one of them.

The first kind of influence is that which manifests itself in the *specification and design* of curricula. Designers implicitly or explicitly derive at least some of their definitions of subject-matter and curricula objectives from the existing practices of examination boards; courses designed to match existing examination syllabuses are necessarily constrained in their selection of content and teaching methods; the importance of public examinations for pupil selection restricts assessment strategies to those commonly accepted as legitimate and fair and limits the range of pupil outcomes that can be successfully promoted. These and other factors affect curriculum reform processes when they are conceptualised and translated into materials and programmes of development.

* Similar instances in Africa can be found in JASPA, 1981, where Lewin and Little compare examination papers with curriculum objectives in eight states; in Boakye and Oxenham, 1982, p. 10 *et seq.*; and Oxenham, 1982. See also Chapter 7, by Angela Little, in this volume.

The second kind of influence manifests itself when new curricula are *implemented.* Whatever the effects of examinations on curriculum design and specification, their impact on classroom practice will be mediated by the priorities and achievement criteria of public examinations. Emphasis on content areas and on the acquisition of particular intellectual skills in curricular materials is likely to be a less important determinant of classroom transactions and pupil outcomes than those promoted by the form and content of selective examinations which control access to further education and employment.

The first case history is concerned with the introduction of new curricula in Sri Lanka after 1972. It focuses on the design and development of an integrated science course, paying special attention to the ways in which its conceptualisation and design were affected and conditioned by public examining structures. The second case history is concerned with Malaysian integrated science and highlights the effects of the examination associated with it on the curriculum in action.

Case History 1: Integrated Science in Sri Lanka

The development strategy of the government elected in Sri Lanka in 1970 stressed the development of indigenous resources and policies for a greater degree of self-reliance (Government of Ceylon, 1971). This was reflected in educational policy which was similarly built around concern for the coherent development of indigenous resources:

The present type of education has also placed a premium on examinations and diplomas rather than the development of skills so necessary for economic development. Thus today in nearly all sectors, there is a tendency to depend on foreign technical skills and resources and the foreign expert, and foreign aid has become a substitute for the development of indigenous skills and resources. The present divorce of education from the world of work has uprooted an entire generation from the type of production which can readily be developed in the country and has pushed the person who would normally have gone into some productive activity into a fruitless search for white collar employment, the expansion of which can no longer be supported by the country's productive sectors. (Government of Ceylon, 1971)

An Education Review Committee was established in late 1970 to report on the restructuring of the education system in line with the new government aims. Before it could do so, its deliberations were interrupted by a widespread insurrection throughout the country, apparently organised by disaffected educated youths who were frustrated by rising levels of unemployment and the educational qualifications necessary to secure those jobs that were available. According to one commentator (Wilson, 1973), over 85 per cent of those ultimately detained as a result of the insurrection were Ceylon GCE O-level graduates. Though this observation has subsequently been revised (Obeyesekere, 1974), most commentators placed the burden of responsibility for the insurrection on the education system and, in particular, its inappropriate orientation towards academic subjects and professional jobs:

> The basic shortcoming of the country's educational system is that the academic type curricula are framed to cater to the needs of that small minority of the output of the educational system who, having reached the GCE 'O' level, compete for the very small number of jobs available as doctors, engineers, administrators or teachers. Of the others a small number obtain employment in the clerical, technical and service occupations, while the rest begin the interminable wait for white collar jobs that are not there. Judging from the results it is no exaggeration to say that returns to educational investment have been negligible, if not to say negative. (Government of Ceylon, 1971)

As a result, the embryo proposals of the Education Review Committee were revitalised and progressively announced, resulting in a restructuring of the education system that was more far-reaching than it would have been had not the insurrection occurred (Wijemanne, 1978). Two new national examinations – the National Certificate of General Education (NCGE), and the Higher National Certificate of Education (HNCE) – were announced to replace Ceylon's O and A levels. NCGE was to be held from 1975 as the first selection examination in the education system, at the culmination of nine years of general education with a 'pre-vocational' bias; HNCE was to be held after two more years of schooling, partly as a university qualifying examination and partly as a school-leaving certificate for those who could not be accepted into higher education.

Other changes included raising the school-entry age to 6 years and reducing the total length of pre-university schooling from twelve to eleven years; and abolishing selection for O-level streams in favour of a common curriculum for all students up to grade 9. New curricula were designed for all levels of the school system with the conscious intention of complementing academic content with that which was related to local occupations and which, it was hoped, would provide a useful basis for students to enter into productive employment. Thus, the five-year plan published in late 1971 argued for

> vocationally oriented curricula which are expected to stimulate an interest among pupils in the opportunities available at all levels for engaging in productive activities . . . [The] aim is to shift labour from its present aimless search for non-existent white collar occupations to economic activities which increase the income of the country. (Government of Ceylon, 1971)

Curriculum development certainly did take place and a large number of new courses was produced in a remarkably short period of time. All subject areas of the secondary curriculum required the production of new teaching material to match the aims established for the restructured educational system and the CDC was given the task of doing this. The pattern of work used to redesign O-level science curricula in the 1960s was extended across the curriculum and subject specialists were recruited to teams which wrote teachers' guides and pupils' texts. Unlike the revision of O-level science, which proceeded at a relatively leisurely pace, it was not possible to pre-test material on a large scale prior to island-wide implementation. Less than six months was available for the writing of grade 6 texts, and these were distributed immediately they were available.

In the 1960s conscious attempts had been made to change O-level teaching and learning through changes in the kinds of question included in the examinations, and this principle was carried over into the rhetoric that accompanied the introduction of integrated science in 1972. The introduction by the Secretary of Education to the *Integrated Science Teachers' Guide* recognised that:

> Since the curriculum for grades 6, 7 and 8 was not examination orientated the interest shown by teachers in teaching and by the pupils in learning was not as strong as was required. It is well

known that most of the periods allocated for English . . . General
Science, Home Science . . . were not effectively used.

The solution to this problem was seen to lie in the development of
examinations for all subjects which closely reflected the priorities
of course designers.

A number of factors were instrumental in shaping the new
examinations, the net result of which seems to have been to keep
them largely within existing O-level practice in spite of intentions
to the contrary. Most obviously, there was public pressure to
retain some semblance of comparability with O level, even though
the pupils who would be taking the course were a non-selected
group and the time allocation for teaching was only one-third that
for single-subject O levels. Concern with the competitive value of
the new qualification in the labour market and for further
education exacerbated these pressures. The desire to retain the
overt objectivity of closed book, controlled condition
examinations also acted to limit further the possibilities for
significant departures from traditional formats of examining and
effectively ruled out active teacher involvement in assessment.
Previous experience with a teacher-assessed component of public
examinations had proved controversial and great difficulty had
been found in devising moderating procedures. In Sri Lanka the
traditional written examination has been officially described as the
only way of 'screening the candidates in such a way that
favouritism, thuggery and low cunning are set at nought in
selecting persons for jobs or further education' (Government of
Ceylon, 1972). Practical examinations were eliminated from
consideration as a result of logistic and administrative constraints.

Thus, the O-level pattern of a two-paper written examination,
the first consisting of multiple-choice questions and the second of
structured free-response essay questions, was retained with
modifications to suit changes in content of the new integrated
science course. It remained the case, however, that despite
statements that integrated science should emphasis teaching
scientific concepts, patterns and processes, rather than facts, it was
possible for pupils to pass the final examination through
performance on factual recall items alone. This is shown by the
analysis of NCGE question papers reproduced in Tables 4.3 and
4.4.

Table 4.3 *Classification of Objective Test Items (Paper I) (Percentages)*

	Physics	O level(1973) Chemistry	Biology	Average	NCGE (1975) Integrated science	O level (1978) Integrated science
Knowledge	25	30	72	42	58	58
Comprehension	32	35	20	29	32	25
Application and higher	43	35	5	28	10	17
Affective	0	0	3	1	0	0

Source: Lewin, 1981.

Table 4.4 *Classification of Component Parts of Structured Questions (Paper II) NCGE Integrated Science, 1975*

	(%)
Knowledge	35
Comprehension	46
Application and higher	19

Source: Lewin, 1981.

Performance on pilot-tests using similar instruments to the NCGE produced mean scores of representative samples of pupils of between 30 and 35 per cent (raw score). Pass rates (percentages of candidates passing) in different districts for NCGE integrated science fluctuated between 30 and 60 per cent with most falling between 40 and 50 per cent. This suggests raw-score pass-marks were of the order of 30 per cent. If this is so, candidates would easily reach pass-marks by scoring most or all of their marks on recall questions.

Decisions on the detailed nature of the integrated science course were certainly conditioned, if not determined, by factors associated with its role as an examinable subject of key importance for selection. Though it is clear that there were other considerations, these played a major role in shaping the programme that emerged. As a former director of education observed:

it is a hard fact that in our country each segment in the educational ladder is viewed by the pupils and parents primarily as a route for entry into the next. These values of the clients naturally influence the order of priorities among school authorities. Stipulations laid down for crossing a hurdle are likely to have a backwash effect on what goes before that hurdle. (Wijemanne, 1978)

By examining three aspects of the course, that is, aims and objectives, content selection and course structure, some strong inferential links can be drawn between the form and content of NCGE and the integrated science curriculum.

The aims for integrated science were specified by the Ministry of Education centrally with little consultation and consisted of a comprehensive list of attributes that the course was intended to promote. These included many with a strongly affective element – for example, welcoming the findings of science as adding to the stock of knowledge, supporting scientific activity and being sensitive to situations that demand further investigation; and a number designed to promote basic scientific skills – for example, recording observations and using measuring instruments. The main stress in these aims is on helping students to acquire fundamental scientific concepts and appreciate common applications of them through the teaching of scientific ideas, patterns and principles, rather than through the acquisition of factual knowledge. Teachers are exhorted to use styles of teaching which are characterised by frequent practical activity, pupil-centred approaches, significant emphasis on attitudinal outcomes and open-ended questioning. To this end large numbers of specific objectives were constructed by writing teams for each section of work to provide detailed guidance to teachers. However, these specific objectives seem to have been derived less from overall course aims than from consideration of the content prescribed and from the previous experience of curriculum-writers with O-level courses. Analysis of specific objectives for integrated science yields the pattern shown in Table 4.5.

The emphasis of unit-level objectives throughout all four years is on those that fall in the cognitive knowledge category. The major course objectives do not share the same quantitative emphasis and address themselves most frequently to outcomes in the affective domain – a category in which only about 4 per cent of unit-level objectives fall. Further, higher-level cognitive objectives (at the comprehension and application and higher levels) account for 17 per cent of unit objectives, though they appear as major parts of at least half of the overall objectives. Psychomotor objectives occur infrequently in both classifications. It might be anticipated that over the four years of the course there would be significant shifts in the type of objectives associated with units of the course. The only pattern that does emerge is that knowledge-level objectives are given more prominence in later years of the course. Other shifts in emphasis are not consistent in direction, except for a decrease in the emphasis on psychomotor outcomes. This interpretation agrees with qualitative judgements derived from reading sample units from each of the years. It is particularly noticeable that grade 8 and 9 materials include considerably greater quantities of information formally presented in a way which suggests that acquisition of scientific knowledge is the primary objective.

Table 4.5 *Distribution of Unit Objectives for Integrated Science (Percentages)*

Type of objective	Year 1	Year 2	Year 3	Year 4	All-Year
Cognitive					
Knowledge	48	71	85	70	69
Comprehension	21	4	5	12	10
Application and					
higher	8	5	3	11	7
Affective	3	7	1	4	3
Psychomotor	21	13	6	3	11

Note: The classification system is from Bloom, 1956.
Source: Lewin, 1981.

The unit-level objectives, therefore, fall into a pattern which quite accurately reflects the requirements of NCGE examining. Affective and psychomotor outcomes are not stressed (and are not measured in NCGE); knowledge-level objectives are most common and those related to higher cognitive behaviours are given little emphasis. This quantitative analysis does, of course, obscure qualitative emphases but further analysis of the course did not lead to the conclusion that it presented a misleading representation. It is, therefore, suggestive that – despite the broad curricular aims established – the detailed specification of the course has placed greater emphasis on outcomes most likely to be measured in NCGE examinations.

From analysis of pupil and teacher texts developed for integrated science some further inferences can be drawn concerning the ways in which their structure was influenced by the

NCGE. Tables 4.6 and 4.7 indicate the frequency with which experimental activities are recommended. Later years of the course contain lower frequencies of pupil activities per period, though the last year of the course does display some anomalies in this respect. (When it was recognised that too much material was included in the course, the quantity of grade-9 work was reduced. Taking account of these changes would effectively reduce the value of year-4 indices of pupil activity.) The frequency of teacher demonstrations follows a contrary trend as it increases during the course. There is no systematic evidence that decreasing frequency of experimental activities is compensated by simultaneous increases in the length of time they are likely to take. Since there is no practical examination, it could be argued that this decline in experimentation was consonant with the implicit evaluation of the importance of practical work made by its exclusion from the NCGE.

Table 4.6   *Pupil Textbook Analysis – Frequency of Activities per Teaching Period (Percentages)*

Activities	Year 1	Year 2	Year 3	Year 4
Pupil experimental	0·83	0·58	0·35	0·38
Pupil non-experimental	1·30	0·48	0·62	0·67
Teacher demonstration	0·21	0·03	0·30	0·47

Table 4.7   *Teacher Guide Analysis – Frequency of Activities per Teaching Period (Percentages)*

Activities	Year 1	Year 2	Year 3	Year 4
Experimental total	1·90	1·62	1·37	1·67
Pupil	1·55	1·02	0·53	1·08
Teacher demonstration	0·34	0·60	0·81	0·53

The pupil text includes a considerable number of questions addressed to pupils relating to the work in individual units. When these were categorised according to the source of information from which they were likely to be answered, the data in Table 4.8 was the result. Most questions are answerable from direct observation. Typically these are questions asking pupils to make simple observations of phenomena and experiments. Questions answerable indirectly are also frequently used and these typically ask pupils to draw on their own experience of events outside the classroom. Text-based questions usually require reference to immediately preceding text for a response. It is noticeable that these appear to increase in frequency through the course, while direct and indirect observation-type questions diminish in frequency. This is a quantitative confirmation of the tendency for later work to be less experimental and more closely based on descriptive text which, incidentally, is more likely to form the basis of examination questions.

Table 4.8 *Pupil Textbook Analysis – Questions by Frequency of Occurrence (Percentages)*

Question type	Year 1 Average no./ period	Year 2 Average no./ period	Year 3 Average no./ period	Year 4 Average no./ period
Direct observation	2·44	1·10	1·05	0·03
Indirect observation	1·41	0·75	0·42	0·18
Text-based	0·52	0·63	0·81	0·85
Revision	0·21	0·02	0·23	0·26
Other	0·55	0·38	0·09	0·06

Analysis of the frequency with which definitions were introduced, and principles and laws stated, confirmed the trend towards more formal presentation and increased emphasis on factual knowledge in later years, as Table 4.9 shows. The proportion of text devoted to factual description increased substantially in later years of the course, as that related to student activities diminished, as Table 4.10 shows. This is a quantitative confirmation of the qualitative observation that the need to include material which is examinable through the conventional methods of NCGE led to the inclusion of much information for later recall in examinations.

Table 4.9 *Pupil Text Analysis – Presentation Categories by Frequency of Occurrence (Percentages)*

	Year 1 Average no./ unit	Year 2 Average no./ unit	Year 3 Average no./ unit	Year 4 Average no./ unit
Definitional statements	4·1	3·8	5·7	11·3
Statements of principles/laws	0·3	0·6	0·2	1·0

Table 4.10   *Pupil Text Analysis – Percentage of Text in Four Categories*

		Year 1	Year 2	Year 3	Year 4
1	Descriptive factual	52	69	70	78
2	Activity-related	37	23	25	17
3	Derivation of principles/concepts	6	6	2	2
4	Application of principles/concepts	5	2	3	3
		100	100	100	100

The process through which integrated science was designed was influenced by a number of factors. Three appear to have been more important than others. First, the new course was constructed by educators steeped in the traditions of O- and A-level teaching and examining, working in a context where the pressure was on to maintain 'academic standards'. Indeed, the new courses were to 'equip students with a good general education together with a basic familiarity with one or more vocational opportunities available to them. This does not mean any reduction in academic content' (Government of Ceylon, 1971). Under these conditions it was not surprising that, although early parts of integrated science were innovatory, later units converged back towards the traditions of O-level-type courses. Presentation became formal and didactic, large quantities of factual information were included, and early stress on conceptual learning and experimentation was dropped. The academic definitions of the subject-matter of science became dominant once again.

The second related factor was the continued refusal of local universities to contemplate changes in their admissions standards. These were firmly grounded in notions of comparability with those in the UK. Though it was unlikely that NCGE and HNCE could represent similar levels of achievement to O and A level, since science was taught for one-third of the time available at O level and to unselected pupils, politically it was necessary to argue that it did.

The third factor is associated with the development of the NCGE itself. The format of the examination finally agreed on favoured the articulate, studious and academic student at the expense of the practically skilled and vocationally committed one, as had O-level examining. Since it turned out not to be possible to move away from closed book, fixed time limit, summative testing, many of the process skills and attitudinal dispositions incorporated into course aims remained outside the scope of public examinations and were consequently accorded low priority by pupils and teachers.

The direct and indirect effects of the examining system on the development of integrated science were, therefore, quite substantial. Examinations also influenced the curriculum in action. A study undertaken in Malaysia, also on an integrated science course, illustrates major characteristics of this process.

Case History 2: Malaysian Integrated Science (MIS)

The MIS programme was first introduced in Malaysia, in 1969, and by 1975 was being taught in almost all lower secondary schools (grades 7–9) as the standard programme. The course is based on a series of worksheets for pupils to use in carrying out classroom activities which are to be supplemented by help from teachers. Pupil textbooks have been widely available since 1973. These closely follow the pattern of the worksheets but include additional information and explanation.

The general approach to science education promoted by this course can best be indicated through some exemplary quotes taken from material recommended to Malaysian teachers:

It is suggested that the 'didactic' method should be minimised and the 'heuristic' method utilised wherever possible. (Malaysian Integrated Science, 1973)

In order to achieve the objectives it is essential that discovery methods should be used, involving pupils in carrying out as much practical work as possible. They must be active participators, not passive receptors. (Mee *et al.*, 1971)

The very process of discovering appears to us to be as important as the knowledge discovered. (Scottish Education Department, 1969)*

Pupils [should be provided] with examples of scientific methods so that with sufficient practice they may eventually use them in

---

* MIS was adapted from the Scottish integrated science course. Its materials refer teachers to Scottish publications for further guidance.

new situations without the support of imposed worksheets. (ibid.)

Course aims include nine of the cognitive domain (intellectual skills) of which two relate to the acquisition of knowledge, two to communication skills and five to comprehension, application, analysis and higher-level behaviours. In addition, six affective aims (attitudinal) are specified along with two which are primarily concerned with psychomotor skills (physical co-ordination and manipulation).

The programme's intended emphasis is clear. Science is not to be approached as a body of factual information to be memorised, but through an exploration of the world of experience. Active involvement of pupils in identifying, observing and analysing phenomena is central to the teaching strategy, and pupils are expected to develop intellectual skills associated with problem-solving, hypothesising, experimental design and interpreting results. Attitudinal outcomes are to be given considerable emphasis (for example, interest and enjoyment in scientific activities, awareness of social and economic implications of scientific activity).

Since the MIS course was to end in a public examination, it was necessary to develop an appropriate test instrument for use in the Lower Certificate of Education/Sijil Rendah Pelajaran (LCE/SRP). This examination takes the form of a 75-item, multiple-choice objectively scored paper with five possible responses to each question. Original Scottish materials emphasise that

> any examinations set should be such that this syllabus is taught as it ought to be; tests should be constructed to examine practical techniques, design of experiments and ability to solve problem situations either by experimentation or by describing the experiment in words. When written answers are required they should not be long essays about remembered details; instead, questions of the multiple choice and one word answer type should be used. (Scottish Education Department, 1969)

Malaysian materials endorse this and further stress that 'testing should be done only to assess whether the stated objectives have been achieved' (MIS, 1973).

Analysis of examination papers during 1972–5 provides some

insight into the extent to which behaviours actually tested reflect the intended emphases of the MIS programme: this is shown in Table 4.11. The classification system used is that of Bloom (1956), referred to in course materials. Over half the items used were classified as testing achievement at the knowledge level (that is, they were questions answerable from recall of information alone). Though some items are related to experiments performed by pupils, there is no provision for any practical examination. Few questions used required the application of knowledge and none were directed towards measuring affective outcomes. Official guidelines suggest that no more than 40 per cent of items should test knowledge recall. Given the intended stress in the programme on higher cognitive and attitudinal outcomes and the deliberate playing down of the importance of factual information, the distribution of item types appears anachronistic.

Table 4.11   *Classification of Items in the LCE/SRP Integrated Science, 1972–5 (Percentages)*

Classification	1972	1973	1974	1975
Knowledge	61	60	51	51
Comprehension	31	31	33	32
Application and higher	8	9	16	17
Affective	0	0	0	0
Psychomotor	0	0	0	0

Note: This overall classification was the result of combining the classifications of four independent, experienced educationists familiar with the course.

It is relatively easy to explain why the format chosen for LCE/SRP integrated science was an objective multiple-choice examination. Other subjects had adapted this pattern of testing in Malaysia and original Scottish materials appeared to advocate it (Scottish Education Department, 1969). In addition, the Malaysian Examinations Syndicate's need to measure the achievement of large numbers of pupils for selection purposes weighed heavily in favour of examining methods that would allow large-scale mechanisation in the processing of scripts. A practical examination was never considered a possibility, because of its costs and administrative problems.

It is more difficult to explain why the papers designed did not more closely reflect the intentions of course designers and stress non-recall based achievement. In some respects, for instance, in experimental design, problem-solving techniques and application of scientific knowledge, there seem no compelling reasons for the lack of emphasis on related questions in the public examination. In other respects, for instance, in relation to affective outcomes, it is plausible that problems related to the construction of appropriate questions provide an explanation.

Part of the conventional wisdom among examiners with whom the course was discussed appeared to be that knowledge-level items were easier to construct and validate than those measuring higher-level cognitive skills. This may be true, but it is not a sufficient reason to justify disproportionate emphasis on the former given the stress in emphasis of curriculum materials. Another reason advanced was that items designed to operate above the knowledge level were too difficult for many candidates and, therefore, the discriminating power of the examination would be reduced. Such items *may* be more difficult for examinees, but not necessarily so – facility values (that is, proportion of candidates producing correct responses) for the 1975 LCE/SRP items clearly show this (Table 4.12). The most difficult question, with only 18 per cent achieving a correct response, was a knowledge item (see also Little, 1978).

Table 4.12   *Analysis of 1975 LCE/SRP (Percentages)*

Item classification	Mean facility	Range of facility values
Knowledge	0·503	0·18–0·75
Comprehension	0·487	0·29–0·86
Application and higher	0·429	0·24–0·61

The LCE/SRP is crucial in the allocation of life chances for Malaysian pupils; it is the first selection point in the education system which limits progression to the next level. Pupils who fail the LCE/SRP are unlikely subsequently to obtain wage or salary employment and will almost certainly find occupational niches in the 'traditional' sector of the economy. Understandably the pupils' anxiety about passing the LCE/SRP is high: over 60 per cent of a sample of approximately 2,000 grades 8 and 9 pupils expressed worry about failing the LCE/SRP; about 75 per cent indicated that they would try and resit if they did fail; 75 per cent claimed that they practised objective tests in order to improve their examination performance; and nearly 40 per cent indicated that the main reason they studied science was to pass the LCE/SRP (Lewin, 1981). These observations, coupled with a recognition that it is easily possible to pass LCE/SRP science on the basis of the recall of information alone, suggest that the pattern of examining is likely to have adverse effects on teaching and learning related to MIS.

In the research on which this chapter draws teachers of MIS from fifty-four schools in the West Malaysian states of Selangor and Kelantan were asked to comment in a free-response questionnaire on the form and effects of the LCE/SRP examination: 105 teachers responded to this invitation and the main remarks made are summarised in Table 4.13. Few teachers responding had positive remarks about the effects of the LCE/SRP on the teaching of MIS. Teachers might reasonably be expected to voice dissatisfaction rather than satisfaction in response to an open question, since those who are dissatisfied may feel more motivated to write comments. Nevertheless, that only four teachers did indicate general satisfaction does suggest that there is widespread and genuine concern with the adverse effects of the LCE/SRP.

Information from semi-structured interviews (43 teachers in 15 schools) followed a similar pattern to the questionnaire responses. Objective tests were the subject of much criticism, the most common assertions being that they discouraged the development of powers of expression and language fluency (six responses); discouraged understanding by rewarding powers of recognition and recall (three responses); increased the bad effects of examination orientation, since weaker students especially perceived performance to be related closely to practice and memory (seven responses). Several teachers referred to a common belief among pupils that objective tests were 'easier' than other types and, therefore, required less work and more luck in their completion. This, they asserted, had adverse motivational results, particularly among the less able. Some (three) teachers went as far as to suggest that considerable proportions of students relied heavily on books of objective test questions for examination practice and neglected the course itself almost entirely.

Though two teachers expressed the opinion that practical work was indirectly useful in enhancing LCE/SRP performance through helping students to remember facts and processes, a larger number (six) explicitly said that they felt practical work had little effect on examination results in the present LCE/SRP. About

Table 4.13 *Free-Response Remarks Made by Teachers Relating to the LCE/SRP Examination (N = 105)*

Summary comments	%age of total comments
Expression/understanding:	21
objective questions inhibit expressive ability	(10)
pupils can do well with little understanding	(10)
Motivation:	29
pupils are only interested in studying for the examination	(11)
pupils need only recognise answers and concentrate on memorisation	(7)
pupils rely on practising objective tests for revision	(6)
pupils guess objective tests and do not study for them	(4)
Effects on teachers:	14
teachers concentrate on facts and discard discovery methods	(10)
Nature of examination questions:	30
few questions relate to practical work and it is, therefore, undervalued	(10)
concentration on factual knowledge restricts teaching and learning	(7)
other forms of questions apart from multiple choice should be used	(5)
General:	6
examination system is satisfactory	(4)

Note: Bracketed figures refer to actual numbers of teachers making substantively similar remarks; where these numbers were small, such remarks have been omitted from the table.

one-quarter of the teachers interviewed referred *unprompted* to examination orientation dominating teaching in their schools, saying, for example, that 'teachers only teach for examinations'; 'the headmaster, parents and pupils are only interested in examination results'; 'good teachers are those who give good notes for examination revision'. One teacher pithily observed: 'the purpose of the integrated science course is to develop the ability to observe and reason; the purpose of the school is to get as many examination passes as possible.'

Another way in which the format adopted for the LCE/SRP seems to have influenced classroom teaching is in relation to methods of internal school assessment. Despite the largely unfavourable perception of the educational consequences of restricting assessment to the use of objective multiple-choice tests, this is in fact what the bulk of teachers do according to their questionnaire responses and interview data, as Table 4.14 illustrates.

Table 4.14   *Test Types by Frequency of Use (Percentages)*

Type	Frequency of use				
	Not used	Less than $\frac{1}{4}$ of tests	$\frac{1}{4}$–$\frac{1}{2}$ of tests	$\frac{1}{2}$–$\frac{3}{4}$ of tests	$\frac{3}{4}$–all tests
Structured	44	85	86	23	5
Short answer	74	75	59	25	9
Essay	141	78	12	7	4
Multiple choice	24	17	30	53	118
Practical	161	66	13	1	1

Note: Total number of teachers responding = 242; total number of teachers in sample 291; response rate = 83 per cent.

Significantly, very few teachers utilise forms of practical testing, though this is the only kind explicitly recommended in addition to multiple-choice objective questions in Malaysian course materials. Moreover, other questionnaire data indicate that the majority of teachers rely on unpublished books of multiple-choice items (usually derived from previous LCE/SRP question papers) in constructing their tests and that most use questions to test knowledge of scientific facts and principles, rather than their application. Teachers' opinions of the purposes served by internal testing give overall priority to measuring the achievement of pupils (52 per cent ranked this first) and providing a motivation for pupils to study (21 per cent ranked this first). Only 17 per cent ranked measuring how effective their teaching had been as a primary purpose, though this seems to be the recommendation in course materials (MIS, 1973; Scottish Education Department, 1969).

Pupils' attitudes to learning do seem strongly influenced by the LCE/SRP examination. In addition to the levels of concern with success, the numbers of pupils practising objective tests and the large numbers asserting that the main reason they studied science was to pass the LCE/SRP noted above, it is clear that pupils perceive multiple-choice objective questions as easier than essay questions that involve expression. They also see such questions as being primarily dependent on recall for their successful completion. Two questionnaire responses from the pupil survey cited above indicate this and are shown in Table 4.15.

Table 4.15   *Pupil Response to Survey Questions*

Question
I like objective questions because they are easier to answer than essay questions:

	No.	%	%
strongly agree	755	36·4	72·2
agree	744	35·8	
undecided	316	15·2	15·2
disagree	153	7·4	11·5
strongly disagree	86	4·1	
omissions	22	1·0	1·0
	2,076	99·9	99·9

Question:
To do well on objective questions all you need is a good memory:

	No.	%	%
strongly agree	497	23·9	57·0
agree	689	33·1	
undecided	369	17·8	17·8
disagree	376	18·1	24·1
strongly disagree	125	6·0	
omissions	22	1·0	1·0
	2,076	99·9	99·9

A large majority of pupils apparently do feel that 'there are too many facts to remember in integrated science': about 62 per cent of the sample agreed with this statement. Moreover, it is disproportionately the less able who feel this. (Of those getting the top three LCE/SRP grades, 40 per cent agreed with this, while the proportion of agreement among those getting the bottom three grades was over 70 per cent. The question was asked before the examination was taken.) Thus, the perception is strong among pupils that science education is concerned very much with the acquisition of factual information.

Data from the observation of forty normal class periods in fifteen of the schools in the sample provides some additional insight into ways in which the LCE/SRP may affect the teaching of the course. An observation schedule was used to record the frequency with which various types of activity took place, with the results shown in Table 4.16.

Table 4.16 *Classroom Interactions by Percentage of Time Spent*

1	Settling the class/administration	4·5
2	General class discussion	32·2
3	Group–teacher discussion	8·3
4	Individual–teacher discussion	0·9
5	Teacher draws/writes/reads	7·0
6	Pupils draw/write	2·9
7	Pupils use text/reference books	2·1
8	Pupils use worksheets, reading/writing	16·6
9	Teacher explains experimental procedure	5·6
10	Teacher demonstrates experiment	4·2
11	Class experiments	15·7

That is, less than 16 per cent of classtime was spent with pupils actually undertaking experimentation as the main activity. Most classtime – over 32 per cent – was spent with the teacher addressing the class as a whole. These interactions were further analysed into categories of discussion types as shown in Table 4.17.

Table 4.17 *Classroom Interactions – General Class Discussion by Percentage of Time Spent*

Introduce facts/principles	21
Recall facts/principles	35
Apply facts/principles	6
Hypothesise	1
Observe	28
Interpret data	7
Infer from data	1

Thus, considerable time was spent in class discussions introducing new information and concepts, and the greatest single number of observations occurred when teachers were requiring pupils to recall such information. Further analysis of other observation data indicated that the 'guided discovery' approach recommended in course materials was used by very few teachers. For example, on no occasion were pupils observed contributing to the design of experiments, and they were rarely asked to hypothesise, predict, interpret, or infer.

The observed pattern of teaching described very briefly here is consistent with an interpretation which holds that the lack of emphasis on practical work and related skills is at least partly attributable to patterns of examining. In so far as these encourage the acquisition of factual knowledge they inhibit teachers from devoting more time to experimentation and the use of 'guided discovery' methods. Interestingly, one teacher did refer directly to public examinations in an observed lesson. For her, this provided a powerful source of motivation for her pupils and influenced her teaching, even though the examination was four months away. The remarks she made included the following:

> 'Come, you are going to sit for the examination.' (The teacher was trying to get the attention of the class at the beginning of the lesson.)

> 'I am fed up with you people, many of you do not work and deserve to fail. Be quiet, and try to pass your LCE. Do not disturb us.' (A large group of boys were misbehaving.)

> 'Do you think you can guess the answers [in the LCE]? If only A and B you could, but with five [alternatives] – ABCDE – you cannot.'

Other explanations of the observed patterns of teaching described are, of course, possible (lack of teacher understanding of new pedagogy, shortage of resources, and so on). However, a brief summary of some of the evidence emerging from a detailed study of MIS does suggest strongly that the impact of a particular pattern of examining has been detrimental to the achievement of the course aims. Patterns of teaching, internal assessment procedures and students' perceptions of the nature of science education all appear to have been influenced adversely by aspects of the LCE/SRP.

In principle, however, there seem no overriding reasons why changes in the LCE/SRP should not be capable of producing an examining pattern that reinforces rather than undermines important emphases of the curriculum. An analysis of examination performance of 744 LCE/SRP candidates suggests that differences between high- and low-achievers are not related closely to differential performance on higher cognitive-level questions (Lewin, 1981). The proportion of marks scored on different types of questions is quite similar between groups of pupils at each end of the ability spectrum. The inclusion of much greater proportions of comprehension- and application-based questions in the examination would not, therefore, penalise poorer pupils disproportionately. It could have the positive effect of shifting the priorities of both teachers and pupils away from the simple acquisition of factual knowledge towards greater concern with the kinds of achievement that the MIS course seeks to promote.

SOME CORROBORATING STUDIES

The main characteristics of the relationships between curriculum, curriculum development and public selection examinations are not limited to the particular programmes considered. In many countries examinations have come to dominate the educational process, despite attempts to mitigate their impact. From Papua New Guinea (Conroy, 1976) to Cuba (Bowles, 1971) the pathology is common. In Japan Dore has identified the consequences of pressure from the 'examination hell' on the process of schooling (Dore, 1976). These include the devastating effects on the curricula of high schools which results from their preoccupation with preparing students for university entrance examinations. This 'backwash' extends down the school system to the extent that primary schools apparently use entrance examinations to select suitable candidates for the long grind through successive selection barriers to higher education. It has even been reported that since it proved impossible to test 2-year-olds for pre-kindergarten schools, mothers have been tested as a proxy measure.

Work in Hong Kong on teachers' attitudes towards, and use of, new secondary economics curricula has shown that examinations associated with the new course have played a powerful role in shaping classroom practice (Morris, 1982). Despite the promotion of new pedagogy for the course which involved movement away from descriptive to more analytical and activity-based presentation and an emphasis on the ability to apply economic concepts to real problems, teaching styles have changed little, notwithstanding a generally favourable reaction from teachers to the new pedagogy. Although many teachers feel that the new methods are preferable, the constellation of pressures on them arising from the school environment and particularly from the pressure to achieve high examination pass rates is such as to discourage or prevent their use. The setting and marking of economics papers continues to reward the descriptive enumeration of key points rather than the creative or original analysis which thoughtfully applies concepts which have been well understood.

More detailed analysis of the impact of examinations on curricula has probably been undertaken in Kenya than anywhere else (Somerset, 1974, 1982). Analysis of examination-performance data over time has provided very strongly suggestive evidence of the influence of changes in types of examination question on classroom teaching and patterns of school achievement. Examinations for the Certificate of Primary Education have been changed over the last decade to assess educational outcomes promoted by new curricula in English, mathematics and science. Papers have been redesigned to incorporate a high proportion of questions requiring the use of intellectual skills apart from the recall of information and to utilise relevant local situations and data which are not familiar only to urban children. Though performance on these papers initially declined compared to performance on those they replaced, concerted efforts over several years have succeeded in transforming expectations of the examination and performances now compare very favourably. From an educational viewpoint the new kinds of question are clearly preferable, since they promote much deeper levels of understanding and more useful skills. In Kenya coupling detailed monitoring of school performance with a sophisticated and detailed system of feedback and support to schools has illustrated the very real potential that exists for using examination reform to lead rather than obstruct enduring curriculum change.

As we have argued elsewhere (Lewin and Little, 1982), examination reform may be seen to be constrained by those factors which more generally can be argued to lead to 'underdevelopment' but the strength of such factors is often exaggerated and misunderstood. Changes are possible given adequate analysis of the dynamics of change.

CONCLUDING REMARKS

The stress in this chapter has been on the effects of public examinations on curriculum reform in developing countries. The intention has not been to argue that other factors are unimportant or that the problems described are not encountered in rich countries. Decisions on teaching methods, content, objectives and the use of the curriculum are clearly not wholly circumscribed by public examinations. None the less, in situations where a primary motive in going to school is to be selected for more schooling and acquire qualifications, examinations are likely to exert considerable influence on the curriculum at both design and implementation stages; more than, for example, exhortation, rhetoric and prescription contained in texts and guidebooks.

Three further conclusions can be drawn. These relate specifically to ways in which selection instruments can be developed to support successful curriculum reform. These consist, first, of developing techniques of assessment and examination which correspond closely to the educational emphases of new curricula. Systematic and sustained investment in the development of high-quality examinations produced by adequately trained staff should reduce difficulties arising from the differing requirements of curricula and examinations. Secondly, close monitoring of the working of selection examinations and their effects on the curriculum in action is desirable in order to ensure that such influence is benign. Support for new curricula through in-service courses, district advisory staff, changes in initial training, resource provision, and so on, must include careful consideration of changes in patterns of assessment, since these are likely to play a central role in determining classroom practice and motivating teachers and pupils. It is worth noting that evidence from several countries indicates that selection examinations can work to test the adequacy and understanding of teachers as much as to provide reliable indicators of pupil potential (Lewin, 1981). Close monitoring could establish the extent to which this is true and whether action is desirable to diminish this effect.

Thirdly, detailed and explicit feedback of examination performance to teachers and pupils has an important role in curriculum reform. Communicating to a teacher that 20 per cent of his class failed tells him nothing of the reasons for his and their failure. Indicating which questions and tasks pupils completed successfully and which they did not provides useful information on which to base future action. If pupils do behave according to what they perceive to be the demands of examinations, then feedback of this kind provides a potentially effective method of reducing misconceptions and using examination 'backwash' to support new curricula.*

Taken together, concerted action on these aspects of examining

* The annual CPE *Newsletter* of the Kenya National Examinations Council provides excellent examples.

does provide an attractive response to some of the problems of effective and enduring changes in the curriculum in action. Though not a panacea, such a tactical shift towards curriculum improvement through examination reform does provide genuine possibilities for action at relatively low cost and in a comparatively short time. This can only be effective if it is part of a broad strategy that includes a reconsideration of educational purposes and a sensitive appreciation of the social functions of educational qualification and selection.

Chapter 5

The Influence of Certification and Selection on Teaching and Learning

NIGEL BROOKE and JOHN OXENHAM

Before this chapter looks at the effects of selection in schools, it will recall four assumptions implicit in Figure 1.1 on p. 32. Briefly, they are as follows:

(1) Education in developing countries is viewed almost exclusively in instrumental, qualification-gathering terms. Conversely, if the schools and universities ceased to offer diplomas and degrees, there would be no demand for them. Scholastic education would wither away.

(2) Equating education with diplomas generates an obsession with academic success. Because this has to be measured, attention seizes upon the mechanics of assessment, to the detriment of the process of education. Chapter 4 has illustrated the point. As selection not only concerns employment, but first determines who continues in the educational system, two important inferences follow. Extending assumption 1 the academically unsuccessful would tend to drop out or be withdrawn from school, simply because they could not satisfy their own purposes. They would form a species of voluntary attrition. Secondly, the drive for academic success would encourage more attrition, but of a less

voluntary kind. If teachers are measured in part by the success of their pupils, they might press the less successful to withdraw from school by means of unfavourable internal assessments. Apparently voluntary attrition, then, disguises the full effects of the frank and institutionalised attrition by examination and selection.

(3) Existing techniques of assessing academic success both militate decisively against reforms in curricula and pedagogy, and more important, are incapable of substantive improvement. Chapter 4 has both illustrated and questioned this assumption. Latent, however, is another: examinations are the only, or at any rate the main, constraint inhibiting teachers from adopting more adventurous and stimulating teaching practices.

(4) A reinforcing constraint stems from assumption 1, namely, the anxiety of parents that their children do well at school. Since the education profession depends on demand for its services and since demand is chiefly for diplomas, teachers need to reassure parents that their teaching promotes success. The implication is that parents affect teachers' behaviour conservatively and constitute an inhibition to reform.

There is much evidence, systematic and anecdotal, to support all four of these assumptions. On the other hand, there is also evidence to suggest that they are much too absolute. This chapter will argue that the array of variables, which affect the demand for and conduct of education, is so complex that it produces not one or two polarised options, but a spectrum of differing situations. Each of these requires that educational theory account for it and that educational policy respond to it appropriately. Although the core of the discussion will be drawn from research in Ghana and Mexico,* findings from a wider field will also be used to assess the issues.

TWO PATTERNS OF EDUCATIONAL PROGRESSION

The convenience of Ghana and Mexico taken together is that they share one set of characteristics central to this discussion, but differ on another. In both the distribution of income and well-being is

* For full accounts, see Brooke and Oxenham, 1980; Brooke, 1979; Boakye and Oxenham, 1982.

very unequal between the modern and other sectors, access to salaried employment is dependent on scholastic credentials and the correspondence between education and income is strong. The societies differ markedly in educational practices, however.

Ghana is a member of the West African Examinations Council and operates a system of centralised examinations. One of these, the Common Entrance Examination (CEE), selects some 6 to 8 per cent of an age cohort for secondary education and eventually the Ordinary or O-level examination of the General Certificate of Education. O level is now virtually essential for all forms of salaried employment. In effect, the bulk of an age cohort is now disqualified from salaried employment. They have instead official access to a ten-year span of elementary education, through which progression is automatic. An examination at the end awards the Middle School Leaving Certificate (MSLC) to the successful. Once useful for entry to a range of low-level non-manual jobs, the MSLC retains scarcely any market value. The fact seems to be reflected in the numbers of young people who take the MSLC and CEE.

The former is intended to be taken by all young Ghanaians, who are not selected for secondary schooling. It is non-selective and normally has a pass rate of 75 per cent. In 1979 just over 100,000 candidates took it, an increase of just 7 per cent over the numbers in 1972, seven years before. The average annual rate of increase was 1 per cent, less than half the population growth rate. By contrast, the average annual rate of increase in CEE candidates during 1973–9 was 7 per cent. Despite its selectivity and the low rate of success in actually securing secondary school places, the number of candidates in 1979 was 135,000, nearly 50 per cent higher than had been planned for in 1971 (JASPA, 1982). A difficult selective examination which offers access to higher education and salaried jobs, albeit to a tiny minority, is clearly much more sought after than one which is universally available and has a high pass rate but offers diminishing access to further education and no access to salaried jobs.

Mexico, by contrast, has almost as many secondary school places as there are students qualified for and seeking them, and puts no hurdles of selection in the way of candidates (Moreira, 1972). There is no centralised and universally applicable set of examinations comparable with Ghana's CEE or MSLC. Instead, each primary school is empowered to test, graduate, or fail its own students. Failure rates are very low, so that simply to complete the six-year course in itself virtually guarantees graduation. Neither selection nor certification appears to present problems to the determined and capable student.

On first appearance, then, the schools of Ghana might be expected to suffer a severe case of the 'diploma disease', while those of Mexico should on the contrary display models of ideal teaching and learning. This chapter will show that such clear polarity does not exist. In fact, choosing between the two would be difficult and it might even be the case that the rural pupils of Ghana receive a more conscientious education than those of Mexico – possibly because of the examinations, certification and selection! The chapter's conclusion will suggest that, although certification and selection do indeed affect teaching and learning, they are by no means the only forces at work. While it may certainly be necessary to transform, if not eliminate, selection in order to achieve better education, it will also be essential to transform other factors simultaneously.

SCHOOLING SOLELY FOR SELECTION

Before looking at what goes on in classrooms, it will be as well to put the foundation assumption of the 'diploma disease' into perspective. How true is it that parents send children to school chiefly, if not solely, to help them get selected for salaried employment? Conversely, how likely would it be that the demand for schooling would wither away, if qualifications were no longer its goal? There is no doubt that the literature does make it clear that selection and salaried employment loom large in most decisions about schooling in most societies where the issue has been studied. Social mobility, 'a better life' for their children, does seem to be a forceful concern of most parents, perhaps particularly mothers.

Also, where social mobility or economic betterment is not a concern, schooling does appear to be in less demand. There are a few slants to be distinguished here. Some societies, for instance, in northern Nigeria or northern Ghana (Blakemore, 1975), judge the Western school alien, even hostile, to their own values and culture. These they wish to conserve, and not being attracted to the modern sector, they withhold their children from schooling. Others, like the Masai of Kenya and Tanzania in times bygone, may simply take no part in the modern sector and see no use for the school. They ignore both. Others may have connections with the modern sector by way of trade, but still not wish either to participate in it themselves or get their children incorporated. Peasants in India, for example, are reported not to send their heirs to school – although they may enrol younger children – simply because a qualification is not necessary to inherit and manage the land. Similarly, the nomadic majority of Somalia, though connected with the modern sector's international network through the export of cattle, sheep and camels, sends few of its children to school. Their decisions may, indeed, be affected partly by the practical difficulties of using fixed schools without a fixed address, as it were. Nevertheless, two other factors have parts, too. The first is obviously that tending the herds and making an adequate living from them in normal times does not require scholastic education. Possibly more important, however, is the second – at least at present. This is simply that, along with a steady decline in the national income per person since 1970, the differentials between the modern and other sectors have been narrowing quite considerably. Consequently, there seems no clear advantage in salaried employment, and hence no compelling reason to send children to school (JASPA, 1981, Vol. 1). In Ghana, too, the economic decline and inflation of the 1970s have reduced the purchasing power of much salaried employment, while rural incomes in contrast have apparently kept abreast of prices. Not unexpectedly, it appears that rural primary school-enrolment ratios have fallen, even as the urban demand for secondary schools has intensified (JASPA, 1981, Vol. 2).

Relatedly, possibilities of access to the modern sector without qualifications may also reduce demand for schooling. Two prime examples of this come from Botswana and Lesotho. Both societies have large numbers of families who are accustomed to wage employment in the mines of South Africa. Not only does this pay better and perhaps offer more opportunities than the lower levels of non-manual, salaried employment within their national borders, it also requires no qualification apart from physical fitness. Most of these families also own cattle and need some of their boys to tend the herds. The two factors of access to wages and labour for herding combine to keep many boys out of school. A very rare phenomenon is produced: in the primary and even secondary schools of Botswana and Lesotho girls outnumber boys (Allison, 1983; JASPA, 1979). Taken together, all this would confirm the assumption that the school is, indeed, used simply as a channel to better and higher incomes.

On the other hand, Botswana and Lesotho raise another

possibility. Although girls outnumber boys in the schools, men outnumber women in most forms of salaried employment. The situation involves the necessity that numbers of schooled women are not in jobs, but occupied instead in some form of domestic or self-employment. The likelihood that they would be so occupied must have been clear to their families before they were enrolled. The inference is that at least some demand for schooling must be at least partially independent of qualifications and selection.

Support for this view comes from some of the parents Allison interviewed in Botswana: they felt it was just good for their daughters to have some education. Modiano in Mexico (1973), Wallace in Peru (1976), Miranda in Brazil (1977) and Foley (1977), more generally, similarly report that many village parents enrol their children in school but have no aspirations for mobility and exhibit no anxiety over their children's success or lack of it. Sufficient for them is that their children are learning something. Considerable proportions of the parents in the IDS studies in some rural communities of Ghana and Mexico took much the same stance. Of 127 Ghanaian parents in six rural communities, 29 per cent talked of the benefits of education only in terms of enlightenment and heightened capabilities:

> I am blind, I do not know how to read. I am deaf, I do not understand the English language. I accept only twopence for uprooting elephant grass, I get only a little for hard work. If I had been to school, I would not have ended up like this.

A further 28 per cent mixed in possibilities of further education and good jobs, but were emphatic also about the simple good of having an education. Only 41 per cent – a substantial proportion, but still a minority – talked only in terms of selection and qualification. That minority was even smaller in the sample of eighty-eight parents in four villages of Michoacan, Mexico: only 18 per cent or one in five. In contrast, 72 per cent mentioned solely the direct benefit of education, literacy and numeracy. A person with education is 'awake', 'someone in life', no longer blind, ignorant, or defenceless against the abuses of short-changing shopkeepers and unscrupulous officials. An additional bonus is the ability to keep in touch with those members of the family who have migrated to the city. These responses indicate that the perceived uses of education and literacy are wider than just getting a certificate. They show that, while parents perceive illiteracy to be a serious handicap in a literate society, and will send their children to school to acquire the basic skills in order to cope, they do not necessarily see schooling as the way to joining the literate society.

Particularly as they come from rural communities, such responses indicate that, even if the school were totally divorced from selection for employment, demand for its services would not disappear. Admittedly, it might shrink, as the earlier mention of Ghana's economic difficulties and declining enrolment ratios suggested. On the other hand, the Mexican experience seems to demonstrate that, when the necessity for literacy is clear for even minimal dealings with the modern sector, the utilisation of the school will take on its own momentum. There seems also to be a social reinforcement to this functional value. As scholastic education spreads, so to be unschooled becomes a disgrace not just to oneself, but more importantly to one's family: only negligent parents would fail to get their offspring some education. This was clearly brought out among the Ghanaian teachers and parents. Such a fusion of economic and social value would probably maintain and promote public demand for schooling independently of selection and certification.

A conclusion of this nature would certainly restrict the force of the 'diploma disease'. However, it must itself be modified in its optimism by an important observation. It is simply that families who are outside the modern sector and/or who are not socially mobile make rather limited use of the school. Some examples can illustrate different aspects of this generalisation. It is well known in the industrialised societies of Europe and North American that families of the less-wealthy social groups tend to make – or to be able to make – less use of educational opportunities than those of the more wealthy. They are almost always severely underrepresented in enrolments for higher education, while the latter are conspicuously overrepresented. Miranda and Schmidt (1977) confirmed a similar situation in Brazil, and Sinclair (1976) and Cooksey (1981) have traced its emergence in Ghana and the Cameroon. Miranda also suggests that working-class parents are less likely to see education as the principal route to progress and so are less likely to push their children beyond what seems a desirable minimum. What that minimum is can vary with the parents' own schooling: the more the latter, the higher the former. More than a primary education, however, is as yet seldom judged necessary.

Somewhat different are the Tarascan Indian parents in two of the villages of the IDS studies in Mexico. They see themselves excluded from the modern sector by the *mestizo* majority of all social classes. They feel discriminated against racially and social mobility is not a real option for them. So they use the school only as far as they think it will equip their children to deal with the hostile larger society. However, although they all feel the same racial bar, these families vary in what they judge to be sufficient schooling.

Their judgement appears to depend much on how the family makes its living and the degree to which it needs to utilise its children's labour. Potters, for instance, seem to get by on only two or three years of schooling: their children can help in the workshop from the age of 10 or so. Furniture manufacturers are more likely to allow their children the full primary course of six years: helping with heavy timber and dangerous machinery is feasible only for children in their teens. Larger landed peasants able to hire labour, and shopkeepers, seem most likely to see that their children do have a complete primary education. This last group, shopkeepers, seem kin to traders in Gujarat, India, who are also reported to send their children to primary school and no further; for that is all that is needed to keep the family business going. What this seems to signify is, first, that families who require education for its own sake need much less of it than families who want education for entry to the modern sector; and secondly, that a family's demand for education for its own sake is determined by its need for labour and by its children's capacity to contribute to its welfare.

A further possible factor in demand is the public norm of an adequate education. In Mexico a diploma is still awarded after six years of schooling. In Ghana, however, that stage is long past and it is now accepted that ten years of elementary school are needed for adequacy. If Mexico were to adopt Ghana's norm, the children of the shopkeepers might well stay in school for ten rather than six years, even though the children of the potters and furniture-makers might continue to quit after three or four years.

A propos the first assumption of the 'diploma disease' it can be said, in general, that probably not all pupils and their sponsors are concerned with selection and certification; and that, were schooling to be divorced from selection, demand for primary schools would probably be sustained at near-current levels. However, demand for secondary and tertiary institutions might well decline, to the extent that they failed to be public norms for an adequate education. For the particular purposes of this chapter, a further inference must be drawn. The fact that considerable proportions of parents concerned with the Ghanaian and Mexican schools studied were not preoccupied with the selection and certification of their children, means that at least one pressure for selection-oriented education was reduced. On the contrary, the parents' expectation of useful skills and knowledge should fortify efforts to make the curriculum relevant to rural life.

OBSESSION WITH ACADEMIC SUCCESS

The implications do not stop here, of course. They go on to undermine the second assumption listed at the beginning of this chapter. First, any obsession with academic success will affect only portions of the pupils and should not infect whole classes. Secondly, voluntary attrition would be an unlikely consequence of academic failure. It would be particularly unlikely in the schools of Ghana and Mexico, since both systems practise virtually automatic promotion from class to class. Thirdly, neither Ghanaians nor Mexican teachers would feel any need to push out slower learners. Both groups observe automatic promotion, which in any case frowns on failing pupils. Although the Ghanaians do teach for the MSLC examination and do bear it in mind, they have experienced such consistently high pass rates* that they would not need to worry that the failures among their students would reflect badly on them. The Mexicans were, of course, in an even more confident position. They themselves decided graduation or failure and had hardly ever failed anyone. The sources of dropout in these schools, then, lay elsewhere than in academic failure. Most of the parents, both Ghanaian and Mexican, thought that simple economic reasons lay behind voluntary attrition.

Parental Pressure on Teachers

The third assumption will be discussed later. The fourth, however, does not escape repercussions from the modifications to the first and second. In general terms parents who are not preoccupied with qualifications are scarcely likely to badger teachers about sticking to and covering prescribed syllabuses. In the particular circumstances of the Ghanaian and Mexican schools the parents had little

* All six schools studied had for years had pass rates above the national average, itself high.

to badger about, because of the high examination pass rates in one group and total pass rates in the other. In all ten communities studied, so it proved, the parents had very little to do with the school. There was simply no question of pressure on the teachers. Such a finding conflicts with reports from India or Sri Lanka that schools and teachers have been stoned for low success in getting pupils through examinations. It also conflicts with tales from Ghana itself of students stubbornly chanting 'Non sylla, non sylla', when a teacher has tried to be innovative. The key explanations for this change may well be the increasing acceptance of education for its intrinsic good and the assurance of success. For the purposes of this chapter, however, it is enough to note that the teachers in the Ghanaian and Mexican samples of schools were not constrained by parents from introducing better content and methods to their pupils.

The Constraint of Examinations

In effect, then, the only apparent barrier to good education in Ghanaian middle schools and Mexican primary schools are the modes and techniques of academic assessment. (What might be meant by 'good education' in the two countries will be discussed in a moment.) There are, of course, two aspects here: the assessment done by the teachers themselves and the assessment that may be applied by authorities external to a school. As observed earlier, only the Ghanaians are subject to the latter. Mexican teachers are deemed capable of doing all the assessment that is necessary without further checks. If the assumption about the force of external assessment is accurate, the Ghanaian teachers can be expected to model their own assessments on the external examination. The Mexicans by comparison might display variety and innovation in their approaches. Further, even though they achieve high examination success rates and have little anxiety about failure, the Ghanaian group can be expected to trim their instruction much more closely to the examination than to any wider values included in the syllabus. The Mexicans, on the other hand, with their greater discretion, might be expected to pay more attention to good education than to good marks. Before these expectations are tested, however, it is necessary to be clear on what was regarded as good education in the two countries and whether the forms of assessment were congruent with those ideals.

The Question of Good Education

During the early 1970s both Ghana and Mexico launched fresh attempts at educational reform. In 1969 Ghana introduced pre-vocational studies to its middle schools in an effort to ease the way to self-reliance and self-employment.* This was followed in 1974 by *The New Structure and Content of Education in Ghana.* It redefined the goals of the successive stages and different forms of education and proposed a restructuring and consolidation of the pattern of schools. Simultaneously, but independently, Mexico was entering a period of intensified reform. During President Echeverría's term of office (1970–6) the volume and rate of change in education far exceeded what had been attempted in the 1950s and 1960s. As in Ghana, the very goals and processes of pedagogy were reconsidered and reformulated from the primary school onwards.

Although the two countries lie a broad ocean apart, and have very different cultures and histories and a very low level of contact with each other, their aims for primary or elementary schooling were remarkably similar. Both concepts of good education embrace the following elements:

- relevance to local society and environment (implying an effort to reduce the urban bias in many of the textbooks);
- formation of attitudes and skills of scientific curiosity, logical thought, creative self-expression, co-operative learning and effort;
- appreciation of all efforts to learn, maximising and diversifying learning activity in the pupils.

Mexico went further and attempted to eliminate notions of failure and even rank-orders of achievement from the primary school. Nevertheless, these four common elements provide a sufficient core of criteria against which to measure the actual teaching in classrooms. If implemented, these standards imply processes of teaching and learning very different from the rote-memorisation of facts, abstract drilling of arithmetical skills and equally abstract dinning-in of science, geography and history so familiar from the stereotypes of traditional primary schools (Beeby, 1966). On the contrary, they connote moves towards forming cognitive and

* The scheme was not shared with the selective secondary schools, which did not have self-reliance as one of their goals.

manual skills vividly from the needs and problems of everyday life, quests on the nature and reasons for local phenomena, and co-operative work by groups of pupils on imaginative projects. Intellectual stimulus, local relevance and co-operation might be the three watchwords to characterise the intended reforms.

Congruence of Curriculum and Assessment

The Mexican textbooks and guides published to support the reforms proposed methods of assessment, which were consistent with these aims. As indicated, they eschewed failure and rank-orders among pupils. Rather, they advocated that each pupil's progress be measured against his or her own previous attainment and that each be allowed to learn at a pace best suited to himself. How individual teachers applied the proposals was, of course, left to their discretion. The same was unhappily not true of Ghana's MSLC examination. Boakye and Oxenham (1982, p. 13 *et seq.*) compared the examinations for 1976 against the array of objectives announced two years earlier in *The New Structure and Content.* What they found suggested that the examiners of the West African Examinations Council had not taken much notice of the reforms. Not only did the examinations fail to incorporate the new objectives in their probing, they also did not test the programme of pre-vocational studies at all.* Their predominant style was such as to support and encourage rote-memorisation, routine drilling, bookishness. In this respect, then, the third assumption about the conflict between reforms and assessment is valid for Ghana. Consequently, the Ghanaian middle school teachers could be expected to pay rather more attention to the examinations than to the reforms, and to orient their teaching content and style more to the one than the other.

It is important to point out that this conflict is not unique to Ghana. In an analysis of examinations from eight African countries (JASPA, 1981, Vols 1 and 2) Lewin and Little found very few which seemed to take into account the goals expressed by Ministries of Education and development plans. They did indeed

---

* This latter fault cannot be laid at the door of the WAEC, for it examines only what its constituent governments invite it to examine. As late as 1980 the government of Ghana had apparently not invited the Council either to devise assessment for pre-vocational studies or to assist with the design of curricula for the projected new junior secondary schools.

single out instances – the Gambia and Kenya – where examiners were beginning to break the mould of the traditional examination. The overall tenor, however, was that examinations simply fail to support efforts to reorient education towards intellectual stimulus, local relevance and co-operation.

It is equally important to point out that what new orientations Lewin and Little did find, question one part of the assumption, namely, that examinations are incapable of substantive improvement. The indications from Kenya and some of the WAEC country offices are that, given thought, ingenuity and time, examinations can actively promote good education (see also Somerset, 1982). The assumption must, then, be restricted to the simple statement that most existing practices in examinations militate against pedagogical reform.

Classroom Practice

It is time now to consider in what ways the MSLC exam might influence teaching and learning in Ghanaian classrooms. Four areas of impact can be distinguished: the curriculum; the pupils; the pedagogy; and the learning. If the diagnosis of the 'diploma disease' is accurate, distortions should be visible in all four.

Distortion of the curriculum The MSLC examination gives greatest weight to the subjects of English and mathematics. It also tests history, geography and, for girls only, home science; in all, four subjects for any pupil. The full middle school curriculum, however, comprises twelve subjects. The expectations would be that the teachers would tend to neglect the non-examination subjects and would in particular stress English and mathematics – even though the official timetable required that the allocations of time be adhered to strictly. Such, indeed, proved to be the case. The teachers themselves freely confessed it, the pupils and actual observations of the classrooms confirmed it. Gardening, arts and crafts, music and physical education were either skimped or ignored. In their place the teachers gave extra lessons in the examination subjects.

Examination backwash was strong. If it were extensive, teachers might even pick and choose topics *within* a subject, according to whether they judged them likely to appear in an examination. Again the teachers were frank. The syllabus of no subject could be covered in a year; indeed, even the examination subjects were lucky to be three-quarters taught even in the extra time made available by downgrading the others. Some selection was unavoidable and the staple examination questions provided a convenient first guide. So although all the teachers interviewed recommended that subjects like agriculture, science and nature study should be given emphasis in the curriculum, practical necessity pushed them in other directions.

Distortion of attention to pupils   It has already been noted that the policy of automatic promotion inclines teachers not to ease slower learners out of the school. In addition, since teachers' careers in no way depend on their pupils' performances, there is no indirect incentive to do so. In these circumstances a concern for good examination results might encourage teachers to concentrate their attention on two particular groups of pupils, the very weak and the very bright. Helping the former to pull up would raise pass rates – a source of professional pride – and boosting the latter might raise the numbers of distinctions in the examination marks. The first prediction was certainly borne out, the second not at all. The teachers said they usually tried to help the weak learners, the pupils and the classroom observations justified them.

However, no teacher said his or her reasons for focusing on the slower had anything to do with pass rates. They were concerned rather that these pupils should be assisted to reach a level close to the average, and should not hinder the progress of the rest of the class.

A propos helping the brighter it is worth remarking that the minority of pupils – about 30 per cent – who were trying for selection to secondary school through the CEE, were given very little special attention in class. Admittedly, special sessions were organised for them after normal school hours, but there was little hint of any other kind of preferential treatment. Examination backwash, then, did not cause these teachers to discriminate either adversely or positively among their pupils.

Distortion of pedagogy   None the less, it might lead them deliberately to adopt undesirable methods of teaching in pursuit of efficient learning for examination success. The evidence collected from six rural classrooms does not support that supposition. The teachers acknowledged that the MSLC could encourage rote-learning and other regrettable practices. They contended that rote-learning was useful for some purposes, as were drills for formulas and simple mathematical operations. None the less, the teachers actually used such methods very little in the periods they were observed. On the contrary, their pains in explaining reasons and discussing phenomena and events in the textbooks, and in eliciting responses from their pupils, more than counterbalanced the bad practices. The teachers' overt approval of methods which encouraged their pupils to think for themselves was generally borne out by their behaviour, whatever the subject they were teaching. They could not be dismissed as stereotypes of traditional instruction.

On the other hand, to absolve these six teachers from extreme orientation to methods to pass examinations is not to declare them models of good teaching. They acknowledged that they fell short of their own ideals, but they had rationalisations to offer. Their teaching relied heavily on 'chalk and talk' not because they were ignorant of other approaches, but because they found them less easy and sometimes more time-consuming. Even without examinations, time was important, simply because there was a syllabus to be got through. The teachers were implying that the 'education' and 'methods' advice of the school authorities was contradicted by the 'content' and 'exam' demands of the same authorities. The teachers felt constrained to defer to the demands rather than to the advice.

The probability that the teachers were putting forward rationalisations rather than solid reasons is strengthened by the variations between them. In the teaching of English, for instance, most of the teachers put the substandard performance of their pupils down to the lack of reading materials, tape-recordings and access to decent libraries. They confined their work mainly to pen-and-paper exercises in grammar and syntax and left oral practice virtually on one side. This fitted, of course, both with completing the syllabus and with the style of the examination, which does not test oral ability at all. By contrast, one teacher, equally constrained by syllabus and examinations, used his classes to create occasions for reading aloud, class conversations or dramatics in order to force his pupils to mobilise and utter their English. Again, in only one school, which had an experimental science curriculum, did a majority of pupils collect things – birds, nests and fish – for investigation in class and for the school's science museum. The overall impression is not so much that the teachers could not implement better methods, although a lack of skill may have been a factor. A rather more powerful support for humdrum – but not exam-mad – teaching seemed to be a broad satisfaction or complacency with current achievements and a consequent inertness in imaginative effort. Since, then, their pedagogy was not heavily influenced by examinations, the conclusion must be: while exam orientation may inhibit good teaching, the absence of exam orientation will not ensure it.

Distortion of learning If the pupils were preoccupied by examinations, they might be expected to resist any content or methods which appeared irrelevant or inefficient for examination purposes, no matter how great or important the intrinsic interest. The 'ideal' opposite would be pupils willing to pursue any topic or problem that offered intellectual stimulus. The Ghanaian sample could not be expected to be dominated by exams, simply because they did not themselves see qualifications as an overwhelming goal and their teachers were only mildly affected. Nevertheless, they were aiming at an examination and, just as their teachers were influenced by the exam's requirements, so they too might be.

Their favourite subjects were those in the MSLC examination: nearly eight out of ten named English or mathematics, while a sprinkling mentioned history, geography, or home science. Fewer than one in ten named an academic subject not in the examination, and fewer than three in a 100 named a practical subject. On the face of it, this is not simply exam orientation, it is more like exam obsession. Yet when asked why a subject was their favourite, fewer than four in 100 mentioned examinations and only twelve in 100 thought the subject might be useful for future employment. In contrast, seventy-seven in 100 said the subject was interesting, easy to learn and useful in daily life – all good, non-instrumental reasons. A similar pattern of responses was given to the question of which subject was likely to be most useful to them. There was an apparently close coincidence between officially prescribed importance, perceived relevance and personal interest. Being examined merely added a reason for doing one's favourite subject better.

On the other hand, there were two complaints from the teachers. First, their pupils did not like learning or working independently: they wanted simply to be given the answers. In line with this, secondly, giving the pupils homework was vain, because they either got their relatives and friends to provide the answers or came to school early to copy from classmates. The implication was that interest and motivation were diluted by a laziness that accorded with what the pupils knew of examinations. As with the teachers, perhaps, there was an inclination to minimise, to do only what was necessary.

Since there was seldom homework, it is not surprising that most pupils did not spend much time on independent study. However, the picture changed dramatically whenever an examination or test was in the offing. Half the pupils then confessed to spending around three hours an evening getting themselves prepared. Two teachers commented in confirmation: 'To be honest, all pupils study only when an examination is near'; and 'Pupils like to study only when there are impending examinations, as they do not do well in class, but perform fairly well in tests'. Apparently, then, despite good intrinsic motivation, the pupils still needed extrinsic goals and incentives to maintain their application. They themselves confessed this, opining that if there were no examinations or certificates, many pupils would simply cease learning, even though what was learned was intrinsically valuable. Falling short of the ideal of learning for interest's sake alone, then, appeared due less to anxiety about the MSLC examination and more to an avoidance of effort beyond what might be necessary.

The Ghanaian study points to a paradoxical conclusion. Where a central examination is the measure of scholastic success, its style of testing will always constrain teaching and learning to some extent. If it is difficult to pass – as, for instance, the Certificate of Primary Education in Kenya – teachers and pupils will anxiously conform to its requirements and disregard other styles out of fear. If, on the other hand, it is easy to pass – as the MSLC in Ghana – they may exceed its requirements in so far as it is convenient to do so, but will disregard objectives and methods which require abnormal effort. If that is indeed the case, the Mexican primary schools may prove not to have made much use of their freedom from central examinations.

THE MEXICAN CLASSROOMS

Two major impressions emerged from the studies of the four rural primary schools in Michoacan. The first was that the reforms of 1972 had not made much headway by late 1976, even though they were known to the teachers and the supporting textbooks had been distributed. Freedom from central examinations as well as from pressures for selection and certification had apparently not enabled the teachers to move far towards intellectual stimulus, local relevance, or co-operation. Their teaching was not very different from that of the Ghanaians, except that they appeared more successful in getting their pupils to ask questions and offer comments. On the other hand, they were somewhat more prone to use grades as incentives to make their pupils work. Freedom from examinations also did not prevent distortions of the curriculum. Of the four major academic areas, the teachers taught Spanish and mathematics above all and almost ignored the natural and social sciences. The minor subjects – art, technological and physical education – were virtually excluded. The only elements of the reforms which appeared to have been adequately acted on were those which required least change to past patterns of activity: reducing rote-learning, reducing questions which require only recall, and reducing reinforcement by bare repetition and drill. The elements on which no action had been taken were the encouragement of independent research by pupils and creating local illustrations for the curriculum.

The second major impression was the differences between the teachers. Put another way, whether and how the reforms were implemented depended very much upon the individual teacher. Of the four teachers observed, in their classrooms, two were obviously conscientious and trying to progress. The other two had a variety of excuses to explain their inertia.

While differences had certainly been observed between the Ghanaian teachers, they seemed more extreme between the Mexicans. While the latter shared a common disregard for the natural sciences and minor subjects, they varied astonishingly in their treatment of the major ones. In a week of observations of each class, for instance, one teacher was seen to devote nearly 80 per cent of his time to Spanish, while another formally spent a mere 10 per cent on the same subject. Similarly, while two teachers gave about one-sixth of their classes to mathematics, the other two allocated nearly half their time to it. Possibly the provision of only general norms for the rationing of time between subjects and the absence of a strict timetable, such as the Ghanaians were expected to follow, allowed greater scope for idiosyncrasy. The teachers themselves seemed to have no reasons other than that each emphasised what he thought important and what he enjoyed teaching.

In short, freedom from qualifications and central examinations appeared not to have promoted better education in these four schools. More alarming, perhaps, it seemed to have permitted the attainments and outcomes of schooling to become more uncertain and arbitrary. They now depended not on standards which, however imperfect, might be justifiable, but on the whims of individual teachers. An argument could be plausibly made that the six Ghanaian middle schools were offering a more reliable and probably better education, precisely because of their somewhat higher concern with qualifications and their frank, if mild, orientation to the MSLC examination.

This possibly sustaining influence of the examination may be detected in a behaviour already remarked among the Mexicans. It is that they were prone to use grades to prod their pupils to more effort. True, the Ghanaian teachers also used periodic tests to assess and galvanise their pupils and modelled their tests largely on the MSLC examination. Nevertheless, they seemed to refer to the exam itself rather seldom. By contrast, all the Mexican teachers used the grades that they themselves would confer both to encourage and to threaten their pupils. And true to the observation of differences, two of the four were rather more prone to do so, and both these were in the Tarascan communities, where intentions for secondary education and salaried jobs appeared lowest.

A possible inference is that teachers need examinations quite as much to keep their pupils learning as to keep themselves up to the mark. Where an external examination does not provide an obvious stimulus for the pupils, the teachers have to fashion one of their own along almost identical lines. Automatically, then, two critical issues emerge: what motivates children to learn well in schools and what motivates teachers to teach well? Both are central to the puzzle set by the preceding paragraphs on the broad similarities between Ghanaian and Mexican teachers: why does freedom to educate well not lead to good education? The phrasing of this question insinuates that only the teachers and pupils need to be considered. However, they are of course influenced by the interaction with their environment and institutions. The following sections, then, will attempt to unravel the connections, taking the teachers first.*

Let it be marked in parenthesis, however, that the focus of enquiry has shifted importantly. It is no longer on the connection

---

* There is a large literature on these issues and no attempt can be made here to summarise it. The Ghanaian and Mexican samples, however, tend to concord with its general tenor that most actors are concerned with several goals, preferences, incentives and sanctions. Persuading them to change behaviour, then, can require action on several connected dimensions.

between the 'diploma disease' and certain educational symptoms. Instead, it is trying to clarify why the symptoms persist, even when the disease is reduced or removed.

Explaining the Similarities

Time-lags in reform A first obvious hypothesis to help account for the similarities between the Ghanaian and Mexican teachers is that the time to bring about large changes in behaviour was simply too little. In Ghana the *New Structure and Content of Education* had been announced in 1974, while the schools were studied in 1976 and early 1977. In Mexico the period was longer (1971–6) but the literature on the diffusion and implementation of educational reforms suggests that even half a decade is a modest period for transforming even a centralised, closely supervised system, which Mexico's was not. On the other hand, the ideas embodied in the reforms had had a rather longer history of circulation in the education professions of both countries. Their promulgation through official documents and programmes was simply an outcome of a fairly lengthy process. It was also just the latest in a procession of educational changes: indeed, both groups complained of being confused by the incessant change. The general aims and principles of the reforms seemed well enough understood and/ accepted by both groups of teachers, and as observed already, some of the easier ones were already being put into practice. All that notwithstanding, the probability that the more difficult measures did need more time was high.

Imperfections in implementation Apart from time, the fact is that neither Ministry of Education had done its full duty in ensuring that the teachers were fully familiar with the reforms, let alone in seeing that they had sufficient material, guidance and training to carry them out. Among the Ghanaian teachers, the level of detailed information was so low that there was no question of their deliberately neglecting the reform. Of the thirteen teachers interviewed in the six schools, seven could not say what the Ghana Education Service was recommending by way of improved teaching. Although ten had had at least an opportunity to see and try out the new texts and were willing to comment (judiciously) on them, none had had any systematic reorientation or training. Only a couple professed sufficient familiarity with the reforms to undertake discussions on them. In their view there was deficient stress on retraining, better incentives, higher pay and improved conditions of service. The implication seemed to be that teaching was after all only one part of a teacher's concerns.

The case in Mexico was not dissimilar, although somewhat more had been done to communicate with the teachers. The reform had been as much a political as a pedagogical project. It obeyed the political need to create the appropriate climate for further reforms, the need for high visibility in the form of the new texts, the need for rapid dissemination, and the preference for a model of teaching and learning that was better judged in terms of its egalitarian ideals than its practicality. All these factors reduced consideration of the method of delivery to the point of compromising the reform's success. The confusion of the first months was only compounded by the continued absence of support facilities, supervision and in-service training. The attitude of the teachers towards the reform four years after its supposed implementation was still one of confusion mixed with an awareness that their preparation had been sadly inadequate.

None the less, the federal government had gone to some pains to publicise the reforms and President Echeverría himself made a number of speeches in their support. The new textbooks, admirable publications, were distributed free by the Ministry of Education. In addition, conferences had been organised in all the states of Mexico at which teachers and other educators were invited to examine and comment on the texts. Not surprisingly, all twenty-five teachers interviewed knew of the reforms and had used the texts in their classes. However, none had attended a conference and five admitted to being cloudy on the objectives of the reform. In addition, up until 1975 there had been delays and scarcities in getting the texts: in 1975, for instance, the fifth-year groups had all had to manage without any materials in mathematics and social and natural sciences. By 1976, however, all four schools had their full quotas – but it had after all taken nearly five years to get even that basic requirement right. Further, the only training furnished was the advice offered in the teachers' guides to the texts – and none of the school directors had thought to attempt self-training sessions for his staff to work out whether that advice was, in fact, practicable. On the other hand, none of the teachers complained that the texts were grossly unrealistic, or that they were being asked to do the impossible. Like the lack of time, then, imperfect implementation provides a partial, if incompletely convincing, explanation.

Conflicts in Central Objectives To some degree the emphasis of the teachers on academic material and their difficulties with using the local natural and science environment is a function of the curricula that give priority to such aims as 'national unity' and 'cultural homogeneity'. The idea of differentiated curricula, designed with the different needs of a heterogeneous population in mind, is rejected by education ministries on the ground that there is a core of society-wide values that are both non-controversial and desirable. As Paulston (1971) notes, the resultant nation-wide textbooks, generally urban in context and orientation, can lead to meaningless ritual and rote-memorisation because of their lack of any real point of contact with local priorities. Vague, if insistent, calls to the teacher to 'adapt the curriculum to the locality' are clearly insufficient to counterbalance such an effect, especially when teachers show a preference for standardised material either because they lack the confidence to improvise or because it represents a less time-consuming option.

This does not imply that differentiated texts are an easily produced alternative. Despite initial enthusiasm, the Mexican reform subsequently abandoned the idea (Bravo Ahuja, 1970; Diaz de Cossio, 1976). One approach that might possibly have been considered was that of different solutions for the different subject areas. The Spanish (or English in Ghana) and mathematics components could, perhaps, be more readily standardised without urban bias. In the science and social science areas the problem is more acute, with the bias towards a 'national' viewpoint more powerful but the need for more local material much greater. The problem of how differentiated texts would be treated in both qualifying and selective examinations is similarly difficult to resolve, especially when these texts are designed to be supplemented by locally generated materials.

Conflicts within the declared curriculum are one constraint. Conflicts between the declared curriculum and the hidden curriculum are less obvious and less considered. The hidden curriculum includes the way the school is organised and run: it signals the sorts of value and behaviour which make for a tolerable and desirable society. The reforms in both countries called for more dynamic, flexible and spontaneous styles of teaching. But the patterns of authority maintained by the headteachers in Ghana and directors in Mexico were virtually unchanged. In Ghana the matter was compounded by the necessity to seek the approval of the district authorities. As one teacher put it:

The procedure for taking pupils out on excursions is so tedious – writing for permission in the first place, making your estimates of finance involved, collecting the money, writing back to the Ghana Education Service about the amount collected before final approval is given and so forth. All this will kill the enthusiasm of most teachers.

In Mexico, too, classroom organisation, whether to stay indoors or go outside for practical work, is still largely a matter for the director. While this authority impinges little on day-to-day classroom activities, it makes clear to the teachers the preference for order and predictability. While it does not totally prohibit a teacher from enterprise, it tends to inhibit spontaneity and flexible response. It abets unadventurous, humdrum teaching.

Similarly hidden in their constraints on good teaching are the patterns of evaluating teachers for promotion. In neither country was a teacher formally assessed on his or her teaching methods or pupils' attainments. In both a teacher could gain promotion simply by improving his paper qualifications through part-time and correspondence study. Ghana's pattern, it is true, did make one path of promotion dependent on an inspection of classwork, once a sufficiently high mark had been scored on a paper-and-pen examination. Mexico's form of assessment, on the other hand, looked only at 'preparation and fulfilment of work plans' and 'coverage of the school programme' as indicators of the style and quality of a person's teaching. Neither had been altered to concord with the spirit of the reforms.

Particularly inimical to the quest for local relevance was Mexico's informal, geographical promotion system which was none the less important for being without any written statutes. Through it the more experienced teachers, with firmer contacts within the teachers' union and the state education secretariats, could secure moves to the larger towns and cities. As a general rule, the younger and less experienced were sent to the remoter areas from where, by diligent lobbying, they also could secure their progress towards the larger provincial towns. The very remote postings were automatically rewarded with town jobs. This system ensured extremely rapid teacher turnover, reaching in some schools 100 per cent in two years, with the majority of teachers spending one year or less in each school. Hopes of developing sufficient knowledge of a locality and its citizens for the purposes of local relevance could only be slight even were a teacher interested. But the system itself provided the teacher with excuses for not wasting his time, as he or she would remain 'only a short while' if he had the mischance of a rural post.

Professional Orientations The preceding paragraph insinuated that at least the Mexican teachers were reluctant to teach in rural schools and assiduously sought escape from them. Such, indeed, was the case. Two particular reflections of the phenomenon were, first, the high turnover rates among the teachers of the sample – over 100 per cent every two years in three schools.* Secondly, the average number of years of experience among the teachers in the school closest to the state capital was 11·3. In the school furthest from a town it was a mere 3·2 years. In the other two schools it was 5·7 and 5·3 years. The drive for urban situations could scarcely be clearer. The distaste for rural schools is, of course, unique neither to these schoolteachers nor to Mexico. The literature on rural schooling has been reporting it for several decades and numerous states have introduced measures to counteract or at least to mitigate it. Ghana is no exception. Crook (1970) reported that schoolteachers posted to the villages 'have a fairly strong contempt for and dislike of their rural situation'.

However, that assessment of the late 1960s is not fully matched in the six schools studied in 1976. Of thirteen teachers interviewed, just six or about half frankly wanted town postings. The others enumerated the difficulties of urban life in Ghana's current economic plight and preferred to avoid them. Nevertheless, the strength of 'urban-bias' can be indirectly gauged from the fact that of the six teachers with ten years' or more experience, four were in the two more urbanised and prosperous localities, while both the officially best-qualified of the youngest teachers were similarly stationed. A legitimate suspicion could be that, were Ghana faring better, more of the rural teachers might want city postings, as in bygone years.

Yearning for city life might adversely affect teachers' attitudes to pupils and families who did not share their aspirations and, perhaps, their valuations of salaried jobs. Certainly, the Mexican teachers tended to dismiss as mere passengers those pupils who did not intend to proceed to secondary school. The teachers themselves were upwardly mobile, valued their professional status and

* Some of the teachers in the fourth school were drawn from the locality. Even so, the turnover rate was about 30 per cent annually.

security of employment, and believed that education could and should promote mobility among their pupils.

They compared 'professionals' who have studied and been justly rewarded with good jobs in comfortable circumstances with the *campesiños*, whom they described as working like animals from dawn to dusk. Pupils who wanted to be animals could, of course, not be taken seriously. Not unnaturally, the equation between school and urban jobs makes it harder for the teacher to see much relevance in the stimulation of a child's curiosity or in the development of investigative skills for the goal of rural development. It means little interest in adapting the course materials to the local environment, in undertaking experiments and making observations of the locality, or in pursuing practical activities. In a word, it means a lack of interest in a major purpose of the progressive methods espoused by the primary school reform.

Matters were rather less extreme with the Ghanaian teachers. While half would certainly have preferred urban schools, three-quarters denied discussing urban living with their pupils. Indeed, more than one-third claimed that they actively discouraged thoughts in that direction. 'The city has not got answers to your problems', as one put it. All of them bluntly appreciated that their pupils were simply not in the running for urban jobs and would perforce have to make their livings in the locality. Consequently, urban bias was not an apparent factor in either their attitudes to their pupils or their failure to incorporate local aspects and events in their teaching.

The drive for social mobility can also affect a teacher's commitment to her/his current functions. At this point, of course, there is an interaction between the aspirations of the individual and the requirements, incentives and sanctions of his institution. In order to realise an aspiration within the institution the individual must take account of it. In both Ghana and Mexico – and elsewhere, as Bude (1982) points out – primary school teachers are naturally eager for promotion: half of both groups studied take part-time and correspondence courses to qualify for it.

Now promotion may take the form of advancement through the primary ranks or of elevation to the corps of secondary school teachers. In both states, as virtually everywhere else, the professional structure strongly encourages the latter route, for secondary teachers enjoy not only higher professional status, but superior salaries as well – and most secondary schools are in the larger urban centres. So primary teachers see little future in primary schools.

Equally powerful perhaps is that neither educational system sets successful teaching as a criterion for advancement. In both the acquisition of paper qualifications alone can bring substantial increments in income and seniority. Consequently, they actually create an incentive for teachers to neglect teaching in order to pursue promotion. Bude (1982) reports that in the Cameroon teachers are known to absent themselves from their classrooms so as to make more time to study for their own promotion examinations. No teacher in either the Ghanaian or Mexican group actually confessed to such delinquency, but absenteeism and unpunctuality were noticeable.

Certainly, the Mexicans were no sticklers for duty. The official minimum of daily teaching was five hours. In none of the four schools observed was that minimum respected on even one day. On most days teaching extended for only three hours or so. Absenteeism for whole days ran at over 10 per cent per month. While complaining that the syllabus was overfull, the teachers themselves made it harder to complete. If this shows less than wholehearted professional commitment, the situation was little better among the Ghanaians: of thirteen teachers interviewed, only one intended to remain in an elementary school. The ambitions of the others were directed elsewhere. The inference can be only that, by and large, rural primary teachers are not deeply concerned with better teaching for better education. While they may certainly approve the ideals of reform aimed at intellectual stimulus, relevance and co-operation, they lack both motivation and incentive to realise them. They are confirmed in their inertia by their education systems or institutions. Doing the minimum necessary to escape censure becomes the norm. Worse, teachers who in their enthusiasm exceed the norm and become 'rate-busters' can provoke persecution from their colleagues: a clear instance was observed in one of the Mexican schools.

Pupils' Orientation At this point, common ground appears for an alliance between teachers and pupils to 'minimise'. So long as a pass in the MSLC was pretty well assured for the Ghanaian pupils, they were not at all concerned with – probably not even aware of – issues of stimulus, relevance, or co-operation and, as the teachers complained, they were reluctant to exert themselves more than necessary. However, the minimum was fixed by the MSLC examination and the pupils had to rely on the teachers to know it, and the teachers had to play safe to ensure an acceptable ratio of passes.

Among the Mexicans, however, the absence of an outside, immutable standard made the minimum rather more negotiable. Not only did it allow the teacher more discretion, it also created among the pupils a bias to minimise further. Because the scope of classroom tests or other 'gradable' activities was determined by what occurred within the classroom, the students had a vested interest in restricting the area of study. Clearly, the teacher could not test understanding of what had not yet been covered. The level of treatment might suffer similar restrictive practices. If the students managed to keep discussion and inquiry to a superficial level by a policy of avoiding deviations or pupil-initiated discussions and not responding to a teacher's attempt to delve deeper, they ensured a superficial treatment of the topic when the test came round. An audience of uninquiring students in this case would not have meant they were disinterested in final grades.

A certain degree of 'risk-spreading' might also appear. High-value assignments, projects, or tests (in terms of the number of points involved and their consequent impact on end-of-semester grades) would not presumably be welcomed, if the major concern of the pupil were the grade rather than the learning involved. The consequences of a significant error or absence on the day of the test would be greatly magnified, and the end-of-year grade put in jeopardy. The preference for small, superficial assignments would be the product of such an attitude.

There is a similar 'risk' justification for a teacher-oriented behaviour among pupils. The negative consequences of this would, of course, depend on the characteristics of the teacher and the degree to which these are known. As pupils are dependent on the teacher's evaluation of them, there is a certain risk associated with any novel or unprogrammed behaviour. When the teacher has already shown an openness to 'creative' behaviour, the risk is reduced; but where the teacher is an unknown quantity, such as at the beginning of the school-year or where team-teaching operates, the pupil is unlikely to take the risk, if he/she is significantly grade-oriented.

Inappropriate Paradigms? A further explanation of the similarity in Ghanaian and Mexican teaching styles might cast some doubt on the viability of the progressive model of education as applied in these countries. In both Ghana and Mexico the teachers were largely unable to arouse the interest and enthusiasm of their pupils because of the latter's passivity and introversion. This lack of communication was exacerbated in the two Mexican communities with Indian populations by the absence of normative support for co-operation and the sharp sense of cultural difference between parents and teachers. This culture gap restricts the scope for parental involvement and for school–community collaboration on learning projects.

The progressive model that underlies both Ghanaian and Mexican reforms makes a number of assumptions about the nature of teacher–pupil relations which may be inappropriate in these countries. Its key words are democracy and equality and its fundamental belief is that all children are good, eager to learn, with a wide range of aptitudes and interests, requiring no more than the correct environment for their full development. This is a humanistic philosophy which draws support from among the affluent and concerns for self-actualisation, rather than from considerations of how best to achieve a maximum of learning among the economically and socially underprivileged. With the severe disjunction between home and school cultures commonly found in developing countries, with poorly fed and under-stimulated children with little understanding of the wider significance of their school experience and perhaps even less motivation, it may be expecting too much to ask these teachers to organise school-life as if their pupils were bursting with the energy, enthusiasm and drive for independent learning of their peers in London or New York.

EXAMINATIONS – GUARANTORS OF EDUCATION?

The foregoing attempt to explain why the symptoms ascribed to the 'diploma disease' persist even when the root of the disease is apparently removed, has at least borne out one general truism; human behaviour is influenced by many factors, so that changing one of them, however critical, may not assure a change of behaviour. In the context of this discussion it indicates that the removal of certification and selection for salaried jobs may be a necessary condition for reorienting education, but is by itself insufficient. Other complementary measures are necessary, too. In particular, desired changes in curriculum and pedagogy need to be supported by concordant changes in assessment, supervision, training, incentives and career structure. Conversely and ironically, the discussion suggests that

- where the professional commitment of teachers is unreliable;
- where skills in teaching and assessment are uncertain;
- where services of support and supervision for teachers are weak and infrequent;
- where educational institutions fail to match their overt goals with the real incentives and sanctions they wield

external examinations for pupils may be the most effective means of assuring a minimally satisfactory education for most and especially rural pupils. A further assertion may be ventured. Since improving the quality of centralised external examinations is relatively easier than improvements in the other areas listed above, an obvious strategy recommends itself: a prime line of reform should bend examinations to fit the wider objectives of education. By that kind of judo trick, examinations – whether for education plain and simple or for certification for salaried jobs or for selection for even higher certification for even better jobs – should promote and reward better teaching and learning. That the notion is sound in principle and feasible – if gradual – in practice has been recently demonstrated by Somerset (1982).

Chapter 6

Severing the Links between Education and Careers: the Sobering Experience of China's Urban Schools

JONATHAN UNGER

Ronald Dore's *The Diploma Disease* (1976) has described how schooling in most of the Third World countries has been distorted by the desperate desires of students to win modern sector jobs. School systems have been expanded rapidly in order to meet the students' demands for the diplomas that lead to jobs; but in a vicious circle, as the growing crowds of young people win diplomas, even higher educational credentials have become necessary to obtain the jobs. In much of the Third World, as Dore points out, the end-results can be crippling. The reputations of schools and the careers of teachers increasingly come to depend upon their students' rate of success in getting through the higher school entrance examinations. Students spend years in rote-cramming for the succession of entrance examinations. Their contest to climb the school ladder implicitly teaches them to view the most common occupations of their society with disdain; and most of them are ultimately consigned to those very occupations as 'failures'.

The mass education programmes of Third World nations have come under critical scrutiny from a separate angle also. Study after study, in country after country, has shown that the children of the educated urban elites, coming from literate homes and with access to better schools, disproportionally have been able to climb the examination ladder into the coveted modern sector occupations. As one comparative analysis has observed, 'Even when an educational system can stay justly selective from generation to generation, it will be governed by the children of the well-to-do, who persistently score better on examinations even when such examinations are not intentionally skewed in their favor' (Bereday, 1968, p. 131). The great expansions in the school systems of the Third World, thus, have not necessarily promoted a markedly greater equality of job opportunity.

SCHOOL ADMISSIONS BEFORE THE CULTURAL REVOLUTION

In the 1960s China's school structure resembled the educational structures of other late-developing countries in both of these respects. Entrance examinations helped determine which of the students were able to enter each higher level of education; the competition among students was tight; and many Chinese high schools especially in the cities competed to attain a high university entrance rate.[1] Moreover, mass education at the elementary school level did not mean equal opportunities to all students at the higher educational levels. Students who came from the educated households of the pre-revolution bourgeoisie and petty bourgeoisie tended to do better on the selection examinations than students from semi-literate working-class families.

Though the political leaderships of most countries would have been content with this state of affairs, in China it was the subject of debate among the highest leaders. National priorities were in conflict. The revolution had come to power in 1949 on the strength of two appeals that had won mass national backing: a patriotic promise to restore Chinese pride and prosperity; and a social revolutionary pledge to increase the opportunities available to China's great majority of have-nots. From the early 1950s onward whenever the party leaders had to determine new policies, controversy arose over where and how to draw the balance between these two sets of goals. The moderates (the several groupings within the leadership which presently share power in China) defined the revolution more in terms of its nationalist/ development goals; Mao and the radicals, on the other hand, seem to have become willing by the mid- and late 1960s to sacrifice fast development, if such development meant abandoning the redistributive goals which favoured the 'proletarian' classes.

This issue of development vs redistribution had begun to focus in the 1960s on China's university admission policies – and for a simple reason. The mass education efforts of the 1950s had allowed greatly expanded numbers of children into the secondary schools; and, thus, for the first time there were far more candidates for enrolment in China's universities than there were university openings available. The Chinese were facing a very common consequence of the 'diploma disease': as in the Third World experience, the provision of increased educational places at lower levels of schooling had served only to move the competition for school seats to a higher point on the education ladder.

In the Chinese case a special political tension was involved in this. Until the revolution's success in 1949 relatively few working-class ('good class') children had been able to attend schools; and thus, throughout most of the 1950s the secondary school graduates had come predominantly from the former upper and middle classes. But by the early 1960s the secondary school student bodies included large numbers of young people from the classes of former have-nots. Though they were offered priority in university admissions in a very strong equivalent of America's 'affirmative action' programme, this did not normally outweigh their generally poorer showings on the selection examinations. With rapidly growing numbers of these families finding their children's expectations disappointed in the tightening contest for university places – and with the revolution's commitment to its redistributive goals thereby put to the test – left-wing leaders in the party began arguing with increasing vigour that the criteria for university admissions had to be shifted further in favour of the 'good class' youths. But until the Cultural Revolution of 1966–8 the majority of China's top leadership remained convinced that the revolution's modernisation goals precluded any policy that markedly discriminated against the chances of the most academically capable of the intelligentsia's children.

This disagreement over admissions standards came to the boil in 1966. In the Cultural Revolution's first months, to the delight of the 'good class' students, Mao pushed a radical decree through the party's central committee proclaiming the abolition of the university entrance examinations, and

a new method of enrolment, a combination of recommendation

and selection in which proletarian politics are right to the fore
... The old examination system is a serious violation of the
Party's class line, shuts out many outstanding children of
workers, former poor and lower-middle peasants and
revolutionary cadres ... and opens the gates wide to the
bourgeoisie to cultivate its own successors. (*People's Daily*
(Beijing), 18 June 1966)

THE RADICALS' PRESCRIPTIONS FOR EDUCATION

By the end of the Cultural Revolution fighting in late 1968 most of
the leaders who had opposed the views of Mao's disciples had been
swept away or politically weakened. New leaders such as Yao
Wenyuan and Zhang Chunqiao (two of the so-called 'gang of
four'), who became Mao's representatives in educational affairs,
were given a free hand to implement a new type of education.

For a start, they did not see any pressing need for the universities
to prepare a corps of highly trained technocrats and experts. In
part, this was because the Maoist radicals wanted to pursue a new
approach to economic development. They were oriented towards
an economic strategy of smaller and technically less sophisticated
factories. They argued that with such industrial development, it
would be enough simply to educate greater numbers of politically
reliable 'socialist labourers' with resourcefulness on the job in
handling relatively simple technologies. The radicals wanted to
gear the new secondary school sciences and mathematics almost
exclusively towards such low-level technical familiarity: how
lathes operate, the principles of levers, and so on. It was to be a
knowledge geared not to theory, but towards the tangibly practical
and the easily practised.

The radicals' preference for this type of economic strategy and
this kind of learning derived partly from their perspectives on
social class or what they called the 'class-line'. Since those best at
handling 'expertise' and theoretical constructs were the pre-
revolution bourgeois professionals and their offspring, neither the
schools nor the factories were to be allowed to be arenas in which
they could excel at the expense of the workers and their children.
At all levels education was to be used as a mechanism for
eradicating the gaps between students from different backgrounds.
No longer was it to serve as a means for sorting and stratifying
students.

To meet these ends the competitive school ladder was

eliminated. In the major cities an education was supplied to all youths through senior middle school. This was made financially possible by shortening the entire school curriculum by two to three years. Then, so as to sever entirely the links between classroom achievements and upward mobility, all the young people graduating from middle school were assigned directly to jobs, with no account taken of their academic records when devising these job postings. The choice of which young people could go on to higher schooling was left to the places of work, purportedly on the basis of a young worker's performance during his or her first several years on the job. The 'good class' party leaders at the work unit could be expected to take class origins strongly into account when appraising the dedication and performance of the applicants.

The radical national leaders had other reasons, too, for divorcing academic achievement from the ladder of upward mobility. The Maoists were concerned that academic competition in the classroom bred individualistic and careerist values; and they were concerned, too, that if some young people entered universities direct from school on the basis of their academic abilities and subsequently moved into specialised careers with the status of experts, their life-experience would have put them out of touch with the political interests of the masses. The radicals wanted to prevent the rise in power of a technocratic 'new bourgeoisie', regardless of class background. In the years after the Cultural Revolution conflicts of 1966–8 the derisory term 'bourgeois technician' became a commonplace catchphrase, referring even to technical personnel who had come from 'red' homes. The new means of recruiting China's higher-trained personnel – chosen in reward for good *blue-collar* work – was supposed to help assure that they saw themselves as 'proletarian technicians'.

This should not imply, though, that the Maoists wanted to focus education principally on vocational training. Instead, it was to centre on character-building, through the frequent immersion of young people in Mao thought. The radicals were both 'redder' and more traditional than the party's moderates. They seemed almost Confucianist in their belief that the principal purpose of schooling lay in the teaching of morals (Munro, 1977).

In light of all of the above, the reopened schools of 1968 were to organise education along the following lines:
(1) schools were to play down the systematic teaching of theory,

and instead were to teach concepts that were relevant to industrial and agricultural work;

(2) a student's academic excellence was no longer to be rewarded or even permitted to be an important source of informal prestige in the classroom. Among other things, learning was to be simplified and slowed, narrowing the gap between good and poor students;

(3) overall the shaping of attitudes was to carry far greater weight in the education system than the imparting of knowledge;

(4) learning was to be combined with labour;

(5) urban schooling would be shortened to a universalised nine or ten years;

(6) selection examinations would be eliminated;

(7) school graduates would be allocated directly to jobs, and the work units would hold the right to determine which of their young personnel deserved a university or technical school training.

Abandoning all entrance examinations and severing the links between academic success and careers were expressly intended to improve the chances of working-class children. These measures also came very close to two of Ronald Dore's (1976, p. 142 *et seq.*) proposals for achieving higher educational quality and greater efficiency in occupational selection. China's experiments provide us with a test-case of remedies prescribed by Dore. But the medicine proved unpalatable – certainly in the dosage offered to Chinese teenagers. Indeed, the programme proved unworkable. Between 1968 and Mao's death, in 1976, most of China's urban[2] students simply stopped paying attention in class.

'STUDYING IS USELESS'

Admittedly, when this new structure of education was introduced in 1968, China's urban schools faced enormous problems that would have hampered any educational venture. Students had been running loose on the streets during the chaotic years of the Cultural Revolution, and the schools were having difficulty getting them readjusted to the routine of school-life. The teaching profession, moreover, was demoralised; the textbooks were haphazardly devised; and the curriculum was subjected to exceedingly narrow ideological constraints. In fact, many of the schools initially played it safe by having their students concentrate solely on memorising Mao quotes (Unger, 1982, ch. 7).

But by the early 1970s China could provide a somewhat better test-case of whether it is feasible to divorce education from the contest for careers. Though China's schools still faced administrative problems, the turmoil and confusion of the Cultural Revolution was receding into memory; the textbooks were no longer heavily burdened with political rhetoric; the coursework was considerably better organised. Yet students continued to play truant, and many of them continued to be rowdy. It was, they felt, 'useless to study'. A former student from Canton remembers:

> In class, many of the kids just chatted or slept or wandered outside to do something else while the teacher lectured. Only about half the students would even be in class. Right after the Cultural Revolution, during my first year of junior middle school in 1969, there'd been some students who wanted a bit to study. But they lost that interest by the time they reached senior middle school. Mainly because they felt it all had zero to do with their futures, that they'd just be sent out to the countryside or a factory regardless.

Occasionally rumours circulated that academic achievement once again would count, and in each recorded case a willingness to study came back into vogue temporarily. A student from Fujian province recalled that in his final year of schooling, 1972–3,

> the attitudes of the students toward studying improved. The teachers that year taught a lot of material. For one thing, things generally were more stable that year, which encouraged more stable schoolwork. Second, though no one did end up going directly to a university, the teachers had hinted to them that this year some could. This spurred the desire to study. We organized maths and science study groups, where the good students helped the bad. There was a study group organized by the students themselves, twelve classmates in all, in which I participated. We met at each other's homes at night. But not that type of stuff now [this interview was conducted in 1975]. The students get worse and worse each year because they again feel that, when last comes to last, they have no opportunities.

The same point consistently re-emerged in the interviews, which I conducted in Hong Kong during 1975–6 with nine former students and five former high school teachers from China.[3] Every one of them insisted that most students had felt it useless to study, because success or failure at their schoolwork would have no bearing on their futures.

At the very same time, though, many students were worried about their futures. In China, as in many other late-developing countries, industrial expansion had not kept pace with the 'baby boom'. To avoid high levels of urban unemployment China had begun assigning growing numbers of the new high school graduates to work indefinitely in the countryside. But life in the villages was known to be hard, impoverished and lonely, and most of the young people tried to avoid going (Unger, 1979). Those who were selected felt, resentfully, that the peasant villages were dumping-grounds for the cities' 'losers'. To help dispel this feeling the authorities decided that the system of career assignments must become patently impartial and equitable. Each city devised its own programme, but Canton's was fairly typical.

Earlier in the high school class that had graduated in 1969 the teenagers selected for the countryside from Canton had been largely from the former bourgeois and petty bourgeois families. But this only had served to strengthen the feelings among Canton's young people that those sent to the villages were second-class citizens. The authorities, therefore, decided in 1971 that class origins should no longer determine who got assigned to a village. Nor did the leadership feel that a student's political activism at school should be allowed to affect his or her job assignment. Settlement in the countryside was something a dedicated student was supposed to *want* to do, not something to avoid. Nor, finally, could a student's academic record be allowed to play any part in the decision of who went. That was precisely the standard that post Cultural Revolution education no longer was supposed to reward.

In 1971, therefore, it was proclaimed in Canton that any graduating student would be assigned to a rural job, if half or more of his brothers or sisters were still in the city. This was indisputably an impartial method. It meant, basically, that elder siblings in each family went to the countryside, and younger siblings got the urban jobs. When in 1973 Canton's leadership decided that urban job openings would become even scarcer during the coming years, all but the last remaining child in each family was supposed to settle in the countryside.

The 'backwash' into the schools from this job assignment policy was profound. Once the students felt their futures were already fated by the order of their births, those destined for the countryside became even less inclined to open their books. They argued to their teachers they would only be able to utilise very rudimentary skills in the villages. Why pay attention to mathematics beyond the multiplication tables, when rural accounting techniques used no mathematics beyond that? Why bother even to learn to recognise rural pests or how to plant rice, when they would be learning that anyway once they were peasants? It was partly that they felt little preparation was needed for the countryside. But it was partly also, according to respondents, that students did not want to lead the hard and poor life of a peasant. They were consequently refusing to orient themselves towards such a future, while still at school. In class some of them openly vented their frustrations and resentments. The final year of senior middle school was 'the worst class to try to control', observed a high school teacher from Yunnan province: 'When kids are imminently facing settlement in the countryside, sometimes on purpose they'll sabotage the class period.'

Students who were heading for urban postings were less obstreperous, but only slightly more prone to give any attention to their schoolwork. For one thing, few of them even contemplated going on to a university education. Word had circulated that without entrance examinations or other standardised means for selecting the new university students, party officials had begun pulling strings and making use of 'old boy' networks. They were getting their children out of the countryside by getting rural officials to nominate the child for a university place. According to a former Shanghai high school teacher, the young people from other backgrounds, including the students from working-class families, no longer saw any possibility of their own further education, 'just like people don't even think about whether it would be nice or not to live on the moon'.

For another thing, many students, even from the intelligentsia, *only* wanted blue-collar work. In earlier times a production-line job had seemed to many youths like the sort of work one took only when there were no other opportunities. But now that students were faced only with the stark choice between becoming a worker or a peasant, the blue-collar urban jobs had taken on a considerably rosier image. The students were aware, moreover, that a worker in the early and mid-1970s held a relatively high political status as a member of a 'proletarian' occupation, at a time when intellectuals were politically vulnerable and sometimes harassed. Workers also enjoyed secure incomes, which stayed about the same whether or not they became skilled and whether or not they stayed workers or became technicians. The higher standing which all of this gave to ordinary blue-collar work probably attracted a fair degree of working-class support. But the adverse side-effect was that for students who were now reasonably content to be production-line workers with no career goals beyond that, most of their school subjects did indeed seem useless.

Teachers found few means to get recalcitrant students to open their books. As a final resort, some teachers turned to 'political' threats against the worst offenders. Recalls a secondary school teacher,

> The kids didn't worry. They knew that if they failed they'd still be promoted. So we sometimes had to use political pressure. We'd organize other kids to criticize them. This would be through a session to criticize the ideology of 'studying is useless', an idea that we attributed to Liu Shaoqi.[4] But actually, there were still some kids who completely refused to study, and to that we had to close one of our eyes.

At the same time, though, the new desirability and improved status of industrial employment encouraged a growing interest among many of the students in modern mechanical crafts. This was even true – in fact, especially true – of young people fated for rural assignments, probably because such crafts represented the type of urban jobs they desired but would not be getting. Students who generally gave little attention to schoolwork often gravitated, out of school, towards radio-building, woodworking, model-plane building, and the like. At the Fujian school where these skills could be practised in 'hobby groups', the interest of students was so great that the school was able to get some of the students to behave better by denying participation to any students who were rowdy during regular classtime.

Some of the students who would be staying in the city had their own reasons for pursuing such hobbies. As part of the new school curriculum, they had engaged in work stints at factories, and interviewees say that they and their classmates had become aware of the monotony of routine production-line work. In reaction the hobbies reportedly reflected a desire for *interesting* blue-collar work, such as shopfloor mechanics, and the like.

But the radicals who until 1976 were in charge of education had mixed feelings about encouraging these desires and hobbies. Before the Cultural Revolution, as they pointed out in newspaper editorials, a high regard for expertise had propped up the prestige and salaries of the old professionally trained petty-bourgeois classes.

However, the Chinese leadership was split. The scientific and military establishments and the economic planners were increasingly alarmed at the absence of a new generation of technicians and scientific personnel. They were convinced that all the radicals' prescriptions for secondary and higher education were endangering China's future. Increasingly as China approached the mid-1970s education was becoming an open arena for debate between the party's moderate and radical factions (Unger, 1980).

Much of the urban population weighed in on the side of the moderates on this issue. Though the radical leaders' proposals for education initially had won some support among working-class families who thought their children's chances of upward mobility would be improved, this constituency subsequently had been alienated by the poor quality of the new schooling, the students' refusal to study and the schools' inability to discipline them.

Parents from all class backgrounds were disturbed at the 'bad' habits of a new teenage subculture (smoking, dating, and so on), their children's materialistic interests and cynical flippancy. By smashing the prior educational structure Mao and his followers had hoped to erect a system that would better allow the schools to teach 'proletarian' and 'revolutionary' virtues, but if anything, the decade of Maoist schooling had very seriously eroded the Maoist ethos among the younger generation.

In more ways than one the radicals' tenacious and dogmatic pursuit of unrealistic educational prescriptions had become (to paraphrase a Chinese saying) a stone that they dropped upon their own feet. They had smothered the 'diploma disease' problem, but as an official recently explained to a visitor, 'though their remedy may have been curing the disease, it was killing the patient' (Smerling, 1979). By providing an inadequate education for all sectors of the urban population they built a massive constituency against their ideas. Inflexible like the Jacobins of the French Revolution, they themselves contributed most to the popular Thermidorean reaction which awaited Mao's death.

To counter the radicals' strangulation of educational standards the new leadership that took power in late 1976 looked back in time to the school system of the 1960s. Indeed, with the momentum of a pendulum swinging back past its initial resting point, the post-Mao system has stressed academic 'talent' considerably more than the pre-Cultural Revolution schools. The middle schools, for example, have begun tracking students into different classrooms on the basis of their academic achievements. China's newspapers belatedly have acknowledged that many of the symptoms of the 'diploma disease' have emerged stronger than ever before: after-school private tutors, rote-digestion of school material, schools sponsoring weekend 'cramming' sessions and ambitious students exhausting themselves.

LESSONS

What can be learned from China's experiences? It might have been hoped that if an educational system could be divorced from the competition for careers and if the threat of selection examinations were removed, students would be better able to learn for other reasons – such as the practicality of their schoolwork for the jobs they later would be most likely to get.

But in this respect China's experience induces little optimism about the effectiveness of such wholesale reforms. Admittedly, even in China's mismanaged school system of 1968–76, many students did focus their attention upon manual craft skills, and to an extent greater, indeed, than the schools encouraged. But it must also be recognised that the social status, political prestige and economic security of China's industrial workers were, all in all, probably higher at that time than the prestige and security of engineers and technicians. This situation was unlike any other country in the world and temporary even in China, soon to be overthrown along with the 'gang of four'. The students, in short, were interested in the skills that were associated with highly desirable jobs; the same students neglected to pay attention to the school lessons on farming. If even China, with a national political ideology that actively promoted the dignity of farmwork, could not persuade urban students destined for the countryside to pay attention to learning agricultural skills at school, how might other countries expect to promote a similar type of vocational coursework?[5]

Reforms to the structure of schooling, I would argue, will not succeed if they do not address students' hopes to climb into desired careers. But there are many partial reforms that Third World nations can employ which realistically recognise students' job aspirations, but at the same time come to grips with some of the diploma disease's ill-effects (for instance, Dore, 1976, pp. 152–63).

China employed an intermediate solution of this type very successfully prior to the Cultural Revolution. China's urban vocational school programme in the 1950s and 1960s was linked to the job market in a way that encouraged the learning of actual vocational skills. The vocational schools' singular advantage was their ability to channel vocational graduates directly into reserved jobs. Unlike China's academic-track senior middle schools, whose graduates had to scramble on their own to find jobs, the vocational system in the 1950s and 1960s was able to *assign* its graduates to be the new bookkeepers for government offices and factories, the new marine pilots, locomotive engineers, machine-shop craftsmen, and so on. These vocational schools' annual enrolments were geared to the projected manpower needs of the various industries and government units: this was to ensure that there would not be any shortages of new skilled personnel.

The results of the programme were impressive. True, the most achievement-oriented urban students in the 1950s and 1960s continued to gamble on the academic-track senior middle schools in the hope of getting into a university. That fact notwithstanding, in 1965 Canton's full-time vocational schools held fully 80 per cent as many students as the academic-track senior middle school system; and the competition to get admitted was fairly tight. Most of these vocational students were purposely made ineligible to take the university entrance examinations so as to prevent them from turning their studies back towards 'examination-prepping'. The vocational school administrators very likely supported this regulation, since they were under pressure to supply the government organs with adequately trained personnel.

During 1968–76, however, the doors of many of these vocational schools were closed.[6] As a recent complaint in China's press observes:

Ever since the Cultural Revolution the ordinary senior middle schools blindly have been allowed to expand, and the secondary level specialist schools and the various vocational schools have largely stopped operating. This type of one-sided development has [meant that] ... each year the number of senior middle graduates is extremely large, and so the ratio of students which the higher educational institutions can admit is very small. This [presently] not only has created a lot of pressure on the institutes of higher education, but also pressures on the senior middle schools to compete for favourable rates of university admissions. Even more noteworthy is that over 90 percent of the senior middle graduates will have to participate in manual labour; but they do not have vocational preparation, which gives rise to an acute ... demand for skilled labour power. (*Guangming Daily*, 5 July 1979, p. 4)

China's vocational programme of the 1960s is being resurrected in its entirety.

Such an approach to vocational schooling would probably be of considerable benefit to other late-developing countries. The Third World governments normally are the employers of a substantial portion of the modern sector personnel: in India, and many states of Africa, nearly two-thirds of the educated labourforce (Blaug *et al.*, 1969, p. 239; JASPA, 1981a, b). Yet the personnel officers of Third World governments all too frequently operate on the premiss that the less capable students are obliged to enter the vocational track, and they accordingly prefer to hire general education graduates instead. Probably more than anything else, it is this which defeats vocational programmes. With vocational graduates so often relegated to the unemployment rolls, it is little wonder that in some countries the vocational students reportedly do not concentrate on their courses, but instead 'prep' to pass the next higher regular-track entrance examinations.

If the Third World governments' regulations stipulated that specified categories of their new middle-level technical, administrative, or even blue-collar government workers were only to be hired from among the graduates of the appropriate vocational schools, their vocational students could be expected to turn their attention more towards their vocational courses. Perhaps as important, students in the lower schools of these countries would be likely to show a greater interest than at present in learning the various skills useful for getting into vocational studies.

Both the success of China's vocational scheme and the failure of the Chinese radicals' drastic reforms provide the same important lesson to educators elsewhere – that any curricular reforms which are aimed at curbing the 'diploma disease' must provide students with positive reasons for study. Brooke, in Chapter 5, shows that these reasons need not be connected with diplomas and jobs when only basic schooling and literacy are the aim. Purposes beyond that, however, will almost certainly need some kind of career inducement.

EGALITARIAN OBJECTIONS

China's vocational programmes of the 1960s did not, however, address the issue that most preoccupied the Chinese radicals. They had been unhappy before the Cultural Revolution that a disproportionate number of the young people from the urban professional classes were climbing the school ladder into the same level of occupations as their parents. The radicals were worried – and accurately – that a modern occupational elite tends to perpetuate itself through precisely the sort of education structure that in most countries is touted as providing for 'equality of opportunity'.

From the vantage-point of distributing opportunities more broadly a vocational programme like that of China's before the Cultural Revolution may, indeed, have been counter-productive. Most of the achievement-oriented children of China's party officialdom, and of the former middle classes, had not been deterred in the early 1960s from the contest to enter a university and gain a high-level career, even when the penalty for non-success increasingly had entailed unemployment or lifetime peasanthood. Most of the Chinese students who withdrew from this competition in order to enter vocational schools were from the urban working classes.

If the linkages between vocational training and job recruitments were similarly strengthened in other countries, it could be expected that there, too, the students of working-class backgrounds would be far more willing to desist from the risky contest for the top than the children from upper- and middle-class families. The opportunities for the already advantaged classes to continue their dominance through the levers of education correspondingly would be enhanced. It is a prospect not likely to be relished by a great many educational reformers.

But there may be no completely satisfactory remedy for the 'diploma disease'. Certainly, the radical surgery of 1968–76 provided no solutions whatsoever. The Chinese vocational programme of the 1960s provides us with only a partial solution and this is coupled to potentially adverse side-effects, yet it *is* a programme that has proved workable. In a situation where no proposed solution is free of drawbacks it helps point one way forward.

NOTES

As part of the Institute of Development Studies project on Third World education and employment, I have written a book on the Chinese case (Unger, 1982). Sections of this chapter borrow from that longer study, with permission of Columbia University Press.

1   The important exceptions to this 'diploma disease' competition, as we shall later observe, were China's urban vocational schools.
2   To avoid misunderstanding note the qualification in the title of this chapter that only urban schools are discussed here.
3   All but three of these fourteen interviewees were legal emigrants. Some were Chinese from South-east Asia who had returned to China with their families in the 1950s and early 1960s and had recently come back out again through Hong Kong. Others were Hong Kong residents whose parents had sent them to socialist China for their education.
4   In a school environment where 'ideology takes command', attributing the phrase to Liu Shaoqi put the erring student in a politically indefensible position. Early on, the national mass media began claiming Liu as the author of the phrase 'studying is useless' so as to oblige students publicly to repudiate their own way of thinking. After 1971, it was revealed in the press that the author of the phrase was actually none other than Lin Biao, and in 1977 the press discovered, *mirabile dictu*, that the gang of four's Zhang Chunqiao had been the originator of that same phrase.
5   The experiences of those countries which have tried suggest that this problem has been common. Repeatedly such programmes have come up against this difficulty: be it the village institutes of 1930s Turkey and Mexico; or Gandhian basic education in India in the 1950s; or the agricultural primary schools of Tanganyika and, later, independent Tanzania.
6   Under the radicals' scheme the vocational schools no longer operated as secondary schools. Instead, if a factory needed improved manpower skills of a given kind, it was supposed to select several young workers to attend the appropriate vocational programme. After graduating, the workers were to return to the factory. The municipal education departments, however, had run into great difficulties finding enough classrooms and teachers for the new universalised ten-year school programme. With this priority in mind, they converted many of the former vocational school facilities into regular schools in the late 1960s. The radicals' vocational training scheme was crippled from the start.

Part Three

Reconciling Efficient
Selection with Good
Education and Equity

At this point, stock needs to be taken of the relationship between the discussions of employers and productivity on the one hand, and the processes of schooling on the other. No defensible correspondence was demonstrated between levels of school and levels of salaried work, and no real association could be demonstrated between levels of school and levels of productivity in salaried employment. The schedule of correspondence and the escalation of qualifications proved highly questionable even on their own terms, without taking into account their effects on social relations and equity. It was possible to regard them as rickety conveniences which, if evil, were by no means necessary. The question, then, was whether they actually were evil in their effects upon education.

The three chapters on schooling have confirmed that part of the demand for basic schooling is for access to salaried employment; and suggested that most of the demand for further schooling is for that same purpose. They have confirmed, too, not only that external examinations for qualifications and selection do affect in harmful ways what and how teachers teach and learners learn; but also that qualification orientation has the same effect, even where external examinations are not used. In doing so, however, they have simultaneously thrown up a problem of human motivation, which makes it debatable whether qualification and selection *per se* distort education, or whether the real culprit is the mechanism chosen to validate them. (It should be noted that the focus here is more on the educational processes of the classroom than on the distribution and equity of educational expenditures and provision.)

The Mexican case suggests that, when schooling is not oriented to salaried employment, the demand for it from parents will be restricted to whatever a family feels is satisfactory. The criteria for satisfactoriness, both the Mexican and Ghanaian cases indicate, will be some compromise between the direct costs of schooling, a family's use of child labour, the prospects of a given child and public norms about what constitutes a decent minimal education. If schooling were wholly separate from selection for salaried employment, the demand for education beyond a minimum, as a consumption good, would be likely to fall steeply. The motivation for demand, then, seems largely oriented to practical purposes and only education efficient or minimal for them will be utilised.

In regard to motivation to learn the Chinese, Ghanaian and Mexican cases suggest that, when schooling is not oriented to salaried jobs, motivation is relatively low. The Chinese case suggests further that, when pupils think their education is more than their futures warrant, their low motivation can degenerate into disruption. The Ceylonese and Mexican cases suggest that, when schooling is not oriented to external examinations, motivation to learn is relatively low. The Mexican case shows further that, if there are no external examinations, teachers are driven to find some substitute for mental coercion. The Ceylonese, Ghanaian and Malaysian cases suggest that, when schooling is on the other hand oriented to external examinations, motivation is raised, but only selectively, sparingly, spasmodically and with little regard to official standards for good education. Two inferences seem reasonable. First, both goals and goods that are tangible and relatively immediate are necessary to help young people sustain their efforts to learn current scholastic curricula. Secondly, young people seem, by and large, to regulate their efforts around satisfying a salient few criteria and to reducing both the criteria and the level of acceptable satisfaction.

Such behaviour may well be imitations or reflections of their parents and teachers. These last certainly appear to need the stimulus of incentives and sanctions to sustain an acceptable level of instruction. They, too, by and large, regulate their behaviour to satisfying minimums, rather than achieving maximums. A not unreasonable inference might be that the teachers are themselves reflections of their supervisors, administrators and trainers.

All three parties interested in education – parents, pupils and educators – seem to share a common tendency to minimise. This is certainly not irrational: it simply calls for a minimum input to assure a satisfactory output. However, it does seem to mean that there exists an endemic bias of alliance towards worse, rather than better, teaching and learning. External standards, incentives and sanctions seem to be necessary to counter it. It also seems to mean that the quality of education – but not the demand – is independent of certification and selection as general institutions of society. Indeed, employers must needs and do make use of whatever comes to them from the schools. But that quality is, indeed, dependent on what is used to certify and to select. In its turn, what is used to certify and to select depends for its power – whether restrictive or sustaining – on the value accorded it by parents, pupils and teachers.

The problem, then, is to devise a framework which will stimulate and sustain good education, but allow for selection – not necessarily by the school – and simultaneously mitigate the absurdities and inequities generated by the schedule of correspondence and qualifications escalation. The final chapter examines a number of devices, in turn, and assesses their possible joint effects.

Chapter 7

Combating the Diploma Disease

ANGELA LITTLE

Social institutions designed to legitimate the allocation of persons to society's adult roles appear to be universal. In some societies this allocation is based on the caste group into which one is born; in others it depends on personal skills, such as horsemanship; while in yet others sex and social-class groups are the dominant criteria.

In Lilliput it was quite different. Gulliver noted that in choosing people for all employment the Lilliputians

> have more Regard to good Morals than to great Abilities: For, since Government is necessary to Mankind, they believe that the common size of human Understanding is fitted to some Station or other, and that Providence never intended to make the Management of Publick Affairs a Mystery, to be comprehended only by a few persons of sublime Genius, of which there are seldom three born in an Age. But, they suppose Truth, Justice, Temperance, and the like, to be in every Man's Power; the Practice of which Virtues, assisted by Experience and a good Intention, would qualify any Man for the Service of his Country, except where a course of study is required. But they thought the want of Moral Virtues was so far from being supplied by superior Endowment of the Mind, that Employment could never be put into such dangerous Hands as those of Persons so qualified, and at least that the Mistakes committed by Ignorance

in a virtuous Disposition would never be of such fatal Consequences to the Publick as the Practices of a Man, whose Inclinations led him to be corrupt and had great Abilities to manage to multiply and defend his Corruptions. (Jonathan Swift, *Gulliver's Travels*)

The modern world would strike the average Lilliputian as a very strange place. Most societies today select persons for employment on the basis of academic achievements, on the basis of a package of educational qualifications collected through a long career in the formal education system. Academic achievement is the main selection criterion used for recruiting, shortlisting and selecting candidates for both government and non-government positions in all but the very lowest levels of employment. Information about moral virtues does enter the selection process but this information is seen as supplementary to, rather than substitutable for, information about educational achievements.

The ills which have been fomented or exacerbated by the predominance of academic credentials have been extensively discussed throughout this book. However, so far only general indications have been offered on what might be done about them. This chapter hopes to probe a little further into the solutions suggested by Dore in his earlier analysis of the 'diploma disease' (1976), to put forward some additional approaches and to evaluate their possible effects and repercussions.

ALTERNATIVES

Some would argue that the roots of the problem lie in the external economic system of reward and status differentials. Remove those differentials and the problems of education would disappear. But it is not, of course, *quite* so simple. Even in those socialist societies where status and income differentials *have* been massively reduced, many problems of qualification escalation, irrelevant basic education and distorted resource allocation remain. Capitalist and socialist societies alike differentiate work roles into those which require higher and lower levels of specialisation. In both types of society access to highly specialised roles is regulated and legitimated via a meritocracy based predominantly on academic achievement.

Others would argue that the heart of the disease lies with the selection and qualification system itself. Could selection be carried out in a way that would combat the several problems outlined above and achieve the pedagogical and social development objectives not currently being met? Six main problems have to be dealth with:

(1) 'unnecessary' qualification escalation;
(2) 'unnecessary' expansion of the formal school system and costs;
(3) examination cramming;
(4) the imbalance of skills taught in schools;
(5) the imbalance between extrinsically and intrinsically motivated learning;
(6) the inequality of resource provision between the different levels of the education system.

It would, of course, be asking a considerable amount of any alternative to solve satisfactorily *all* the problems listed above, problems whose importance will be judged differently by different groups of decision-makers.

What kind of alternatives can be offered? There are at least four possibilities. All but one have been proposed in detail by Dore (1976), though not discussed explicitly in terms of the problems listed above. For Dore, the essential elements of an alternative way of linking education and work are twofold:

1. Start careers earlier – around the ages of 15–17 doing as much of the selection as possible within work organisations, and transforming all tertiary education and training into in-career learning, either part-time or full-time, in special educational institutes.
2. At all points where there has to be selection particularly for the all-important decision as to which work organisation people are to enter initially at the end of their period of basic schooling – avoid using learning achievement tests: whether the alternative be aptitude tests, lotteries, special 'encapsulated' tests . . . the essential thing is that they be tests which cannot be (or cannot much be) crammed for. (Dore, 1976)

To make the following discussion clearer we shall examine the first proposition separately from the second. The second, which has to do with selection mechanisms, will be examined in detail in two forms, aptitude tests and lotteries. We shall then discuss a reform not considered by Dore, but presented here as a much less radical but possibly more acceptable and efficient reform. This alternative is examination reform. The four alternatives to be discussed, then, are as follows.

(1) Earlier selection into jobs – later selection for promotion or further training by the employer or the market.
(2) Abolition of educational qualifications – selection for jobs through aptitude-tests.
(3) Selection through restricted lotteries.
(4) Selection through reformed examinations.

EARLIER SELECTION INTO JOBS

The essential idea of earlier selection into jobs is that students destined for high-level jobs would not spend extensive periods in the formal education system. After a basic education accessible to *all* and of a length determined by local resources and preferences, students would be apprenticed and would learn specific job skills mainly through on-the-job training. Prospective engineers, for example, could work first as craftsmen apprentices, then as craftsmen, then perhaps as technicians and then as engineers. Interspersed with the on-the-job training would be short-course training in educational institutions. The university could run a series of short courses for engineers. Engineers would not attend theory courses for long stretches of time as they currently do in many developing countries. Rather, they would mix their practice with their study through attendance at university for several short periods of time. Decisions about who would eventually become an engineer would be left to the employing organisation.

From the point of view of solving the 'diploma disease' problem, this alternative has many attractions. It could certainly reduce 'unnecessary' qualification escalation at the top end of the qualification range, simply because the ceiling of qualifications awarded by the formal education system would itself be much reduced.

However, there *would* be increased costs to employers, both large and small, and to those educational and extension services designed explicitly to train individuals in specific skills. These total costs would vary enormously, of course, between different kinds of job functions (for instance, between an engineer where specific skills are required, and an administrator where rather more general skills are required) but whether the proportion of costs borne by the employer would differ between job function is difficult to predict. However, it is worth remembering that, whatever the costs, since the state is the largest employer in many Third World countries, then the costs to an employer would be no more than a transfer of tax resources from one form of manpower development to another. It is also difficult to generalise about the overall impact on education and training costs (both private and social) but the likely long-term productivity returns to a system where most of the job-specific training takes place in the workplace, rather than in the school or university, may well be greater than at present (Fuller, 1972). The balance of skills taught in schools, the balance between extrinsically and intrinsically motivated learning and the amount of examination cramming (see Table 7.1) would be little affected by the earlier job selection *per se*. These factors would be affected more by the type of selection system which allocated students to employment at the end of the ten years of education. This point will be discussed in subsequent sections. The final problem, equitable distribution of resources *within* the education system, would have a high chance of being dealt with. Ministries of Education would be able to resist the pressures of politicians, parents and students for increased secondary and tertiary education, simply because those institutions would not exist or would exist in a very different form. With this pressure from the top much reduced, the potential for a more equal quality of educational service for students in both rural and urban areas could be realised. The quality and quantity of basic education *for all* could be enhanced. The likely impact of this alternative on these problems are summarised in Table 7.1. Public resistance to such a scheme would be marked not least because at least one university and upper secondary school has already been established in almost every country in the world. Even those few countries without them (mostly small and island economies) have a tradition of a small group of graduates attending universities in other countries. Resistance would come from educators and clients of the education system with entrenched interests in its survival in its present form and from employers. Despite their repeated criticism of the 'education of today', employers do regard the education system as a selector of their personnel as well as a trainer (as Chapter 2 makes clear).

But before rejecting the idea as too fantastic, one should pause a little and observe just three reforms which are being implemented around the world and which represent attempts to socialise students into the world of work at an age earlier than before. The Tanzanian reforms for entry to university only *after* the completion of one or two years of work experience were initiated by the 1974 Musoma Declaration. They were modelled on and have outlived similar reforms in China in the mid-1960s. Papua New Guinea has recently introduced community and work education experience into the secondary school curriculum. The government of the Seychelles is implementing a national youth service scheme in which students from secondary schools will engage in community projects for two years before being readmitted to the formal education system for further academic training. These are just a few examples of attempts to recruit students to the idea of work, if not to work itself. They have involved the real world of work to varying degrees. Their 'success' remains to be seen, but if they do succeed and are accepted by the public as having succeeded, then the way is open for an even further shift of the job-training responsibility from the educators to the trainer-employers, and for the idea that universities provide 'in-career training', rather than 'pre-career training'. Lifelong education has long been the call of the 'non-formal' educators. The universities, with the weight of status, could transform that call into a reality.

Table 7.1   *The Impact of 'Earlier Selection into Jobs' on the Diploma Disease*

Alternative	*Educational and Social Goals*					
	Reduce 'unnecessary' qualification escalation	Reduce 'unnecessary' expansion of the formal school system and costs	Reduce exam cramming	Improve balance of skills taught in schools	Improve the balance between extrinsically and intrinsically motivated learning	Increase equity of resource distribution within the education system
A.1 Earlier selection into jobs, later selection by employer or market	Reduced at top ends of current spectrum of qualifications	Yes, but training costs would shift to employers. Resultant costs could be greater or similar	No impact	No impact	No impact	Could do

Of course, earlier selection still demands selection, so that its problems would continue to dominate discussions about the acceptability of such a reform in exactly the same way as it dominates current discussions about slightly less radical reforms. Would not the selection device used to recruit people to the world of work distort the curriculum and quality of learning in schools in precisely the same way as now? This problem is fully recognised by Dore, when he insists that the early selection into jobs would have to be coupled with 'tests which cannot be (or cannot much be) crammed for'. This condition is important – if the objectives of balanced skill-learning and of intrinsically oriented learning are to be met, given the distorting influence on both of exam-cramming. Aptitude tests are discussed by Dore as one way forward, because they are thought to 'give more weight to the way innate potential had been developed by the accumulation of learning experiences likely to be common to the majority of children in a society . . . than to the way it has been developed by recent classroom learning experiences which may be more highly variable' (Dore, 1976). We turn now to a discussion of them.

APTITUDE TESTS

It is not entirely clear who would administer aptitude tests for employment. It would be a very inefficient system, were it left to individual employers. Most likely students would sit a battery of tests at the end of their school career. These would be administered either by the school or by a centralised testing agency. The only educational qualification which people would need to sit these tests would be a certificate of satisfactory completion of basic education. Aptitude tests are seen by Dore (1976) as a *substitute for*, rather than a supplement to, conventional achievement tests.

For some time now a fairly clear distinction has been drawn in the American and British psychological literature between achievement and aptitude tests. A substantial literature describes the development and use of occupational and educational selection tests in the Third World and the West (Ord, 1972; Schwarz and Krug, 1972; Ghiselli, 1966; Goslin, 1963). Goslin describes how 'it was the vision of being able to measure inherited differences in intellectual ability between individuals which had much to do with the beginning of the testing movement' (1963, p. 132).

Achievement tests are generally thought to measure acquired

abilities susceptible to environmental influences, whereas aptitudes are thought to be less susceptible to environmental influence and more a characteristic of innate, underlying ability. This distinction between acquired characteristics vs innate characteristics overlaps with the distinction between tests which provide good and poor predictions for future achievement. Because an achievement test is intended 'to measure a students' grasp of some body of knowledge or his proficiency in certain skills', and an aptitude test is intended 'to determine the potential of an individual for development along a special line' (Ebel, 1972), then it follows that achievement tests are much poorer predictors of future performance than aptitude tests.

Tests of verbal and mathematical aptitude became synonymous with tests of intelligence but the distinction between both types of test and achievement was maintained. Tests of intelligence and aptitude formed the major part of the 11-plus examinations introduced in Britain after the 1944 Education Act, while tests of achievement were used for certifying school performance at the end of the secondary cycle of education. The distinction between tests of aptitude and tests of achievement is maintained today by the West African Examinations Council. Entrance to secondary schools in Ghana, Sierra Leone and Gambia, for example, is based on performance of four examinations: English language (achievement), arithmetic (achievement), verbal reasoning (aptitude) and quantitative reasoning (aptitude).

There are, of course, major controversies within the testing profession over the various claims made for achievement and aptitude test scores. These include controversies about their relative predictive values, their relative dependence on innate potential and the relative effects of cramming on them (Goslin, 1963). It is not necessary to examine these issues here. They are, perhaps, rather less important than an examination of how teachers and students are likely to *interpret* the meaning of an aptitude test and how this affects subsequent behaviour. Would a substitution of aptitude tests for achievement tests *really* lead to a change in the beliefs about how one achieves job success and would it, in turn, lead to a reduction in examination or test-cramming?

There are three reasons for believing that a substitution of aptitude tests for achievement tests would neither be desirable nor lead to substantial changes in the examination-cramming attitudes and behaviours of students, teachers and parents. These three stem from (1) current beliefs about the causes of academic success and failure and the dominant mode of evaluating them; (2) the web of meanings associated with the term 'aptitude'; and (3) the implications of the ideology of 'aptitude' for future behaviour. These three sets of constraints will be examined in the next three sections.

Current Beliefs about the Causes of Academic Success and Failure

The IDS education research programme generated a considerable amount of data on parent, teacher and student beliefs about the causes of academic success and failure. It did so because it recognised the importance of establishing the nature of prevalent beliefs in order to assess the acceptability of substituting aptitude tests for achievement tests. We called these beliefs the 'perceived ingredients of success':

> Do parents view the success or failure of their child in selection tests as chiefly dependent on their child's efforts or on the quality of the teachers' coaching, or on the child's native ability? . . . It is important to establish this in order to assess the acceptability of substituting aptitude tests. (IDS, 1973)

In the research we attempted to assess not only parents' beliefs, but also those of teachers and students. While parents may well determine whether or not an educational reform like aptitude-testing is 'acceptable' or not, it is teachers and students who will determine whether or not examination-cramming is reduced in the classroom. It is they who determine how the reform is implemented.

We have research data on the beliefs about the causes of success and failure from Sri Lanka, Ghana, Mexico, Malaysia and England. In Sri Lanka 140 urban parents and 40 rural parents were asked whether they knew a child who had failed the GCE O-level examination and whether they knew a child who had passed. If so, what did they think was the main reason why one child passed and one child failed? The largest single explanation for the different performance was the effort and interest of the student: 53 per cent of the urban parents' responses and 40 per cent of the rural parents' responses were of this kind. Other explanations were environmental in nature. These included factors outside the personal control of the child (for example, economic reasons, parental interest and changes in the education system). These accounted in total for another 30 and 34 per cent of the urban and rural parents respectively. Only 2 per cent of the urban parents and 4 per cent of the rural parents attributed the difference to intelligence (*Buddhia*), an attribution that was as frequent as 'good fortune' (*waasęnaawen*)*. Among the children, too, effort and interest were very frequent explanations of success and failure. Thirty-five 14-year-old students in an academically 'average' high school in Colombo were interviewed about school success and failure. All but one explained success and failure in terms of personal effort. And all ten of a smaller group of rural 14-years-olds did so. Fewer gave 'ability' explanations (Little, 1982).

These findings were similar to those from a parallel study of English school-children. Some 90 per cent of English 14-year-olds (N = 42) produced effort explanations for academic success and failure. The importance of effort was confirmed in a series of closed-ended questions. Students were asked to rank-order alternative explanations for success and failure (for instance, effort, ability, help from others and luck). Effort was always ranked consistently as the most important explanation. When an ability explanation like 'clever' was offered as one of the alternatives, it was usually ranked second or third; but when it contained an explicit reference to 'native ability', its importance declined sharply. A small survey of British primary school teachers (N = 6) also revealed that the child's own effort was perceived to be the most important explanation of both success and failure out of a list which included native intelligence, parents, luck and teacher help. Native intelligence came a close second in the explanation of success but a rather lower third in the explanation of failure (Little, 1982).

In Ghana a similar pattern emerged. Over 60 per cent of parents chose 'working hard' as the 'most important determinant for good marks', compared with 15 per cent who chose 'being bright naturally' (N = 127). Interestingly, the proportions of parents who believed that working hard was the best explanation for good marks was inversely related to the economic level of the community. The poorer the community, the greater the parental belief that effort explained success. The belief in the efficacy of effort was echoed by their middle school form-3 children: 77 per cent of these 15-year-olds claimed that hard work was the main

---

* The value of 'ę' is approximately 'er' with the 'r' unsounded.

ingredient of academic success, while only 13 per cent attributed success to 'natural gifts' (Boakye and Oxenham, 1982).

In rural Mexico 84 parents of primary school children were asked what were the most important factors in helping their children to learn well and earn good marks: 40 per cent felt that the main factor was studying hard and motivation; 20 per cent felt that the main factor was having good teachers; 19 per cent, help from parents; 13 per cent, the intelligence of the child; and 7 per cent, the child's ability to get on well with teachers. The main attribution for failure was similar: 69 per cent attributed school failure to lack of effort and study; 17 per cent, the child's 'lack of capacity'; 11 per cent, poor teaching; and 3 per cent, lack of parental support (Brooke and Oxenham, 1980).

In Malaysia 246 science teachers were asked to rank in order of importance eight factors for student performance on internal classroom tests and the grade-9 selection examination. Hard work and general intelligence of pupils were the most frequent first choices made (Lewin, 1981).

In summary, then, individual effort is perceived to be a major determinant of both academic success and failure by students, parents and teachers. How would aptitude tests reduce examination practice and cramming when effort is currently perceived to be of such importance? If aptitude tests were introduced, would effort and practice be transferred to them?

We have scattered evidence from a number of countries to suggest that they would. In the UK, for example, the famous 11-plus examination was introduced after the 1944 Education Act to select students for secondary school. That examination largely comprised tests of verbal and mathematical aptitude. Although schools were not supposed to coach their pupils for this examination, many did and strenuous efforts had to be made by education authorities in the UK to restrain schools from allowing students more than one practice attempt for the 11-plus exam. Note also the practice and coaching which goes on in the USA for the Scholastic Aptitude Tests (SAT), a pattern repeated in some states in India where aptitude tests imported from the USA are now used for admission to some colleges of higher education, and where private tutors thrive, coaching students to improve their aptitude. We also know that upper primary school curricula in anglophone West Africa are almost totally geared to practice for the Common Entrance Achievement and Aptitude examinations (Hawes, 1980; Bray, 1981).

Since effort is perceived to be such an important attribution for success and failure, it is not surprising to find that effort is also highly valued and rewarded by others. The criteria used for *evaluating* academic success and failures have been investigated in the context of American schools. Weiner (1973), for example, found that the dominant criterion for evaluation varied with age. Young children (4–5 years) based their evaluation on the achievement outcome. In their opinion academic success should be rewarded and academic failure punished, irrespective of either the ability or effort of the child. Things changed around the age of 7. Effort became the main criterion for reward and punishment. Effort should be rewarded, even if the result is failure. This was true also for the 10- and 12-year-olds. None of the age groups rewarded or punished high or low ability. This high degree of reward and punishment for effort was also reflected in an American experiment designed to simulate teacher behaviour (Kukla, 1972).

Both studies suggest that a selection reform which tried to reduce the value attached to effort and practice would be at odds with current evaluations of achievement. The effort invested by a student is valued both by teachers and students more than ability in the school classroom. It is, therefore, rather difficult to see how teachers could themselves be encouraged to discourage students from expending effort and practice on aptitude tests.

The Web of Meanings Associated with the Terms 'Intelligence' and 'Aptitude'

In the last section we saw how the attributions made by students, teachers and parents for academic success and failure were dominated by effort attributions. It was suggested that since effort attributions are so dominant, then they would probably be transferred to performance on aptitude tests. Success and failure on aptitude tests would probably also be explained in terms of high and low degree of effort, the implication being that performance could be improved if the student tried harder.

However, even if students were to attribute performance on aptitude tests to intelligence or special aptitudes, what precisely would they *mean* by those words? In this section we explore the possibility that the terms intelligence, ability and aptitude are themselves perceived to be factors determined by effort. If this is so, then the tendency to practise or try hard to improve one's aptitude will be reinforced.

The advertisement in Figure 7.1 is for a Sri Lankan 'crammer', designed to help the student improve her or his aptitude for the primary grade-5 scholarship examination. The Sinhala word used here for aptitude makes the point. The word is *shishathwa abhiyōggathāwa*, which means 'a challenge to test one's level of scholarship'. Another word often used as a translation for aptitude is *kusalathāwa*, which connotes the status or level of one's 'merit'. Here merit (*kusal*) derives from its religious context and means good deeds and actions achieved through effort. The meaning of the term is closer to achievement than it is to aptitude as used in a Western context.

Help your child to face
the Scholarship exam with
confidence

APTITUDE TEST

by

W. O. T. Fernando

Rs. 16.00 Postage 2.00
Try nearest book shop or
send
M/O.N.H. Fernando
21/21, Fernando Road
Dehiwala

Figure 7.1

The suggestion here is that when a Western technical concept like aptitude is grafted on to another language and culture, much of the original meaning is likely to be lost. There are other examples (Wober, 1974; Kingsley, 1977; Goodnow, 1980; Maehr and Nicholls, 1980). Wober (1974), for example, contrasted the meanings attached to the word 'intelligence' by traditional Baganda villagers in Uganda, by Baganda village teachers, by the

210/*Education versus Qualifications?*

urban Baganda elite and by urban Baganda university medical students. The web of meanings associated with the English word 'intelligent' and the closest Luganda translation *obugezi* were examined through the use of the semantic differential technique. The roots of the word can be traced to several sources, including the Islamic concept of *al'aql*; *aql* means 'to tie' or 'to bind'. Those who stray from religion are considered to be those whose intelligence is impaired. Supreme intelligence is attained when one enters the community of Islam in a state of peace and surrender. For the Baganda, *obugezi* is an acquired, rather than an inherited, characteristic. It is also associated with slowness, with delay and with care. It is a view that contrasts markedly with the views ɔf psychologists like Jensen (1969).

Intelligence carries a similar connotation in the Sinhala language in Sri Lanka. The best translation appears to be 'buddhia'. Its very sound indicates its close connection with the Lord Buddha, the central figure of Buddhism. Buddhia connotes the psychological state of ultimate or final knowledge. It is a state which *all* in theory can achieve. It is achieved through personal effort, through meritorious deeds and actions and is a manifestation of a good 'karma'. Karma accumulates through effort and actions performed, not in one single life, but during a progression of different lives. Thus, in any one life, the degree to which one achieves buddhia is determined both by one's karma and effort during this life and by the karma brought from previous lives. It is not a question, therefore, of buddhia being either predominantly acquired or predominantly inherited in the Western psychological sense. It is both acquired *and* inherited simultaneously. Interestingly, the Sinhala translation for an IQ test is grafted on to this concept. It is called *buddhipareekshana*.

The general point is that prevailing beliefs in some societies reinforce the view that ability, aptitude and intelligence *can* be gained through effort and practice. They contradict the view that an aptitude is *largely* innate and uncontrollable. It should not surprise us, therefore, to find students and teachers practising to improve their aptitude. The behaviour is perfectly consistent with the meaning of aptitude. Not that meanings and cultural beliefs can by themselves determine the sucess or failure of a change in the selection system, but they will encourage the adoption of one interpretation of the system rather than another, especially if that particular interpretation is seen to be profitable. And effort and cramming are certainly more hopeful behaviour strategies than a reliance on an uncontrollable aptitude to get one through the selection hurdle.

Wober (1974) recognises that the different conceptions of intelligence held by village Baganda have important applications for education but the tenor of his advice is that the Western model of intelligence is by far superior. But perhaps what Wober overlooks is that the Western psychologists' conception of intelligence is itself changing. The growth of interest over the last few decades in Piaget's work draws attention to at least one alternative definition of intelligence within psychology. And even within the dominant psychometric tradition of psychology there are signs that the meanings attached to words like ability, aptitude and intelligence are changing, particularly on the acquired vs inherited dimension. The following quotations, the first from a manual for the American Otis–Lennon test of mental ability and the second from the famous Educational Testing Service of Princeton, USA, are instructive:

[The Otis–Lennon test claims to] provide a comprehensive, carefully articulated assessment of the general mental ability or scholastic aptitude of pupils – emphasis is placed upon measuring the pupil's facility in reasoning and dealing abstractly with verbal, symbolic and figural test content sampling a broad range of cognitive abilities ... [the test] is constructed to yield dependable measurements of the 'g' or general intelligence ability factor [but] it should be clearly understood that the Otis–Lennon tests do not measure the innate mental capacity of the pupil. (Otis and Lennon, 1969)

A common misconception is that these [scholastic aptitude] tests somehow measure innate, unchanging abilities. In fact, they measure learned skills ... they measure intellectual skills that students are expected to have developed through both school and non-school experiences, apart from the particular courses of study they may have pursued. (Educational Testing Services, 1980)

Carefully spelt out these claims may appear contradictory to those who equate the 'g' factor with innate mental capacity. Clearly, Otis and Lennon are themselves now doubtful about the once clear-cut distinction between tests of achievement and tests of ability and aptitude.

Conceptions and meanings vary across time and across cultures. This suggests at the very least that the assumptions of meaning attached to an aptitude test by a Western psychologist are unlikely to be identical with those of a teacher or student or parent in a Third World country – or an industrialised country for that matter. The small effects of practice on test scores may be 'evident' to a Western psychologist (though the research evidence is difficult to locate). They are likely to be less evident to a teacher or a student whose future depends on test success.

The Implications of Beliefs about Aptitudes for Future Behaviour

The third and final concern over the proposal to substitute aptitude tests for achievement tests has to do with long-term motivation. Suppose there are four students who sit an aptitude test. We shall call them SE, SA, FE and FA. SE and SA are both successful (S) on the test. However, SE believes that the success is due to the *effort* she/he has made. SA, on the other hand, attributes the success to *ability*. FE and FA both fail (F) the test. FE attributes the failure to a lack of *effort*, while FA attributes it to a lack of *ability*. Would these four students differ in their expectations about what their future success or failure will be? Will they continue to try and achieve in the future? The research literature offers a few clues.

A student's expectation of future success seems to be determined, in part at least, by the way in which she/he explains past success and failure. If we consider our four students above (SA, SE, FE and FA), then we shall find differences between them in their expectations of future success. Research evidence suggests that it is SA – the student who attributes success to ability – who has the greatest expectation of success in the future. SA is followed by SE – then by FE – then by FA. Ability attributions for success and failure lead to the greatest *and smallest* expectations for the future. Effort attributions, on the other hand, lead to medium-level expectations. The difference in expectations between those who have failed and those who have succeeded in the past test is not very wide. The widest gap emerges for those who attribute success and failure to ability (Weiner, 1974, 1979).

There also seems to be some evidence that future behaviour (as well as expectation of behaviour) is determined by how one explains past behaviour, especially if one is explaining past failures on a test. Consider again the case of FE and FA referred to above. FE fails a test but attributes the failure to lack of effort. FA fails the same test and attributes the failure to lack of ability. Both FE and FA are then observed to see who performs the next test more quickly and with greater zest. FE outstrips FA (Weiner, 1974).

Theory suggests that the reason why we find these differences is that ability is perceived to be an enduring and uncontrollable factor, while effort is perceived to be less stable and more controllable. If aptitude is perceived in the same way as ability, then these findings (based on American schoolchildren) suggest that the effects on motivation of failure on an aptitude test would be more negative than failure on an achievement test. Conversely, the effects on motivation of success on an aptitude test might be more positive than success on an achievement test.

Those labelled as having high aptitude would benefit from high levels of confidence in their own abilities and might, indeed, reach great heights. But at what cost? What are the implications for those labelled as having low aptitude? What would be the attitudes of those labelled as 'being of a high aptitude' to their less fortunate brothers and sisters? How much more deeply entrenched would income and status systems become, if elite groups believed that they were intrinsically better and more capable than others? And how long would it be before those less fortunate give up the achievement game completely? If the test of aptitude reveals an intrinsic unchangeable part of the self, then where lies the motivation and the effort to succeed? The Brave New World would be here at last.

One qualification, however. A distinction is made in the literature between general aptitude and specific aptitudes. Specific aptitudes are qualities like musical ability and manual dexterity, whereas general aptitude would refer to something like scholastic ability, that is, a general ability to do well in all school subjects. If specific aptitude tests were substituted for achievement tests at the selection stage, then one might argue that while a student's motivation to achieve in a specific area might be reduced if she/he fails a specific aptitude test this would *not* affect the desire to achieve in other areas. No single person will excel on all aptitudes; and conversely, no person will fail on all aptitudes.

However, it is this author's contention that, while modern sector job opportunities remain few and while those few remain highly prized, then the specific aptitudes which gain those specific jobs become all-important for the individual student. The value attached to those specific aptitudes which do not lead to desirable jobs will be very low. The situation is probably best summed up by the observation that no one in the West has found it necessary to develop an aptitude test for dustbinman skills. Similarly, in an agricultural economy with a tiny modern sector, how many students will be convinced by the information that they have a specific aptitude for farming paddy?

In summary, then, it has been argued that aptitude tests would probably not have the desired effect of reducing 'cramming' in schools for several reasons. First, students, parents and teachers believe very strongly that effort is the prime-determinant of academic success and failure. More than this, effort lies at the very heart of interpersonal reward and punishment. People reward effort with praise and punish lack of effort with blame. Given these dominant beliefs, it is difficult to see how teachers and students could be 'persuaded' to view their abilities and aptitudes as uncontrollable, as things which they cannot improve through effort and practice. Secondly, it was suggested that even if people could be persuaded to view aptitude in this way, it might lead to unintended consequences. A selection test which claimed to be a test of innate, uncontrollable and stable abilities could widely affect the confidence of those groups who 'succeed' and 'fail' in society.

But what of the impact of aptitude tests on the achievement of the other 'diploma disease' problems listed earlier on p. 199 – the problems of 'unnecessary' qualification escalation, 'unnecessary' expansion of costs, the balance of skills taught in schools, the balance between extrinsic and intrinsic motivation and the equitable balance of resources within the education system (see Table 7.2). They could contribute to the reduction of qualification escalation. Faced with ever-more applications employers would probably increase the number of aptitude tests employees had to sit, or ask for higher grades of performance on the same test. If the additional tests or grades indicated skills unrelated to productivity on the job, then the test escalation could be deemed unnecessary. Alternatively, if the tests had all been validated against job productivity, then an increase either in the number of tests or in the grades demanded on a single test would potentially lead to higher productivity. In this case the qualification escalation could not be deemed unnecessary.

Provided that the escalation of tests or test scores was confined to graduates of the same level of the basic education system, then the unnecessary expansion of the system could be held at bay. Recall that the 'unnecessary' expansion of the system referred to that expansion which was a response to employers' escalation of qualifications which, in turn, was a response to an oversupply of labour.

Table 7.2   *The Impact of Aptitude Tests on the 'Diploma Disease'*

Alternative	Educational and Social Goals					
	Reduce 'unnecessary' qualification escalation	Reduce 'unnecessary' expansion of the formal school system and costs	Reduce exam-cramming	Improve balance of skills taught in schools	Improve the balance between extrinsically and intrinsically motivated learning	Increase equity of resource distribution within the education system
A.2 Abolition of achievement test qualifications. Selection exclusively through aptitude tests	Could do	Could do	Unlikely	Could do if teachers and students orient their activities towards aptitude test items	Could do	No impact

What about the problem of skill development in a school system oriented to aptitude tests? Recall that the aptitude-test selection reform assumes that selection for employment would be based on aptitude-test performance alone. School grades would not be used in the selection process. Only a certificate indicating 'satisfactory' completion of basic schooling would be a necessary minimum educational qualification. Inevitably schools would seek out whether they could do anything to improve their students' chances on the aptitude tests. It was suggested that aptitudes would be regarded like any other skills – as skills which can be learned, developed and practised. However, this interpretation could lead to an unintended but none the less positive outcome. If the items in aptitude tests tested more than the rote-memorisation found so frequently in achievement tests, then new skills could be developed. It is generally recognised that the skills tested by aptitude items *are* different and cover a very wide range. Similarly, the balance between extrinsically and intrinsically motivated learning would only be affected if the sorts of items included in aptitude items stimulated a self-sustained interest in the problems and skills tested. In other words, the quality of education could be affected, provided that teachers and students respond to aptitude tests in the *unintended* rather than intended way. The impact on resource distribution within the education system would probably be little affected.

A COMBINATION OF EDUCATIONAL CRITERIA AND LOTTERIES

The third alternative worth considering is a lottery used in combination with educational achievement test scores. Dore's example (1976) describes how one might use lotteries to select the 10 per cent of each age group for whom a modern sector non-manual job will be available. In order to guarantee some minimum level of academic achievement a national certificate examination would be used to select, say, the best 30 per cent of the age group. Out of this 30 per cent, opportunities for further study and for access to the prized jobs in the modern sector would be allocated on a lottery basis. One out of every three students would be chosen by lot. Four benefits flow from this proposal. The first is that cramming would be reduced. The second benefit is that a number of very high-achievers would be channelled into the traditional and self-employed sectors of the economy and away from the modern sector. This injection of educated personnel into the traditional and self-employed sectors of the economy would have beneficial effects on the development of the *whole* economy. Thirdly, the wider span of ability admitted to work organisation in the modern sector would make later selection *within* that organisation easier – 'the fairness of the choices made would be more obvious, if there was a wider span of ability in the initial intake' (Dore, 1976). Finally, any fears about the efficiency of the lower-achieving student who had succeeded in the lottery should be allayed. The lower-level clerical jobs which would be performed by these students would probably be performed very efficiently. Dore (1976) points to the fact that there are precedents for the use of lotteries. In Japan and Korea lotteries have been used to select students for high schools, and in Holland lotteries have been used to select students for higher education. And if we are to believe Jencks's thesis in *Inequality* (1972), then luck accounts for a very major proportion of the variance in men's occupational incomes. If life *is* such a lottery, then why shouldn't we institutionalise the lottery?

There are objections to the use of lotteries. First, it's one thing to discuss lotteries in the context of a society where the differences between the winner's gains and the loser's losses are not great - and quite another in a society where the difference between having a job in the modern sector and one outside is quite marked.* Where income differences are great, the size of the gains and losses allocated by chance would also be great. This doubt is related to the issue of whether one could persuade high-achievers who were not successful in the lottery to enter traditional and self-employment. The Chinese experience during the Cultural Revolution suggests that high academic achievers would resist very strongly any attempt to move them away from the modern sector (Unger, 1980b). It might not be unreasonable to suggest that the acceptance of a lottery system bears an inverse relation to the size of the income and status differentials between lottery winners and lottery losers. The greater the loss, the less likely the acceptance. The less the loss, the more likely the acceptance.

Secondly, lotteries are based on luck, and luck tends not to be perceived as a major cause of academic success and failure by students, teachers and parents. Luck means many things to many people, but if it is understood to mean a factor which is both unpredictable and outside one's control, then few people explain success and failure in these terms. Those who do favour luck as an explanation of success and failure tend to be those who are low in achievement motivation (McCelland *et al.*, 1953; Weiner *et al.*, 1971; Weiner, 1974). Deliberately using luck to allocate life-chances may well be at the expense of non-random rational effort and sap the will to work and achieve.

In our Ghanaian research parents (N = 127) were asked their reaction to selection by lottery: 91 per cent of them were very unfavourable to the idea. A farmer summed up his feelings:

A child's chance of further studies should be based on his or her ability to study. Any selection based on considerations other than this is not fair. Take a lottery for example. A dull child may just be lucky and get a chance while a bright pupil who is not

---

* Recall Lewin's comments on Malaysia in Chapter 4.

lucky does not get a chance. This is not fair. (Boakye and Oxenham, 1982)

Thirdly, the suggested impact of lotteries on the quality of education is also questionable. Even if lotteries *were* to be acceptable, would they really have the anticipated impact on cramming? It is doubtful whether cramming would be reduced. The lottery would take place only after an achievement test and would involve only, say, the top 30 per cent of achievers. For those below the 70th percentile, and certainly those around it, cramming would probably remain at its same high level. Students and teachers do not give up easily – and anyway why should they? The Tanzanian Primary Examination provides a good example. Currently only about 4 per cent of the primary school cohort enter government secondary schools. A maximum of only one or two children from a single primary school can expect to be selected for secondary school each year and many schools achieve zero success. But even in those schools where no student has succeeded in getting to secondary school during the past few years, there is still very high degree of examination orientation. There is always the hope that this year things will change (see also JASPA, 1978).

In any case what is the alternative to *not* cramming for the exam? It is assumed in both the lottery and aptitude-test proposal that if the examination goal is removed, then teachers and students are freed from its harness and 'real' education can take over. But our research on Mexican primary schools, Chinese middle schools and Liberian secondary schools suggested that this would not happen automatically (Brooke and Oxenham, 1980; Brooke, 1980; Oxenham, 1981; Unger, 1980b). Remove exam motivation and a great deal of total motivation seems to disappear. Alternative motivational goals and models do not emerge readily. An 'interest-oriented' education system does not easily substitute for an examination-oriented education system. We shall return to this point later.

Finally, the suggestion that lottery selection would make it easier for employers to select among employees for promotion seems to contain a contradiction. On the one hand, it is suggested that students between the 90th and 70th percentile would perform their initial jobs no worse than the students between the 100th and 90th percentile. On the other hand, it is suggested that employment organisations would find it easier to select for promotion, because the span of ability and therefore performance

differentials is wider. It is difficult to see how one can have it both
ways.

We should also consider the extent to which a lottery proposal
would meet the solution of the other problems listed on p. 199 (see
Table 7.3). We have already discussed the likely impact of lotteries
on the reduction of cramming. If cramming is unlikely to be
reduced, then the balance of skills developed by schools and the
balance between intrinsically and extrinsically motivated earning
would be little affected.

The impact on 'unnecessary' expansion of the school system
and 'unnecessary' qualification escalation could, however, be
more positive. A lottery system, if acceptable, could vary its
selection ratio from year to year according to the number of
modern sector job-slots available and could, therefore, enable both
the education and the occupational system to avoid an
'unnecessary' expansion of costs on the one hand, and
'unnecessary' qualification escalation on the other.

Table 7.3   *The Impact of Lotteries on the Diploma Disease*

Alternative	*Educational and Social Goals*					
	Reduce 'unnecessary' qualification escalation	Reduce 'unnecessary' expansion of the formal school system and costs	Reduce exam cramming	Improve the balance of skills taught in schools	Improve the balance between extrinsically and intrinsically motivated learning	Increase equity of resource distribution within the education system
A.3 Selection through restricted lotteries	Could do	Could do	Unlikely	Unlikely	Unlikely	Could do

A more equitable distribution of resources within the education
system would be achieved only if lotteries were used as a selection
device at various stages within the education system and if the
numbers progressing to different stages could, therefore, be
controlled. The greatest impact on equity would be equity of a
different kind – the improved access of low-status economic and
social groups to further education and higher-level jobs. Given the
link in most countries between social class and both educational

and occupational achievement, then any system based on chance would favour those from the lower and larger social classes.

The benefits of a lottery system, then, are mainly those of allocation. It could be used to control the numbers of entrants to the modern sector and to allocate job opportunities more evenly across society. These benefits are, of course, very important and would probably be considered to be more important in some contexts than in others. The problem really arises with the productive aspect of schools, as opposed to its allocative aspect. The impact on the quality of the day-to-day interaction between teacher and student would probably be unaffected.

EXAMINATION REFORM

We turn, finally, to a fourth alternative selection procedure, examination reform. The diagnosis of the 'diploma disease' described in the introductory chapter pointed to the examination and qualification system as a root of the current educational and employment problem. The examination system, it was argued, distorts the quality of the educational experience, encourages a concentration on some parts of the curriculum at the expense of others, encourages a cramming of facts and creates an overwhelming dependency on extrinsic goals, rather than intrinsic ones. In short, it encourages a wholly negative backwash on the rest of the educational system.

Does the backwash need to be *so* negative? Does the quality of backwash not vary? Could we not exploit the fact that students, teachers and parents are motivated by examinations and alter the examination system in such a way as to combat some or all of the problems listed on p. 199. Could we not perform a 'judo trick' (Jolly, 1974) by identifying the crucial points of balance in the relationship between formal education and the job market and in exerting new forces at these points, thus changing the direction of development. Is cramming necessarily a bad thing? Does it not depend, perhaps, on the sorts of thing one is cramming and how one goes about the process of cramming? It may be the case that the backwash effects of exams are bad, because the exams themselves are bad.

We return now to our earlier discussion about aptitude tests. It was argued that they probably would not have the desired effect in reducing cramming, because teachers and students would continue to believe that effort and practice on test items were important. It is instructive to observe what has happened in one African country which did introduce modified forms of aptitude tests into its educational selection system. In line with the educational selection policies of other African countries the Kenyan Ministry of Education introduced 'reasoning items' into their primary school selection examinations in the early 1970s. These items are of the kind often found in intelligence and aptitude tests. The Kenyans' main objective was not primarily to reduce the exam-cramming that went on in schools, but to provide a more efficient and fairer selector of students. They argued that if aptitude tests really were immune to the effects of socioeconomic background and to school quality, then they could be used to identify 'bright' but underprivileged pupils in low-quality schools. 'Gifted pupils who had been badly taught would no longer be excluded from secondary school' (Somerset, 1977).

A comparison was made of sixteen schools with a high average level of English test scores with sixteen schools having a low average level of achievement. All the schools were drawn from the same rural district in Kenya and were matched for geographical location, distance from urban centres and types of cash-crop grown. The performance of the 'high-quality' and 'low-quality' schools was analysed to determine from which types of examination item the high-quality pupils built up their advantage. If the verbal reasoning items were more immune to the effects of the environment than traditional comprehension items, then the two groups of school should show greater performance differences on comprehension than on the reasoning items. But the prediction was not borne out. The performance gap between the rural high-quality and rural low-quality schools was similar for *all* types of item. The home backgrounds of the pupils were similar.

Since the socioeconomic background factors of the students were similar, the only other environmental factor to which the results could be attributed was the school environment and the quality of teachers. So if the reasoning items traditionally associated with tests of aptitude and intelligence are not as immune to the effects of teaching as was once thought, and if reasoning skills are those skills which we want to encourage, then why not test them? Why not *use* the examination system to encourage the skills one values? If skills now being encouraged are not relevant, then why not make the examinations more relevant? If the examinations do not test students' abilities to solve problems, then why not include problems in the examination and encourage them to solve them?

Evidence from a large number of national examination systems points to an enormous potential for change. An analysis was carried out recently of 122 primary and secondary school examination papers from eight African countries (Little and Lewin, 1980; Little, 1981a). The main questions asked of each examination in each country were:

(1) What types of skill are being examined?
(2) What proportion of the items test anything more than the recall of memorised factual information?

The examination papers were almost entirely devoted to the testing of cognitive skills. Affective and psychomotor skills were rarely, if ever, tested. Within the group of cognitive skills three levels were identifiable. These coincided with the categories of knowledge, comprehension and application outlined in Bloom's (1956) well-known *Taxonomy of Educational Objectives.* *Knowledge* questions require only the recognition or recall of facts, generalisations, or principles. *Comprehension* items, on the other hand, require more than recall or recognition. They require the ability to grasp and understand the meaning of concepts of symbols. The dividing line between comprehension and the third category, *application,* is often a difficult one to draw. Application items generally require the ability to apply and to use rules, concepts and principles in *new* circumstances.

The proportion of items falling into each category varied enormously by country, by subject, by year of examination and by level of education. Somewhat surprisingly, perhaps, examination papers coming at the end of the primary cycle contained higher proportions of items testing comprehension and application than secondary-level papers. A comparison revealed that of a total of the 1,734 items contained in the primary-level papers reviewed from Zambia, Tanzania, Kenya, Sierra Leone, Ghana and the Gambia, some 55 per cent (961) were application items, 25 per cent (434) were comprehension items, while only 20 per cent (339) were knowledge items. At the secondary level, by contrast, the majority of the items in the papers from Liberia, Somalia, Zambia, Kenya, Sierra Leone, Ghana and the Gambia contained a majority 55 per cent of knowledge items (1,585), 16 per cent comprehension items (461) and 28 per cent application items (807). The main explanation for this discrepancy is the fact that it is mainly subjects like mathematics and English which are being tested in the primary-level examinations and these subjects tend to contain higher proportions of items classifiable as application. It was of some concern that so few items in subject areas like geography, history, chemistry, biology, civics and religion tested anything other than the recall or recognition of factual knowledge.

The experience of one country in examination reform stood out among all the others. These were the efforts of the Kenyan Ministry of Education to reform its primary school examinations during the 1970s, some aspects of which were described earlier. In Kenya students sit the Certificate of Primary Education (CPE) at the end of seven years of primary education. The changes during 1971–9 in the distribution of items testing knowledge, comprehension and application have been dramatic. This has come about through a planned effort on the part of the Ministry of Education to make the CPE a more effective terminal examination; to develop powers of reasoning among primary school students; and to include items which have useful local application, especially for rural students (Makau and Somerset, 1978; Somerset, 1982).

There are many other examples: Malaysia, Sri Lanka and India, for example, have in the past changed the proportions of items testing application skills in a deliberate attempt to change the quality of teaching for the better (Lewin, 1981; Little, 1978). Other countries, too, are planning even more major changes in examination strategy. The examinations in Papua New Guinea already contain a very high proportion of items testing the skills of application and comprehension, but the examination system proposes to go even further. Papua New Guinea has recently introduced a new secondary school project known as the Secondary School Community Extension Project (SSCEP). It is a trial project involving five provincial high schools in grades 9 and 10. The project is intended to encourage students to apply skills to the solution of rural community problems. The selection system is being designed specifically to encourage such an application and will involve school-based assessments of social development. The Papua New Guinean experiment is an important one, because it is deliberately trying to manipulate the extrinsic goal of the examination in order to achieve a greater degree of intrinsic motivation on the part of students.

The relationship between extrinsic motivation and intrinsic motivation has long been a concern of psychologists. It has been the implicit assumption of the 'diploma disease' model that a large dose of extrinsic motivation in the form of examinations and qualifications kills off intrinsic motivation or the desire to learn about a subject for its own sake. Recent and provocative evidence is available from the American psychological literature to support this assumption (see, for example, Deci, 1976; Maehr, 1976). The alternative view, however, advanced long ago by Allport and called 'functional autonomy', is that extrinsic motivation can facilitate and encourage intrinsic motivation. Examinations can be used to create a lasting interest in a subject area which otherwise would not have been studied. McNamara applied the argument to Papua New Guinea, expressing it in local terms:

> we can use carrots to induce a donkey, which has never eaten sorghum, to eat sorghum and to learn to enjoy it, so that at some later stage when carrots are no longer available, he will happily amble in the direction of sorghum which he would otherwise have ignored. In such cases the learning survives the extrinsic motivation of the carrots, so that the sorghum itself becomes intrinsically motivating. (McNamara, 1980)

Which view approximates the reality of the classroom more closely is unlikely to be resolved definitively in the near future. However, one is reminded once again of the IDS research in Mexican primary schools and in Chinese middle schools of what happens when the external goals of the examination and qualifications are pulled away from the structures supporting an education system. Intrinsic motivation did not appear to bear a simple negative relation to extrinsic motivation. The removal of extrinsic motivation led to a high degree of demoralisation. The removal of examinations is likely to lead to a high degree of demoralisation.

The removal of examinations is likely to lead to a high degree of demoralisation in *all* countries, not just the Third World. In this chapter we have concentrated on the 'diploma disease' in the Third World. But we in the North also suffer and though we may not have suffered to the same degree in the past – as our unemployment problems increase, so does the importance of examinations and qualifications.

In 1981 a group of 17-year-old sixth-formers in an English comprehensive school were asked whether they would have entered the sixth form if it were not for examinations and if job selection was left to employers. They said:

'I don't think anyone would come to school if there were no exams ... most people associate exams with working hard and getting something out of working, so if you are going to come to school and stay on for an extra two years and then get nothing for it you think, God, what a waste of time.'

'If there were no exams there'd be nothing to work for.'

'If you've got exams you've got something to aim for at the end of it.'

'If there were no qualifications at the end of sixth form, well, I think education is necessary but I don't think the incentive would be there.'

'There has got to be exams somewhere along the line so therefore to get exams you have to do the work. It's as simple as that.'

This is not to say, of course, that students are motivated *solely* by external examinations, that they do not derive any motivation from an interest in the subjects they are studying. It is to suggest that external motivation may be a necessary though not sufficient condition for other kinds of motivation to develop. For many students, an interest in a subject and a concern with the examination go hand in hand:

'Economics is so interesting because you wouldn't believe what goes on and how the stock exchange is run and things like that ... I was only doing economics for a month and was quite pleased because I got 47 per cent, in the mock, which I was pleased about.'

'I do the subjects I do because I like them best. I'm doing them because I want to go to university, but I wouldn't be going to university if I didn't like these subjects.'

'It wasn't a case of I really liked geography, but I have to have another one [at A level] and so I chose that. Now I quite enjoy it.'

Examinations and other forms of assessment are an integral part of meritocratic and economic organisation whether that organisation

226/ Education versus Qualifications?

be of a 'capitalist' or 'socialist' form. Perhaps the radical reform of the examination system itself is the most we can hope for, if we wish to change the quality of education.

Table 7.4   *The Impact of Examination Reform on the 'Diploma Disease'*

Alternative	Educational and Social Goals					
	Reduce 'unnecessary' qualification escalation	Reduce 'unnecessary' expansion of the formal school system and costs	Reduce exam cramming	Improve balance of skills taught in schools	Improve the balance between extrinsically and intrinsically motivated learning	Increase equity of resource distribution within the education system
A.4 Selection through reformed examinations	No impact	No impact	No, but cramming and practice could have beneficial outcomes	Yes	Could do	Could do

How would examination reform match up to the achievement of the six problems listed at the beginning of the chapter? (See Table 7.4.) It would have little impact on either qualification escalation or on the reduction of unnecessary expansion of the formal school system and costs, or on the equitable distribution of resources within the education system. Employers would probably use the examination results as convenient selection devices in the same ways as at present. The biggest impact of examination reform would be in the classrooms. The carrot of the examinations could be used to promote problem-solving skills of relevance. And the items might just also be of interest into the bargain.

Table 7.5 consolidates Tables 7.1–7.4 and shows each of the problems presented at the beginning of the chapter and the likely impact of each of the alternatives on their solution. Table 7.5 makes it clear that none of the suggestions advanced here, if taken alone, satisfies *all* the objectives one desires. Clearly, the question of costs, reduction of qualification escalation and resource allocation within the education system are best catered for by the proposal to select people for modern sector jobs after a shorter period of schooling than now. National lotteries could also put a

Table 7.5 *Summary of Effects of Alternatives for Selecting Employees for 'Modern' Jobs*

Alternative	Educational and Social Goals					
	Reduce 'unnecessary' qualification escalation	Reduce 'unnecessary' expansion of the formal school system and costs	Reduce exam-cramming	Improve balance of skills taught in schools	Improve the balance between extrinsically and intrinsically motivated learning	Increase equity of resource distribution within the education system
A.1 Earlier selection into jobs, later selection by employer or market	Reduced after basic open-access school	Yes, but training costs would shift to employers; resultant costs could be greater or similar	No impact	No impact	No impact	Could do
A.2 Abolition of educational qualifications; selection exclusively through employer aptitude tests	Could do	Could do	Unlikely	Could do	Could do	No impact
A.3 Selection through restricted lotteries	Could do	Could do	Unlikely	Unlikely	Unlikely	Could do
A.4 Selection through reformed examinations	No impact	No impact	No, but cramming would have beneficial outcomes	Yes	Could do	No impact

brake on qualification escalation, though their acceptability to a society where the stakes in the achievement and selection game are so high must remain doubtful. They are also unlikely to reduce cramming in schools. So, too, are most of the other reform proposals. But there is cramming and cramming. It depends what you're cramming for and how you go about cramming. Certainly, the epigram of Ghanaian students who chant 'Chew, pour, pass, forget' as they approach examinations is a recipe for disaster. But some types of learning simply cannot be chewed, poured out and forgotten. Some items require more than a simple chewing. They must also be swallowed and digested into a more complex system of knowledge. And once digested it is less easy to regurgitate and forget them. They remain in the body for longer than that. They are items which can be used by the body to grow and to develop. And it is these sorts of items which could very easily turn an examination system into one which encourages, rather than stultifies, desirable outcomes.

References

Allison, Christine (1983), 'The economics of household demand for children's schooling: a study of the Kweneng district of Botswana', PhD thesis, London University Institute of Education.

Arrow, K. J. (1973), 'Higher education as a filter', *Journal of Public Economics*, vol. 2, pp. 193–216; also in K. G. Lumsden (ed.), *Efficiency in Universities*, The La Paz Papers (Amsterdam: Elsevier, 1974), pp. 51–74.

Aryee, G. (1976), 'Effects of formal education and training on the intensity of employment in the informal sector: a case study of Kumasi, Ghana', World Employment Programme Research Working Paper, International Labour Office, Geneva.

Aryee, G. (1980), *Employment, Incomes, and Production in the Informal Sector in The Gambia* (Addis Ababa: ILO/JASPA).

Avalos, Beatrice (1978), *Educational Change in Latin America: The Case of Peru* (Cardiff: University College Cardiff Press).

Avalos, Beatrice, and Haddad, W. (1981), 'A review of teacher effectiveness research in Africa, India, Latin America, Middle East, Malaysia, Philippines and Thailand: synthesis of results', International Development Research Center, Ottawa.

Bautista Villegas, L. E. (1981), 'The effect of various forms of education in the productivity of farmers dedicated to seasonal agriculture – a case study in the state of Michoacan, Mexico', M.Phil. thesis, University of Sussex.

Becker, G. (1964), *Human Capital* (New York: Columbia University Press).

Bediako, T. A. (1979), 'Teacher drain', *West Africa* (London), no. 3248, 15 October, p. 1909.

Beeby, C. (1966), *The Quality of Education in Developing Countries* (Cambridge, Mass.: Harvard University Press).

Bennell, P. S. (1981), 'Earnings differentials between public and private sectors in Africa: the cases of Ghana, Kenya and Nigeria', *Labour and Society*, vol. 6, no. 3 (July–September), pp. 223–41.

Bennett, N. (1977), 'The need for educational change and the basic criteria for planning such change', Division of Educational Policy and Planning, UNESCO Reports/Studies S43, Paris.

Bereday, G. (1968), 'School systems and the enrolment crisis: a comparative overview', *Comparative Education Review*, vol. 12, no. 2 (June), pp. 126–38.

Berg, I. (1970), *Education and Jobs: The Great Training Robbery* (Harmondsworth: Penguin).

Berry, A. (1980), 'Education, income, productivity, and urban poverty', in Timothy King (ed.), *Education and Income*, World Bank Staff Working Paper No. 402 (Washington, DC: World Bank), pp. 153–230.

Blakemore, K. P. (1975) 'Resistance to formal education in Ghana: its implications for the status of school-leavers', *Comparative Education Review*, vol. 19, no. 2 (June), pp. 237–51.

Blaug, M. (1974), *Education and the Employment Problems in Developing Countries* (Geneva: ILO).

Blaug, M. (1978), 'Economics of education in developing countries: current trends and new priorities', London University Institute of Education, mimeo.

Blaug, M., Layard, R., and Woodhall, M. (1969), *The Causes of Graduate Unemployment in India* (London: The Penguin Press).

Bloom, B. S. (ed.) (1956), *Taxonomy of Educational Objectives. Handbook 1, The Cognitive Domain* (London: Longman).

Boakye, J. K. A. (1977), 'The continuation school programme in Ghana, a preliminary assessment', Centre for Development Studies, Cape Coast, mimeo.

Boakye, J. K. A. (1983), 'Unemployment among elementary school leavers in Ghana and its solution through vocationalisation of formal education: an evaluation of the continuation school system', D.Phil. thesis, University of Sussex, Brighton.

Boakye, J. K. A., and Oxenham, J. (1982), *Qualifications and the Quality of Education in Ghanaian Rural Middle Schools*, Education Report No. 6 (Brighton: IDS).

Bowles, S. (1971), 'Cuban education and the revolutionary ideology', *Harvard Educational Review*, vol. 41, no. 4, pp. 472–500.

Bowles, S., and Gintis, H. (1976), *Schooling in Capitalist America* (London: Routledge & Kegan Paul).

Bravo Ahuja, V. (1970), 'Proposicion de una reforma al sistema educativo nacional', No Sonra, mimeo.

Bray, M. (1981), *Universal Primary Education in Nigeria, a Study of Kano State* (London: Routledge & Kegan Paul).

Brooke, N. (1979), 'The quality of primary education: the implementation of reform in Mexico', D.Phil. thesis, University of Sussex.

Brooke, N. (1980), 'The quality of education in rural Ghana and Mexico', *IDS Bulletin*, vol. 11, no. 2, pp. 42–8.

Brooke, N. (1982), 'Relevance in pedagogy and the problem of educational quality in Latin America', *International Journal of Educational Development*, vol. 2, no. 1 (Spring), pp. 73–80.

Brooke, N., and Oxenham, J. C. P. (1980), *The Quality of Education in Mexican Primary Schools*, Education Report No. 5 (Brighton: IDS).

References/231

Brooke, N., Oxenham, J. C. P., and Little, A. (1978), *Qualifications and Employment in Mexico*, Education Report No. 1 (Brighton: IDS).

Brozek, J. (1978), 'Nutrition, malnutrition, and behaviour' *Annual Review of Psychology*, vol. 29, pp. 157–77.

Bude, U. (1982), 'Towards a realistic definition of the teacher's role in primary schooling and the conditions for integration with local communities: experiences and research evidence from Cameroon', London University Institute of Education, mimeo.

Carnoy, M. (1972), 'The political economy of education', in T. J. LaBelle (ed.), *Education and Development – Latin America and the Caribbean*, Latin American Studies (Berkeley, Calif.: UCLA), Vol. 18, pp. 177–215.

Carnoy, M. (1974), *Education as Cultural Imperialism* (New York: McKay).

Ceylon Daily News, 6 June 1971.

Chaudhri, D. P. (1974), 'Rural education and agricultural development: some empirical results from Indian agriculture', *World Yearbook of Education, 1974* (London: Evans), pp. 372–86.

Cochrane, S. H., O'Hara, D. J., and Leslie, J. (1980), *The Effects of Education on Health*, World Bank Staff Working Paper No. 405 (Washington, DC: World Bank).

Colclough, C. (1980), *Primary Schooling and Economic Development: A Review of the Evidence*, World Bank Staff Working Paper No. 399 (Washington, DC: World Bank).

Collins, R. (1972), 'Functional and conflict theories of educational stratification', in B. R. Cosin (ed.), *Education, Structure and Society* (Harmondsworth: Penguin/The Open University), pp. 175–99; also in *American Sociological Review*, vol. 36, no. 6 (December 1971), pp. 1002–19.

Conroy, J. D. (1976), 'Education, employment and migration in Papua New Guinea', Research Monograph No. 3, ANU Development Studies Center, Australian National University, Canberra.

Cooksey, B. (1981), 'Social class and academic performance: a Cameroon case study', *Comparative Education Review*, vol. 25, no. 3 (October), pp. 403–18.

Court, D., and Ghai, D. (1974), *Education, Society and Development* (Nairobi: Oxford University Press/University of Nairobi Institute of Development Studies).

Crook, R. (1970), 'The Broker model and local politics in Ghana', Institute of Commonwealth Studies, Oxford, mimeo.

Cunha, L. A. (1978), *Educação e Desenvolvimento social no Brasil* (Rio de Janeiro: FCO/Alvis Editora).

Deci, E. C. (1976), *Intrinsic Motivation* (New York: Plenum Press).

Denison, E. F. (1962), 'The sources of economic growth in the United States and the alternatives before us', Supplementary Paper No. 13, Committee for Economic Development, New York.

Deraniyagala, C., Dore, R., and Little, A. (1978), *Qualification and Employment in Sri Lanka*, Education Report No. 2 (Brighton: IDS).

Diaz de Cossio, R. (1976), 'Los libros de texto', *SEP Educacion 1970–76* (Mexico City: SEP).

Dore, R. P. (1976), *The Diploma Disease* (London: Allen & Unwin).

Duby, C. E. (1966), *The Quality of Education in Developing Countries* (Cambridge, Mass.: Harvard University Press).

Dweck, C. S., Davidson, W., Nelson, S., and Bradley, B. (1978), 'Sex differences in learned helplessness: II The contingencies of evaluative feedback in the classroom and III An experimental analysis', *Journal of Developmental Psychology*, vol. 14, no. 3, pp. 268–78.

Ebel, R. L. (1972), *Essentials of Educational Measurement*, 2nd edn (Englewood Cliffs, NJ: Prentice-Hall).

Educational Testing Services (1980), 'Test use and validity: a response to charges in the Nader/Nairn report on ETS', ETS, Princeton, NJ.

Finniston, M. (1980), *Engineering Our Future*, report of Committee of Inquiry into Engineering Profession (London: HMSO).

Foley, D. E. (1977), 'Anthropological studies of schooling in developing countries', *Comparative Education Review*, vol. 21, no. 2–3, pp. 311–28.

Foster, P. J. (1965), *Education and Social Change in Ghana* (London: Routledge & Kegan Paul).

Foster, P. J. (1977), 'Education and social differentiation in less developed countries', *Comparative Education Review*, vol. 21, no. 2–3, pp. 211–29.

Fuller, W. P. (1972), 'Evaluating alternative combinations of education and training for job preparation: an example from Indian industry', *Nanpoon Journal*, vol. 8, pt 1, pp. 7–38.

Ghiselli, E. E. (1966), *The Validity of Occupational Aptitude Tests* (New York: Wiley).

Gillette, A. (1979), 'Structural changes in education since 1954: a slow motion explosion', *International Review of Education*, vol. XXV, no. 2–3, pp. 267–96.

Godfrey, M. (1977), 'Education, training, productivity and income: a Kenyan case study', *Comparative Education Review*, vol. 21, no. 1, pp. 29–35.

Godfrey, M., and Bennell, P. (1980), 'African pay structures in a transnational context, the British connection', Research Report No. 9, IDS, Brighton.

Goodnow, J. J. (1980), 'Everyday concepts of intelligence and its development', in N. Warren (ed.), *Studies in Cross Cultural Psychology* (London: Academic Press), Vol. 2, pp. 191–220.

Goslin, D. (1963), *The Search for Ability: Standardised Testing in Social Perspective* (New York: Russell Sage).

Gould, W. T. S. (1982), 'Education and internal migration: a review and report', *International Journal of Educational Development*, vol. 1, no. 3 (January), pp. 103–11.

Government of Ceylon (1971), *The Five Year Plan* (Colombo: Ministry of Planning and Employment).

Government of Ceylon (1972), *Interim Report of the Committee to Inquire into and Report on Public Examinations at Secondary School Level in Ceylon* (Colombo: Government Printer).

Government of Kenya (1972), *Report of the Commission of Inquiry on the Public Service Structure and Remuneration, 1970* (chairman, P. Ndegwa) (Nairobi: Government Printer).

Government of Kenya (1973), *Scheme of Service – Clerical Officer Grade*, Personnel Circular No. 4 (Nairobi: Directorate of Personnel Management).

Government of Kenya (1979), *Teaching Service Salary Scales* (Nairobi: Teachers' Service Commission).

Government of Liberia (1978), *Civil Service Examinations for Administrative Positions*, Circular Letter, 78–1, 2 January (Monrovia: Civil Service Agency).

Government of Liberia (1979), *Draft Second National Socio-Economic Development Plan: Education Sector Analysis* (Monrovia: Ministry of Planning and Economic Affairs).

Government of Liberia (1980), 'Report on the first civil service expanded exam services to rural areas', *Civil Servant* (Monrovia), vol. 1, no. 2, pp. 8–11.

Government of Malaysia (1971), *Second Malaysia Plan* (Kuala Lumpur: Government Printer).

Government of Malaysia (1972), *Educational Planning Committee Paper No. 3* (Kuala Lumpur: Government Printer).

Government of Malaysia (1973), *Seminar on Science and Mathematics Education Held at the University of Malaya*, Working Papers I, II, III (Kuala Lumpur: Ministry of Education).

Government of Malaysia (1976), *Third Malaysia Plan* (Kuala Lumpur: Government Printer).

Government of Malaysia (1977), *Economic Report, 1977–78* (Kuala Lumpur: Ministry of Finance).

Government of Sierra Leone (1957), *Report of the Commission of the Civil Service of Sierra Leone* (Freetown: Government Printer).

Government of Sri Lanka (1973), *Medium Term Plan for the Development of Education, 1973–77* (Colombo: Ministry of Education Planning and Programme Division).

Government of Sri Lanka (1974), *Report of the Salaries and Cadres Commission, Pt II* (chairman, L. B. de Silva), Sessional Paper No. IV (Colombo: Government Printer).

Government of Sri Lanka (1976), *The Curriculum Development Center* (Colombo: Government Printer).

Government of Tanzania (1975), *Scheme of Service for Civil Service Technicians*, Establishment Circular Letter No. 9 (Dar es Salaam: Government Printer).

Government of Tanzania (1981), *Long Term Perspective Plan 1981-2000* (Dar es Salaam: Government Printer).

Government of Zambia (1975), *Revision of Salaries and Conditions of Service*, Personnel Circular No. B11 (Lusaka: Government Printer).

Halim, A. (1976), 'The economic contribution of schooling and extension to rice production in the province of Laguna, Republic of the Philippines', Ph.D thesis, University of the Philippines, Los Baños.

Hallak, J., and Caillods, F. (1980), *Education, Work and Employment* (Paris: UNESCO/International Institute of Educational Planning).

Hallak, J., and Caillods, F. (1981), *Education, Training and the Traditional Sector*, Fundamentals of Educational Planning No. 31 (Paris: UNESCO/International Institute for Educational Planning).

Hawes, H. (1980), *Curriculum and Reality in African Primary Schools* (London: Longman).

Heider, F. (1944), 'Social perception and phenomenal causality', *Psychological Review*, vol. 51, pp. 358–73.

Heider, F. (1958), *The Psychology of Interpersonal Relations* (New York: Wiley).

Heijnen, J. D. (1968), *Development and Education in the Mwanza District (Tanzania) – a Case Study of Migration and Peasant Farming* (Amsterdam: Centre for Study of Migration and Peasant Farming).

Hoerr, O. D. (1970), 'Education, income and equity in Malaysia', *Economic Development Report, 1976* (Harvard, Mass.: Center for International Affairs).

IDS (1973), 'Qualifications and selection in educational systems in developing countries', IDS, Brighton, mimeo.

IDS (1980), 'Selection for employment v. education?', *IDS Bulletin*, vol. 11, no. 2, *passim*.

Illich, I. (1971), *Deschooling Society* (London: Calder & Boyars).

ILO (1971), *Employment, Incomes and Equality: A Strategy for Increasing Productive Employment in Kenya* (Geneva: ILO).

ILO (1972), *Matching Employment Opportunities and Expectations: A Programme of Action for Ceylon* (Geneva: ILO).

ILO (1978), *Towards Self-Reliance: Development, Employment and Equity Issues in Tanzania* (Addis Ababa: ILO/JASPA).

Inkeles, D. V., and Smith, M. (1974), *Becoming Modern* (London: Heinemann).

Jallade, J. P. (1977), 'Basic education and income inequality in Brazil: the long term view', Staff Working Paper No. 268, World Bank, Washington, DC.

Jamison, D. T., and Lau, L. I. (1982), *Farmer Education and Farm Efficiency* (Washington, DC: World Bank).

JASPA (1979), *Options for a Dependent Economy: Development, Employment and Equity Problems in Lesotho* (Addis Ababa: ILO/JASPA).

JASPA (1980), *School Leavers, Unemployment and Manpower Development in Liberia* (Addis Ababa: ILO/JASPA).

JASPA (1981), *The Paper Qualification Syndrome and Unemployment of School Leavers. Vol. 1, Kenya, Somalia, Tanzania, Zambia* and *Vol. 2, Gambia,Ghana, Liberia, Sierra Leone* (Addis Ababa: ILO/JASPA).

JASPA (1982), *Paper Qualification Syndrome and Unemployment of School Leavers, a Comparative Sub-Regional Study* (Addis Ababa: ILO/JASPA).

Jay, A. (1980), 'Nobody's perfect – but a team can be', *Observer Magazine* (London), 20 April, pp. 26–38.

Jayasuriya, J. E. (1969), *Education in Ceylon before and after Independence* (Colombo: Associated Educational Publishers).

Jayasuriya, J. E. (1979), *Educational Policies and Progress* (Colombo: Associated Educational Publishers).

Jencks, C. (1972), *Inequality: A Reassessment of the Effect of Family and Schooling in America* (New York: Basic Books).

Jencks, C. (1979), *Who Gets Ahead? The Determinants of Economic Success in America* (New York: Basic Books).

Jensen, A. R. (1969), 'How much can we boost IQ and scholastic achievement', *Harvard Educational Review*, vol. 39, no. 1, pp. 1–123.

Jolly, R. (1974), 'The judo trick', in F. Champion (ed.), *The Bellagio Conference Papers* (New York: Praeger).

Kelly, G. A. (1955), *The Psychology of Personal Constructs* (New York: Norton).

Kingsley, P. (1977), 'The measurement of intelligence in Africa – some conceptual issues and related research', Human Development Research Unit Reports, University of Zambia.

Knox, David, and Castles, Stephen (1982) 'Education with production: learning from the Third World', *International Journal of Educational Development*, vol. 2, no. 1 (Spring), pp. 1–14.

Kukla, A. (1972), 'Attributional determinants of achievement related behaviour', *Journal of Personality and Social Psychology*, vol. 21, no. 2, pp. 166–74.

Layard, P. R. G., Sargan, J. D., Ager, M. E., and Jones, D. J. (1971), *Qualified Manpower and Economic Performance: An Inter-Plant Study in the Electrical Engineering Industry* (London: Allen Lane/London School of Economics and Political Science).

Lee, E. (1972), *Educational Planning in West Malaysia* (Kuala Lumpur: Oxford University Press).

Lehmann, R., and Verhine, R. (1982), 'Contributions of formal and non-formal education to obtaining skilled industrial employment in north-eastern Brazil', *International Journal of Educational Development*, vol. 2, no. 1, pp. 29–42.

Leichmann, G. A. (1976), 'The effect of age and educational environment on the development of achievement, evaluation and moral judgements', Ph.D thesis, London School of Economics and Political Science.

Levine, R. A. (1980), 'Influences of women's schooling on maternal behaviour in the Third World', *Comparative Education Review*, vol. 24, no. 2, pp. 78–105.

Lewin, K. M. (1981), 'Science education in Malaysia and Sri Lanka: curriculum development and course evaluation, 1970–78', D.Phil. thesis, University of Sussex.

Lewin, K., and Little, A. (1982), 'Examination reform and educational change in Sri Lanka: dependent development, evolutionary change or dependent self-reliance?', IDS, Brighton, mimeo.

Lewin, K., Little, A., and Colclough, C. (1982), 'Adjusting to the 1980s – taking stock of educational expenditure', in *Financing Educational Development*, proceedings of IDRC International Seminar, Mont Sainte-Mar e, Canada, 19–21 May.

Lewis, W. A. (1977) 'The university in developing countries: modernisation and tradition in higher education and social change', in K. W. Thompson, B. K. Fogel and H. E. Danner (eds), *Higher Education and Social Change* (New York: Praeger), Vol. 2, pp. 516–29.

Lillis, K., and Hogan, D. (1981), 'Attempts to diversify secondary school curricula in developing countries in vocational directions: a literature review and some additional hypotheses concerning the causes of failure', University of Sussex Education Area Centre of Educational Technology, Brighton, mimeo; see also 'Dilemmas of diversification, problems associated with vocational education in developing countries', *Comparative Education*, vol. 19, no. 1 (1983), p. 89 *et seq.*

Little, A. (1974), 'The correlation between job performance and pre-career qualification', IDS, Brighton, mimeo.

Little, A. (1977), 'The rise of educational qualifications in labour markets – an annotated bibliography', Occasional Library Guide No. 11, IDS, Brighton.

Little, A. (1978), *'Types of examinations and achievement'*, Education Report No. 4 (Brighton: IDS).

Little, A. (1980), 'Is education related to productivity?', *IDS Bulletin*, vol. 11, no. 2, pp. 20–7.

Little, A. (1981a), *Content Analyses of Examination Papers in Tanzania, Gambia, Ghana, Sierra Leone and Liberia* (Addis Ababa: ILO/JASPA).

Little, A. (1981b), 'The development of the child's understanding of the causes of success and failure: case studies from England and Sri Lanka', *Development Research Digest* (IDS, Brighton), no. 4 (Winter), pp. 58–61.

Little, A. W. (1982), 'The development of the child's understanding of the causes of academic success and failure: studies of English and Sri Lankan schoolchildren', D.Phil. thesis, University of Sussex.

Little, A., and Lewin, K. (1980), *Content Analyses of Examination Papers in Zambia, Kenya and Somalia* (Addis Ababa: ILO/JASPA).

Lockheed, M., Jamison, D., and Lau, L. (1980), 'Farmer education and farm efficiency: a survey', in Timothy King (ed.), *Education and Income*, World Bank Staff Working Paper No. 402 (Washington, DC: World Bank), pp. 111–52.

McCelland, D. C., Atkinson, J. W., Clark, R. A., and Lowell, E. L. (1953), *The Achievement Motive* (New York: Appleton-Century-Crofts).

McNamara, V. (1980), 'School system structure, curriculum, SSCEP and functional motivation for learning, Papua New Guinea', *Journal of Education*, vol. 16, no. 1, pp. 12–28.

Maehr, M. L. (1976), 'Continuing motivation: an analysis of a seldom considered educational outcome', *Review of Educational Research*, vol. 46, pt 3, pp. 443–62.

Maehr, M., and Nicholls, J. (1980), 'Culture and achievement motivation: a second look', in N. Warren (ed.), *Studies in Cross-Cultural Psychology* (London: Academic Press), Vol. 2, pp. 6, 221–67.

Makau, B., and Somerset, H. A. C. (1978), 'Primary school leaving examinations and basic intellectual skills and equity: some evidence from Kenya', Research Report No. 3, Kenya National Examinations Council Research Unit, Nairobi.

Malaysian Integrated Science (1973), *Syllabus* (Kuala Lumpur: Curriculum Development Centre).

Mee, A., Boyd, P., and Ritchie, D. (1971), *Science for the 70s*, Teachers' Guide Books 1 and 2, Pupils' Work Sheet (London: Heinemann).

Miranda, C., and Schmidt, I. (1977), 'Determinantes de escolarizacao', FAE/UFMG, Belo Horizonte, mimeo.

Modiano, N. (1973), *Indian Education in the Chiapas Highlands* (New York: Holt, Rinehart & Winston).

Molen, G. van der (1976), 'Economic impacts of education and personnel management: case studies from the industrial sector in Iran and Surinam', *Development and Change*, vol. 7, pp. 45–6.

Montemayor, A. (1980), 'Educación y distribución del ingreso en México', *Revista Latinoamericana de Estudios Educativos*, vol. X, no. 2, pp. 33–68.

Moreira, J. R. (1972), 'Educational development in Latin America', in T. J. LaBelle (ed.), *Education and Development – Latin America and the Caribbean*, Latin American Studies (Berkeley, Calif.: UCLA), Vol. 18, pp. 7–44.

Morris, P. (1982), 'The New Economics course, Hong Kong's curriculum: rhetoric and reality', D.Phil. thesis, University of Sussex.

Munro, D. (1977), *The Concept of Man in Contemporary China* (Ann Arbor, Mich.: University of Michigan Press).

Nash, M. (1972), 'The role of village schools in the process of cultural and economic modernisation', in T. J. LaBelle (ed.), *Education and Development – Latin America and the Caribbean*, Latin American Studies (Berkeley, Calif.: UCLA), Vol. 18, pp. 483–98.

Obeysekere, G. (1974), 'Some comments on the social backgrounds of the

April 1971 insurgency in Sri Lanka', *Journal of Asian Studies*, vol. XXXIII, no. 3, pp. 367–84.

OECD (1970), *Occupational and Educational Structure of the Labour Force and Levels of Economic Development* (Paris: OECD), Vol. 1.

OECD (1974), *Research into Labour Market Behaviour*, ed. J. Vin and D. Robinson (Paris: OECD).

Ord, I. (1972), 'Testing for educational and occupational selection in developing countries', *Occupational Psychology*, vol. 46, no. 3, pp. 125–82.

Otis, A., and Lennon, R. (1969), *Technical Handbook* (New York: Harcourt, Brace & World).

Oxenham, J. (1974), 'Education and employment in Indonesia', Asian Regional Team for Employment Promotion, ILO, Bangkok, mimeo.

Oxenham, J. (1981), *The Paper Qualification Syndrome and the Unemployment of School Leavers: The Case of Kenya*, report (Addis Ababa: ILO/JASPA).

Oxenham, J. (1982), 'An analysis of examinations in Lesotho', technical paper for Education Sector Survey Task Force, Ministry of Education, Maseru, mimeo.

Oxenham, J., Dore, R., Jolly, A., Little, A., and Mook, B. (1975), 'Qualifications and selection in educational systems', Discussion Paper No. 70, IDS, Brighton.

Palmer, C., and Barber, C. (1981), 'Mental development after intervention, a study of Philippine children', *Journal of Cross-Cultural Psychology*, vol. 12, no. 4, pp. 480–8.

Panchamukhi, P. (1978), 'Employment and education policy, the Indian experience', *Manpower Journal* (Institute of Applied Manpower Research, New Delhi), vol. XIV, no. 1 (April–June), pp. 31–56.

Paulston, R. (1971), 'Sociocultural constraints on educational development in Peru', *Journal of Developing Areas*, vol. 5, no. 3 (April), pp. 401–16.

PREALC (1978), 'Funcionamiento y politicas', Programa de Empleo para America Latina y el Caribe, ILO, Santiago, mimeo.

Psacharopoulos, G. (1973), *Returns to Education: An International Comparison* (New York: Elsevier/Jossey-Bass).

Psacharopoulos, G. (1978), 'Educational planning: past and present', *Quarterly Review of Education*, vol. VIII, no. 2, pp. 135–42.

Psacharopoulos, G. (1980), 'Returns to education: an updated international comparison', in Timothy King (ed.), *Education and Income*, World Bank Staff Working Paper No. 402 (Washington, DC: World Bank).

Psacharopoulos, G., and Sanyal, B. (1981), *Higher Education and Employment: The IIEP Experience in Five Less Developed Countries* (Paris: UNESCO/International Institute of Educational Planning).

Rama, G. (1978), 'Notas acerca de la expansión universitaria, el mercado de empleo y las práticas academicas', Projecto DEALC Fichas/5, UNESCO, Cepal, PNUD.

Ramos, L. (1980), 'Enseñanza pre-escolar, primaria, media-basica, normal superior y superior durante el ciclo 1978–79', *Revista Latinoamericana de Estudios Educativos*, vol. X, no. 4, pp. 163–88.

Rodriguez, P. G., and Muñoz, J. B. (1976), 'La enseñanza media en México en 1974–75', *Revista del Centro de Estudios Educativos*, vol. VI, no. 2, pp. 155–75.

Rodriguez, P. G., and Ramos, P. (1979), 'Presupuesto educativo y piramide escolar en México 1976–77', *Revista del Centro de Estudios Educativos*, vol. VIII, no. 4.

Salmi, J. (1981), 'Educational crisis and social reproduction: the political economy of schooling in Morocco', D.Phil. thesis, University of Sussex.

Schultz, T. (1961), 'Investment in human capital', *American Economic Review*, vol. LI, no. 1 (March), pp. 1–17.

Schwarz, P., and Krug, R. (1972), *Ability Testing in Developing Countries* (New York: Praeger).

Scottish Education Department (1969), *Science for a General Education*, Curriculum Paper No. 7 (London/Edinburgh: HMSO).

SEP (1971), 'Aportaciones de estudio de las problemas de la educación', Comisión Coordenadiva de la Reforma Educativa, Secretaria de Educación Publica, Mexico City.

Sheffield, James R. (ed.) (1969), *Education, Employment and Rural Development* (Nairobi: East African).

Sinclair, J. (1976), 'The changing composition of university enrolments in Ghana', University of Cape Coast, mimeo.

Sinclair, M. E., with Lillis, K. (1980), *School and Community in the Third World* (London: Croom Helm).

Smerling, L. (1979), 'Admissions', in R. Montaperto and J. Henderson (eds), *China's Schools in Flux* (White Plains, NY: M. E. Sharpe), pp. 92–105.

Somerset, H. (1974), 'Who goes to secondary school?', in D. Court and D. P. Ghai (eds), *Education, Society and Development* (Nairobi: Oxford University Press/IDS), pp. 149–84.

Somerset, H. (1977), 'Aptitude tests, socio-economic background and secondary school selection: the possibilities and limits of change', paper presented to Conference on Social Science Research and Educational Effectiveness, Rockefeller Foundation, Bellagio, NY, 1976.

Somerset, H. (1982), 'Examinations reform; the Kenyan experience', report prepared for World Bank, IDS, Brighton, mimeo.

Srivastava, H., and Oxenham, J. (1978), 'Employers and schools –a sounding among some employers in India', *Manpower Journal*, vol. XIV, no. 1, pp. 58–69.

Stolzenberg, R. (1978), 'Bringing the boss back in: employer's size, employee schooling and socio-economic achievement', *American Sociological Review*, vol. 43, no. 6 (December), pp. 812–8.

Tibble, J. (1969), 'The educational effects of examinations in England and Wales', *UNESCO Education Yearbook* (Paris: UNESCO).

Torrance, E. (1965), *Rewarding Creative Behaviour* (Englewood Cliffs, NJ: Prentice-Hall).

Turner, R. (1967), 'Modes of social ascent through education: sponsored and contest mobility', in R. Bendix and S. Lipset (eds), *Class, Status and Power* (London: Routledge & Kegan Paul).

UNDP (1972), *Project Proposal for Educational Development Centre, Malaysia* (Kuala Lumpur: UNDP).

UNESCO (1971), *New Trends in Integrated Science Teaching* (Paris: UNESCO).

Unger, J. (1979), 'China's troubled down-to-the-countryside campaign', *Contemporary China*, vol. 3, no. 2 (Summer), pp. 79–92.

Unger, J. (1980a), 'The Chinese controversy over higher education', *Pacific Affairs*, vol. 53, no. 1 (Spring).

Unger, J. (1980b), 'Severing the links between education and careers: the sobering experience of China's urban schools, 1968–76', *IDS Bulletin*, vol. 11, no. 2, pp. 49–54.

Unger, J. (1982), *Education under Mao: Class and Competition in Canton Schools, 1960–1980* (New York: Columbia University Press).

Wallace, J. (1976), 'Progress without development – rural education at the cultural interface in highland Peru', *Council on Anthropology and Education Quarterly*, vol. VII, no. 2 (May), pp. 14–18.

Walsh, V., Townsend, J., and Senker, P. (1980), 'Technical change and skilled manpower needs in the plastics processing industry', report prepared for the Rubber and Plastics Processing Industry Training Board and the Polymer Engineering Directorate, Science Research Council (Brighton: University of Sussex Science Policy Research Unit).

Wanasinghe, J. (1982), 'A critical examination of the failure of the junior secondary school curriculum and prevocational studies in Sri Lanka', *International Journal of Educational Development*, vol. 2, no. 1 (Spring), pp. 61–72.

Warren, N. (1973), 'Malnutrition and mental development', *Psychological Bulletin*, vol. 80, no. 4, pp. 324–8.

Watts, A. G. (1973), 'The qualification spiral', *Sunday Times Magazine* (London), 7 October, p. 85.

Weiner, B. (1973), 'From each according to his abilities: the role of effort in a moral society', *Human Development*, vol. 16, pp. 53–60.

Weiner, B. (ed.) (1974), *Achievement Motivation and Attribution Theory* (Morristown, NJ: General Learning Press).

Weiner, B. (1979), 'A theory of motivation for some classroom experiences', *Journal of Educational Psychology*, vol. 71, no. 1, pp. 3–25.

Weiner, B., Friez, I., Kukla, A., Reed, L., Rest, S., and Rosenbaum, R. M. (1971), *Perceiving the Causes of Success and Failure* (New York: General Learning Press).

Wells, K. S. (1982), 'Migration to the capital: primary school leavers in Botswana', *International Journal of Educational Development*, vol. 1, no. 3 (January), pp. 115–16.

Wijemanne, E. L. (1978), 'Education and reform in Sri Lanka', Report Studies C.70, Division of Educational Policy and Planning, UNESCO, Paris.

Wijemanne, E. L., and Sinclair, M. E. (1972), 'General education: some developments in the sixties and prospects for the seventies', *Marga Quarterly Journal*, vol. 1, no. 4, pp. 1–26.

Wiles, P. (1974), 'The correlation between education and earnings, the external-test-not-content hypothesis', *Higher Education*, vol. 3 (February), pp. 43–57.

Wilson, A. B. (1972), 'General education and unemployment in West Malaysia', *Journal Pendidekan* (University of Malaya), vol. 3, pp. 42–8.

Wilson, A. J. (1973), 'The People's Liberation Front and the revolution that failed', Reprint series, No. 23, Centre for Developing Area Studies, McGill University, Montreal.

Wober, M. (1974), 'Towards an understanding of the Kiganda concept of intelligence', in J. W. Berry and P. R. Dasen (eds), *Culture and Cognition. Readings in Cross-Cultural Psychology* (London: Methuen), pp. 261–80.

Wong, R. (1969), 'Educational effects of examinations on pupils, teachers and society', in *World Yearbook of Education, 1969* (London: Evans), pp. 360–7.

Wong, H. K., and Gwee, Y. H. (1972), *The Development of Education in Singapore and Malaysia* (Kuala Lumpur: Heinemann).

World Bank (1966), *Preliminary Survey of Education in Ceylon* (Washington, DC: World Bank).

Index

For Product Safety Concerns and Information please contact our
EU representative GPSR@taylorandfrancis.com Taylor & Francis
Verlag GmbH, Kaufingerstraße 24, 80331 München, Germany